'Fabric of a Nation' Series

*Telling the amazing real life stories of Australians
who, in their own way, have made a significant
contribution to the culture, history and reputation
of our great Nation.*

*Congratulations Richard, you're an esteemed scientist
and teacher whose dedication to your students
and desire to succeed is an inspiration. You have
a boundless energy for life and everything you take on.*

Tony Powell, Lexington Avenue Press.

'Fabric of a Nation Series'

Lots of Scars by Richard Collins

© Copyright Richard Collins 2004

Published by Lexington Avenue Press
2 Oceano Street, Copacabana, NSW Australia 2251

Managing Director: Tony Powell
Phone: (612) 4381 0353
Email: books@lexingtonavenue.com.au

National Library of Australia
Cataloguing-in-Publication Data
Collins Richard
Australian Story - Australian science - Physics

ISBN- 0 9751510 2 9

Cover design: KDR Graphics, Avoca Beach, NSW
Illustrations: Kathryn Collins
Book design: Ec in Ourimbah
Printed in Australia by McPherson's Printing Group

Lots of Scars

Richard Collins

To my students who kept me young
and to my family who mean more to me
than anything else in the world.

Published by Lexington Avenue Press
Copacabana

Foreword

By Leonie Kramer

Samuel Butler wrote "Life is the art of drawing sufficient conclusions from insufficient premises". That, Dick Collins might agree, distinguishes it from science. Within this book science and life rub along together, with some collisions, but always good results. Reading a life, whether it is recorded as autobiography or as biography is very different from living it. Life seems messy and disorderly and unplanned. It just happens. But on reflection it begins to take on a shape, and to suggest explanations which have eluded the subject at the time the events recorded took place. The voice of the autobiographer reveals much of the person, who can appear smug, evasive, bombastic or simply unbelievable. None of these terms and many others one could list, applies to Dick Collins' account of himself. If you have never heard him give a lecture to students, or entertain an audience with stories and demonstrations about science, or engage in conversation, you can rest assured that the voice you hear in *Lots of Scars*, is the man in real life.

His story shares a pattern of experience with other Australians of his generation. Here is a man who was brought up in an outer suburb of Sydney, who enjoyed a carefree childhood, and went to the local primary school and then on to high school. It was there that he discovered his special talent, though he didn't recognize it at the time It was the ability to test theoretical problems in physics by making gadgets. He had no specific ambitions as a young man, and like so many teenagers wasn't at all sure where he was going. Circumstances and his own willingness to take chances and seize opportunities opened doors to a world far beyond his dreams.

With hindsight, he can identify moments of discovery about himself, and meetings with others, often accidental, which led him to further study and employment. Eventually, in 1980, he was appointed to a Chair in Physics in the University of Sydney, and became the Head of School. He brought to this position long experience in industry, a doctorate from New York University, and exceptional talents as a teacher. His enthusiasm for his subject and his inventiveness are infectious, and they inform this book Readers will understand why "physics is fun".

Albert Facey, who suffered a lonely and often miserable childhood, and who was expected to do the work of a man at a very tender age, often without the support of family or friends, called his autobiography *A Fortunate Life*. Why does Dick Collins call his autobiography *Lots of Scars*? That is a puzzle for each reader to unravel, for despite his forthright account of the stages in his life, there remain elusive mysteries each one of us can probe. This is a refreshing change from the "warts and all" school of autobiography which pretends to full revelation, but merely sensationalises superficial events. Dick Collins gives his readers access to those qualities of character and influences from others which determine the shape of the individual life, and the rest is for us to interpret. Curiously, he does not emphasize his quite exceptional capacity for invention. But then, despite his successful career he is a modest man, and like his youthful self, is not quite sure even now how much he has achieved. That is a most engaging scepticism.

About the author

He is known as:
    Richard, to his family;
    Dick, in his professional life;
    Rich, to those who worked with him as a graduate student;
    Sensei, to several colleagues in Japan;
    Biggus, Dags, Gangle, and just plain Dad, to his children;
    Gramps, to his grandchildren.

He loves:
    Food in general, and especially potatoes;
    Inventing things;
    Physics;
    Continual achievement;
    Mathematical puzzles;
    Telling jokes;
    His students;
    Doing useful things;
    Standing up in front of people and talking;
    Woodwork;
    His family.

He hates:
    Long flights in Economy Class;
    Hypocrisy;
    The neglect of students;
    Prostate examinations;
    Ginger;
    Parsnips;
    Onion weed.

He is most proud that:
    He was asked to resign as Chairman of ANSTO;
    People did not want him to retire from the University;
    He received an Award for Excellence in Teaching;
    He can play several brass instruments (not all that well);
    His grown children are his friends.

Contents

Preface

I have always liked telling jokes. I seem to be able to remember lots of them, without effort, even the first crude bum jokes that I learnt when I started school. I also enjoy watching comedians who make their living from telling jokes. I admire their techniques – the way that they can grab an audience, hold them, and send them away feeling great. I have used their methods, and developed some of my own, during my long career as a professional lecturer. Standing up in front of a crowd and manipulating them is a real turn-on. It's probably a control thing, and certainly something of an ego trip, but I like to make people feel good, and it does that to me too.

Of all the amusing stories that I have told or made up over the years, the ones that get the best laughs are those that are true – usually things that have happened to me personally. It was probably when I was in my thirties that I first recognised the correctness of this slight variation of the old adage – truth really is funnier than fiction. Actually, everyone knows this. Many people say that they can't remember any jokes, let alone tell one, and then they recount some hilarious personal experience that sends you into stitches. The beauty of such stories is that they get better with the telling – they grow, and become more polished over the years. And people love to hear them, because these things happen to us all.

I have often been asked to give after-dinner speeches. Having sat through some truly diabolical dirges as a victim, I recognise that if you wish to present a message at such a time and place, it must be well disguised, given with a light touch, and wrapped in something entertaining. People who are full of food are in no condition to absorb additional heavy material. For me, the only realistic way of presenting to a crowd of potential sleepers is to make them laugh. I have found in my own personal experiences a fertile source of amusing stories that I can string together into something entertaining with at least a pretense of continuity, and to work in a message, however loosely connected, if I want to. Moreover, since these things actually happened to me personally, I don't have to write them down in order to deliver them. I know them. All that I need to do is to recall the trigger word for the next story, and I am away. So I can give this sort of presentation without notes, just like a professional comedian. I have to admit, however, that I always have the list of trigger words in my pocket!

After one of these performances, a victim said to me that I should turn these stories into a book. Although I have produced many scientific papers over the years, I had never written a book. It looked like an awful lot of hard work, and my professional life at the time was full of more serious stuff, so such a thing was quite out of the question. But the idea intrigued me. I realised that, if I ever got around to doing this, the principal challenge might not be the actual writing. Rather I would need to extract the stories from within the deep recesses of my aged mind. So I started to write the triggers down on scraps of paper whenever they occurred to me – usually only a word or two for each incident. When I began this process, a lot of them simply tumbled out, and I immediately filled a couple of pages with these entries. Many others emerged over the succeeding years, often unexpectedly and without reason, and sometimes in the most unlikely situations. The only discipline that I exercised was to write the words down *immediately* onto anything handy, and subsequently to put them into a manila folder entitled *JOKES* that I kept in my office. I used to refer to this folder occasionally to obtain material for my after-dinner performances, but otherwise it sat, unread and steadily growing, for over a decade.

I chose the date of my retirement from the University of Sydney, 31 December 2000, long before it came. Although I would have been only 60 years old at that time, I was determined to get out before others wanted me to go. Also, I had a lot of things, not related to my professional interests, that I was keen to do, and I knew that this would never happen unless I escaped from full-time employment. In addition, because I loved my work at the University, I was concerned that I would not be brave enough to make the decision to leave when the time arrived to retire. So I burned my bridges by trading in my tenure several years before my retirement date, and I planned things so that my work, including my graduate students, would get to a reasonable state of completion by that time. Shortly before the end of 2000, I made a trip to Europe, and I took with me my precious manila folder containing the access codes to my memory. I recall feeling quite nervous about this – it was the only written record of my stories, as I had never bothered to take a copy. I clearly remember the excitement as I sat in the aircraft, sifting through the trigger words on all sorts of scraps of paper, eliminating the inevitable multiple entries, and ordering them into some sort of logical sequence. By the time that I returned to Australia, the structure and content of this book had been largely determined. Although I have added a few things, and made some minor changes, what you read here is quite closely based on the outline that I developed on that trip.

Of course, as with everything in life, the writing didn't go entirely according to plan. Specifically, my wife Marilyn and I were in the middle of building our retirement home when I actually left the University, and this completely consumed our time for most of the next year. Marilyn was the designer and owner-builder, and together we did rather more of the actual work than we had anticipated. So I had little time for frivolous things like writing. Actually this was an excellent thing. I had been quite concerned that I might experience withdrawal symptoms after my retirement, but our total immersion in the challenges of house building left no time for such matters. In fact, I strongly recommend that all retirees leave their employment while utterly consumed with an orthogonal task in order to ease themselves into their new mode of living.

After a year or so, the building pressures eased to the point that I could start to think about the writing without guilt feelings. As an incompetent typist, I retired at just the right time, because the wonders of voice recognition made getting the words into my computer relatively straightforward. This technology was particularly useful for me because, for the last 20 years or so, I have done most of my writing by dictation, having had the luxury of excellent secretaries to transcribe my words. A voice recognition package is no substitute for a good secretary – it doesn't order your life, or make tea – but it is a remarkably effective aid, and it gets better with use.

As the chapters were completed, my family generously acted as critics and censors. I am most grateful to them for their comments and feedback, even if at times the advice from different people was completely at odds. What you read here is much improved as a result of their input, and I thank them for that.

I had often heard novelists comment how the characters and plots in their books develop as the writing progresses. I did not understand this at all at the time, but I do now. In my early conception, this book was to be just a series of amusing personal incidents. Indeed, this is how I ordered things when I originally structured its content. Even during the writing of the first chapter, however, themes emerged that I had not anticipated. Essentially, I started to reflect on how I had got from there to here, why I remembered particular experiences, and how they had influenced my development. This book is not an autobiography, however – it contains little about the professional activities that have consumed so much of my life. In addition, I would be astonished if anyone ever described it as a serious work. It is possible that it began as an exercise with a significant component of self-indulgence, and maybe some of that remains. Certainly, writing it was a most enjoyable experience. However, it quickly became much more a process of self-discovery. As is always the case when I write a scientific paper, I came to know much more about the subject as the book took shape. And a few of the things that I learnt astonished me. For example, I found that some events that had occurred decades ago had touched me so deeply that, when I came to speak about them into the computer, I couldn't get the words out, and I had to peck them in.

I should also comment about the title. My original working title for this book was *Physics is a Funny Business*. Although this reflected my intention at the commencement of the writing, I never liked it, and I would have been most disappointed if I had needed to use it in the end. This feeling strengthened as the writing proceeded, and the themes developed. The title that I have chosen emerged after I had written about four chapters, and actually came to me early one morning in a Japanese hotel room. It is obviously based on the ringworm story in the first chapter. Although some of my family reviewers feel that it is a bit negative, I like it. Obviously I think of scars as much more than physical marks on my body, although I have many of these. Memories are really no more than scars on the mind. And scars need not have just negative connotations. Many scars can be worn with pride, and that is how I feel about most those that form the content of this book.

I hope that reading this gives you as much pleasure as I have obtained from writing it. If you find yourself in here, either individually or collectively, I thank you for the scars that you gave me.

Richard (Dick) Collins
MacMasters Beach
March 2004

Retirement

Starting from Zero

When did it all begin? Scientists, philosophers and fanatics have pondered this question ever since the start of thought. There is now general consensus that things kicked off between 10 and 20 billion years ago, although a few enthusiasts continue to cling to the belief that the actual figure is more like 6000 years. Although I have never heard anyone argue that it was even more recent than this, a tiny part of my supposedly scientific brain would like to believe that the precise date was 23 April 1940 – the day (so I am told) that I first squinted uncomprehendingly at the primitive surroundings of the hospital at Mt. Isa, Queensland. I realise that admitting this may lead you, dear reader, to think that you are dealing with a nutter. And maybe you are, but I ask that you wait a while before reaching that conclusion. However, events that occurred before I was around seem to me to be just a bit unreal – like the fragments of the fossil record put there to tempt the unfaithful when the 6000 year argument was all the go. Perhaps even more alarmingly, it is only since the time that I can actually remember things that I become entirely comfortable about the reality of history. I find my earliest memories intriguing because of what they would have predicted, should I or anyone else have bothered to consider the matter, about the path that I would follow later in my life. My story starts with these memories …

Well, not quite. I have to begin just a bit before the memory limit. A few months after I was born, I was deported from Queensland in a clothesbasket during my family's move to Chatswood in Sydney. A year or so later, we moved to St. Marys where my Father worked as the resident electrical engineer at the Commonwealth Munitions Factory. My earliest memories are from there. We lived in a house not far from the factory. Across the road from us lived our good friends and neighbours, the Farrow family – the parents, whom we called Uncle Morris and Aunt Mary, and their sons, David and Robin. These two boys were respectively about the same ages as my one-year-older brother William and me, and so Robin and I were mates. Beyond the Farrows was The Bush – an infinite expanse of unexplored heaven for us two sub-five year olds.

1

In those days, I seemed to be left much to my own devices for a lot of the time, so Robin and I often used to meet up after breakfast and work our way through the day in an unplanned, idyllic ramble. One of my earliest memories concerns the troops of soldiers who marched, seemingly quite often, past our house towards the munitions factory. I have no idea what they did there, but they usually marched back again later in the same day. Once, I recall sitting in the gutter with Robin watching a group of them march back from the factory, rifles on their shoulders. A few minutes after they had passed us, two more soldiers ran along the road, obviously trying to catch up with the others. Upon seeing us, one of them pointed his rifle at me, and said, "Bang, you're dead!" I remember thinking that this was the best thing that had ever happened to me. I still find it hard to believe that the horrors of war were occurring in other parts of the world while I was enjoying the first few halcyon years of my childhood. It seems so unfair.

Even in those early days, I was often in strife with my parents. I remember going on an exploration sortie into The Bush with Robin, and not coming home. In fact, we had wandered into a deep drain and become stuck in the mud. I am sure that we were not in any danger but, when we failed to return, a search party was sent out. I can still recall seeing my Mother standing on the bank above the drain, staring down at us with a look of thunder on her face. We were summarily hauled out and herded back home, to be cleaned up with high-pressure water from the garden hose. This didn't upset me – it just seemed to be part of the price of the freedom that we enjoyed.

Robin, who comes back into this yarn much later on, recently told me of another incident that had been completely removed from my memory by the erosion of time. Apparently, after some cows had broken into his father's yard and helped themselves to the family vegetables, he and I appeared looking over the repaired fence holding cricket stumps on either side of our heads. When asked what we were doing, we replied, "We're them bloody cows!"

An interesting aspect of this story is that I do not recall knowing the word *bloody* at the time. My Father never swore in our presence, and he maintained this discipline for as long as he lived. My clear recollection is that I only learnt these words a couple of years later when I was at Eastwood Infants' School. I therefore must have been about five years old when I became aware of the wonderful power and expressiveness of this part of the vernacular. One day, I was sitting on the back porch of our home with my infant brother Angus, teaching him the word *shit*. Even though my Father was extremely deaf, he figured out what I was saying. (In fact, he was a superb lip-reader – I once observed him sitting in a tram, smiling to himself. I asked him what was amusing him, and he told me that he was "listening" to the conversation of a couple sitting at the far end of the tram!) But I digress. Dad picked me up (he was immensely strong) and shouted at me, "What did you say to Angus?"

In all innocence, I replied, "Shit." And because I assumed that he didn't know, I added helpfully, "It's another word for job."

He roared, "I know what it means, you dirty little boy!" Whereupon, he drop kicked me down the stairs.

I learnt several lessons from this experience. Firstly, *shit* was not a word to be repeated when my Father could hear or see me. Secondly, I figured out that I had better be a bit cautious about trying out at home *any* of the new words that I learnt in the school playground. In addition, the experience reinforced what I already knew quite well – that I could get into strife at home without even trying. Finally, I began to suspect what has been confirmed again and again over the years – that Life is neither fair, nor just.

I was one day short of four years old when my younger brother Angus was born. My Father was doing essential war work, so he could not take time off to look after us. William and I were therefore packed off to a boarding house while my Mother was in hospital. I can clearly remember a couple of things about that experience. We were bathed communally, under a shower I think, and this was the first time that I saw a naked girl. I thought that she looked quite interesting. I also remember that we were both often in trouble because we did not flush the toilets after we had peed in them. At St. Marys, there was a water shortage, and this is what we had been taught to do. It was confusing that what was correct at St. Marys was naughty and disgusting at the boarding house. I do not recall ever discussing this experience with William. However, it is perhaps telling that, in the excellent and moving eulogy that he gave at our Mother's funeral in May 2003, he referred to this experience, describing it as "most unpleasant."

One of my Father's jobs was to turn on the streetlights in the evening. I often walked up with him to the box where the light switch was located, and sometimes he would let me operate it. On one of these occasions, the sun was very low in the western sky and I remember standing there looking at my extraordinarily long shadow, and wondering why it was so much taller than I was.

Just after the end of the war when I was about five, we moved from St. Marys to live at Eastwood. Immediately after the move, I started school. After only one or two days, I remember saying that I could not see the writing on the blackboard in our classroom. I was immediately taken to see a doctor, who discovered that I had very poor eyesight. I have tried and tried to recall the world becoming sharp when I first put my spectacles on, but I have no recollection of this occurring. However, I do remember being pointed at a lot, probably because at that time it was quite unusual for kids of my age to wear goggles, as my classmates described them. I also remember that I broke my spectacles with monotonous regularity – in fact the optometrist that we frequented gave my Father a quantity discount.

Many years later, I talked to my parents about their failure to discover that the first few years of my life had been a blur, but they had no explanation. They said that they used to point out things to me, such as birds in the sky, and I would say that I couldn't see them, but they put this down to my inattentiveness. It's hard to know how the early environment in which you find yourself affects your personality. If I couldn't see very well in my first few years, it might possibly explain why I was a proper little bastard and, indeed, why I developed into such a single-minded person later on. Even now, I drive my wife Marilyn crazy when I fail to respond to her if my mind is on something else. However socially dysfunctional this behaviour might be, single-mindedness and being able to concentrate completely are very useful attributes for a scientist.

At the age of five or six, William and I were taken to see Santa Claus. I recall standing in line in a stinking hot department store, waiting to get up to the gentleman in red. When I was finally introduced to the very hot and flustered Santa, he put me on his knee and said, "What do you want for Christmas, Sonny?"

Unfortunately, nobody had bothered to tell me that this was the deal or, if they had, I had not paid attention. I therefore had not given any thought to such matters, and replied, "I don't know."

He placed me roughly on the seat beside him saying, "Well, you can sit there until you find out." I desperately tried to dream up something that I wanted, but my mind was blank. After what seemed an eternity he turned to me and said, "Well, have you figured out what you want yet?"

In fact, I was quite keen on drawing, so I replied, "A pencil and a piece of paper."

He looked quite surprised, and said, "I think I can manage that," and I escaped. I have never been too keen on Santa since.

When I was at the infants' school at Eastwood, I was in a scripture class that misbehaved so badly that the elderly visiting minister was reduced to tears. The gentleman in question reported us to the Headmistress, who came into our classroom and had him point out the principal offenders. Both William and I were amongst the group of pupils, all boys I think, who were summarily marched down to stand in the corridor outside the Headmistress' office. We were all given the cane – it was two strokes each on the hand, as I recall. We were then kept in over playtime before being allowed to go outside to use the toilet. I remember all of the other students in the school standing in line, ready to march in for the resumption of classes, and looking at us as we walked across the playground. My hands were stinging, and I felt like a hero.

The most significant thing about my time in infants' school was that a fellow student in my classes was Marilyn, whom I ultimately married. The extraordinary aspect of this, however, is that even though we both have the class photos that show us there together in all three years, and we are both able to name most of the other students in these classes, neither of us can remember the other. I have often wondered if there is some deep psychological thing going on here, or whether it's just one of those amazing chance occurrences. As it happened, when we entered primary school in 1948, we went our separate ways for another decade or so before our lives became inexorably entangled.

Things were quite different in primary school or, to give its actual name, Eastwood Central School (Boys' Primary Department). Firstly, there were only boys in our classes. The girls were taught separately in the Girls' Primary Department, directly next to ours. Indeed we shared the same playground, except that the girls were required to stay on one side of a yellow line on the asphalt, and we boys were on the other. Another significant difference was that getting the cane became a way of life. Now I don't want to give the impression that I personally was beaten excessively in primary school, although I certainly received the cane several times in each of the years that I was there. However, some of my classmates were caned regularly, often each day, and sometimes more than once in a day. The worst of my teachers was Mr Harival – Horrible Harival as we called him – for good reason. He particularly set out to break the tough guys in the class, and he often managed to reduce them to tears. These days, teachers would be put in gaol for some of the things that were done to my classmates.

Harival, in common with all teachers, was very economical with words when he provided comment on the performance of his charges in our regular half-yearly and yearly reports. I still have my reports and, in fairness to the teachers, there is only enough space in them for a very few words each time. The comments that I received during this period included: *Suspect eyes need testing*; *Can do better*; and *Squints*. Teachers' comments have clearly come a long way over the years.

Towards the end of my primary schooling, my brother Angus and I suffered a most unfortunate affliction that, if it did not significantly scar our psyches, it certainly should have. We were both infected by ringworms on our heads. The ringworms came from a cat that we had at the time. I was a proper little bugger with this cat. Although I was forbidden to take it into my bed, I regularly did this, sometimes forcing it down under the sheets with my feet and holding it there, only to be released when I fell asleep. I was finally cured of this habit when it shat on me one night. After this cat infected us, it had the good sense to be run over by a car before it could be destroyed.

The treatment for our ringworms was pretty awful. Our heads were shaved, and ointment was rubbed into our scalps for half an hour, both morning and evening. My Mother would sit on a chair with me on a cushion between her knees, and Angus would sit between my legs on the floor in front of me. Mum would put on rubber gloves to protect her hands and rub my head with ointment, and I would do the same for Angus, who would read a book.

Because we were infectious, we could not go to school. I think that work must have been sent home, but I don't actually recall this occurring. After many weeks, although we still looked like Yul Brynners and the shaving and ointment treatments continued, we were permitted to return to classes. In order to keep our heads clean, and for aesthetic reasons, we were required to wear little skullcaps. Ultimately it was decreed that the ointment treatments could stop, and our hair was allowed to grow again. The most traumatic time of all for me was when my hair had grown sufficiently that it was decided that I need no longer wear my skullcap to school. I did not want to give it up. In hindsight, I have no idea why this was such big deal for me, because I had played tennis and gone to Cubs without the skullcap over the preceding few weeks. However I would not part with it for school. Eventually, as I found out later, one evening my Mother secretly told William to hide it, and not to tell her where it was. The next morning when it was time to go to school, I could not find the bloody thing. I put on all sorts of tantrums, but my Mother was adamant – she did not know where it was, and I was going to school without it. End of story. I set off with a heavy heart, wishing that the ground would open up and swallow me. When I arrived in the schoolyard, nobody said anything. Finally, when we got into the classroom, the teacher remarked, "Look at that! Collins has lost his veranda!" And that was the end of the whole thing. Well, almost. A few weeks later, I found the skullcap, but by then I had lost interest in it.

The transition from infants' school to primary school was also accompanied by another major change – we graduated from pencil to ink for our writing. At the time, this did not seem to be a very positive step. The ink was made by combining powder and water in a big earthenware bottle, and this mixture was then dispensed into porcelain inkwells that fitted into little holes in the middle of each two-seat desk. The pens that we used had post office nibs (whatever that meant) and, of course, had to be dipped frequently into the inkwells to charge them. All of this process was astonishingly messy, and ink got everywhere.

When kids first try to write, they will grip the implement any which way. We, however, were only permitted to use one holding style for our pens, and all variants were ruthlessly expunged. Horrible Harival was particularly insistent about eliminating any occurrence of "Mount Vesuvius" in our class. A Mount Vesuvius occurs when the pen is held too tightly, and the first knuckle of the index finger of the writing hand is bent inwards. This causes the second knuckle (the Mount Vesuvius) to stick up in the air. Harival corrected our writing style by the simple technique of hitting offending knuckles with his cane as he prowled around the classroom. Although this method resulted in all of us having excellent pen-holding techniques, it exacerbated the mess problem.

The introduction of the ballpoint pen shortly afterwards presented the opportunity to overcome the negative aspects of writing with ink. For some years, however, it was decreed that students would not develop a proper writing style with a ballpoint pen because it did not permit a heavy down stroke, followed by a light up stroke – a supposedly essential feature of good handwriting at the time. Eventually sanity prevailed, however, and the messy inkwells and post office nibs were consigned to oblivion.

The ballpoint pens of the day were quite rudimentary. We quickly discovered that removal of the ink tube from one end and the cap from the other gave one a nifty little blowpipe, and that grains of rice were just the right size to fit through it. An epidemic of blowpipe/rice warfare ensued. These battles would reach their peak when the teacher was out of the classroom. My teacher at this time was a chubby little man called Mr Wallace, known universally to all the kids (behind his back, of course) as Georgie Wallace. There was a nice piece of doggerel about him:

> Georgie Wallace is a good boy
> He goes to church on Sunday,
> And prays to God to give him strength
> To wallop the kids on Monday.

Although this verse was quite appropriate, Georgie was actually an excellent teacher, and a good bloke. During a particularly torrid fight, one of my classmates filled his mouth with rice, and managed to get going an excellent imitation of a machine gun. Of course, the good times could not last, and one day Georgie burst back into the room when the war was in full swing. He hauled out the culprits, identifying them simply by looking at everybody's ballpoint pen. As it happened, about half of the class ended up standing out the front. Of course we were all caned (two strokes each), but this brought us very little pain, because we were so many that Georgie had to pace himself. Even so, he was completely buggered by the time he had finished. My recollection is that this ended the blowpipe fad, but I suspect that it had just about run its course anyhow.

One of my most memorable experiences at primary school was playing a minor role in a stage performance. In this case, I know the dates exactly: 23 and 24 April 1951 – my eleventh birthday and the day afterwards. The pageant, as it was grandly called, was one of a series of identical extravaganzas that were organised in schools around the State to celebrate 50 years of Federation. I was selected to play the role of William Farrar in this show because I was the tallest kid in the class and, like Farrar, I wore spectacles. Unlike Farrar, however, I did not possess a beard at the time, but my Father made up for this deficiency by constructing an excellent false one. It consisted of hanks of imitation hair that looked a bit like pieces of dead rat, glued onto a sheet of unbleached calico with a little hole to speak through. The whole affair was held in place with a loop of elastic around my head. My part in the pageant was simple enough, and followed a discussion about how difficult it was for the early farmers to grow crops in the harsh Australian climate. I was required to walk on stage, clutching a sheaf of imitation wheat stalks in my right hand, turn and face the audience, raise the stalks high, and say, "What use to try and grow wheat that needs much rain in a land as dry as ours? Ah! *(Action here – raise left hand high with index finger extended.)* But I found a wheat that would grow where rain is light." Turn and exit.

There were four performances. The first was on the afternoon of my birthday, and my participation was unmemorable, in the sense that I don't remember anything about it. Apparently, I therefore approached the evening performance on that day in a relaxed state, and with a high degree of confidence. At my cue, I walked on-stage, turned to face the audience, raised my wheat stalks high, and started my spiel: "What use to try and grow wheat ..." Now at this time I was quite inexperienced at treading the boards, but one thing that I knew quite well was that mine was *not* a comedy spot. This was deadly serious stuff, commenting about the difficulty of growing food in the early days of the colony, with the prospect of failure leading to starvation. I was therefore quite astonished when, as I progressed with my lines, the audience began to laugh – first a little titter here, then a giggle there, but as I ploughed on, the laughter grew until I found myself shouting into a veritable gale of it. Of course, I was concentrating on what I was saying, and so not much of my mind was available to try and figure out what was happening. However, about half way through I glanced downwards and there, to my horror, in my left hand, hanging from the elastic, was my beard. I do not have a clear recollection of what happened next, but one of my classmates filled me in the next day. Apparently, I immediately put my left hand, and the offending object that it carried, behind my back, and stoically continued on to the end of what I was supposed to say, albeit quite rapidly, but having the great presence of mind to omit the left hand/index finger action bit. I then turned and started to exit from the stage at high speed, rather than in the scripted stately walk, my departure being only slightly delayed by tripping on a protruding floor board and falling flat on my face.

Next day at school, I got a pretty bad time from Harival but, to my surprise, I was not caned. The remaining two performances of the show on that day went without a hitch. After an experience like that, you would not expect that I would select a career that required me to stand up in front of crowds and speak. It just goes to show that some people are slow learners.

I have mentioned that I seemed to have a propensity for getting into strife at home. This continued right up to the time when I finally left to get married in my early twenties. In hindsight, I believe that few of the things that I did wrong were planned with malice aforethought – they just seemed to happen. For example, in our backyard at Eastwood were two liquid-ambar trees that had a large number of horizontal branches, like the rungs of a ladder. I was very keen on climbing these trees, and I loved to swing around in them right up to the highest possible levels. Inevitably, I sometimes fell out. On one of these occasions, I hurt my right arm quite badly and took it up to Mum in great pain. It happened to be my Father's birthday, and she was distracted preparing a special evening meal, so I received no sympathy at all. Over the next few days, the pain continued and I kept complaining about it. Finally my parents took me to the doctor who discovered that it was broken. They felt terrible about this, and I experienced a certain vicarious pleasure in their discomfort because they had been so unsympathetic.

It was not a bad break and only required splinting. A flexible wooden sleeve was wrapped around the arm, and bandaged on. Needless to say, this did not slow me down at all – so much so that one day I went swimming and got it saturated. My Mother had to take it off to dry out the bandages and then replace them. Unfortunately for her, she put the splint on incorrectly so that, when we went to the doctor for its removal, he was able to tell that the bandages had already been off. While this was entirely my fault, it was my Mother who got into trouble on this occasion.

Most of my injuries were self-inflicted. At the back of our house at Eastwood, a set of twelve wooden steps ran from a landing down to a concrete pad below. One afternoon, I was showing off to one of my friends and progressively jumped from higher and higher steps down to the concrete pad. My final leap was from the landing at the top. Immediately I hit the concrete, I felt great pain, and could barely move. I managed to crawl up the steps and into the house, to be greeted with appropriate outrage. In fact I had injured my back quite badly, and I was required to lie on a flat board for about three weeks. Although the back recovered reasonably well, from that day on I had bouts of acute sciatica and chronic back pain – problems that recurred for the next 40 years until the damaged disk finally ruptured.

Another time, I recall wandering off the beaten track on my way home from school. My parents frowned on this, but I seemed to be unable to obey simple instructions about such matters. On this occasion, I was playing in long grass with a friend when I cut my arm quite badly – "on a sword" as I insisted later. I still recall looking into the wound and seeing some structure inside, so it must have been quite deep. It hurt a lot, a matter not eased when my mate helpfully informed me that I would probably get blood poisoning. I beat it for home, wailing at the top of my voice, "I've got blood poisoning!"

Everyone in the street heard me, so it was no surprise that my Mother was waiting for me at the front gate, looking very angry. She said, "I'll give you blood poisoning, my boy." I suppose that the doctor looked at my wound and stitched it up, and that I received an anti-tetanus injection and all that stuff, but I am sure that did not get any sympathy.

I think perhaps the best indicator of the extent of my self-harm was evident immediately after our heads had been shaved during the ringworm saga. We went along to the specialist who examined my bald pate, then looked at my Mother sternly and said, "This boy has lots of scars on his head." My Mother later told me that she took this as an implication that I had been physically abused. I think this upset her a lot, and I was sorry about that, because none of the scars had come from her – not on my head anyway.

Of all the areas in which I gave my parents trouble, eating was not one – I loved my food. I was particularly fond of potatoes (and still am), and I would always leave them until last. Nothing my parents could say would dissuade me from doing this. I recall once a discussion at the dinner table (in hindsight it was probably stage-managed) in which a guest recounted a story of someone who left their favourite food until the end, and then had it taken away, on the presumption that they did not want it. Once they tried to do this to me, but I kicked up such a stink that it was never attempted again. And I kept leaving my potatoes to last. (Many years later, I read that leaving your favourite food to last is indicative of feeling secure, and I think this is consistent with the way I felt.)

On only one occasion do I recall giving my Mother trouble over food. One Sunday at our main meal in the middle of the day she had made a mulberry pie for dessert. For some reason, I had it in my head that I did not like mulberries, and I told my Mother that I would not eat it. She said, "You are going to sit there until you do."

I replied, "Well, I will sit here forever."

In fact, it was about four o'clock in the afternoon when I finally realised that she was not going to give in, so I scoffed the stuff down in order to escape. It's hard to know which of us was more tense during this little confrontation, but my Mother never made mulberry pie again.

The house in which we lived at Eastwood was on one acre of land with a clay tennis court down at the bottom. Each weekend, William and I played tennis, and it was my job on Saturday morning to prepare the court. This involved watering and rolling it, and then marking the lines. I undertook this responsibility with great diligence and possessiveness – I believed that it was something that I did better than anyone else. While this was usually the case, there were occasions when the exercise was not without incident. Once I recall pumping up the marking machine so vigorously that the end of it blew out. This made my Father very angry. I remember on another occasion pushing our heavy tennis court roller at high speed towards the fence of the court, and then being unable to stop it. It careered through the wire netting and down a steep slope, coming to rest in a one-metre deep storm water drain at the bottom of the hill. It took my Father the best part of a day to get it out using levers and blocks.

There was a long path leading from the house down to the tennis court, and I often mowed this before the Saturday afternoon tennis. Quite frequently, I managed to cut through the old steel water pipe that lay above the ground here and there. This happened often enough that I should have learnt to be more careful, but I never seemed to remember. However, I became a dab hand at fixing these breaks, using my Father's stocks and dies.

Just like at St. Mary's, beyond the tennis court at Eastwood was another world having exploration potential. The gateway to this paradise was the storm water drain, and my mates and I often used it. On one of these ventures into the wilderness, I had my first experimentation with smoking. The thing that I attempted to smoke was dried paspalum wrapped in newspaper. I lit the end and, instead of taking a tentative draw, I sucked in with full force. The paper flared, causing my mouth and throat to be quite badly burnt. This cured me of the habit for all time, and I have never had a cigarette to my lips since.

I remember another sortie down the drain that finished up with me falling in the water and getting soaked. I had been away from the house for some hours and had lost all track of time. But time was not the thing that caused me concern – it was disguising my soaking wet clothes. I hit on the idea that if I rubbed dry dirt onto them, it might take the water out, and my Mother would not notice anything. When I eventually returned to the house, the rest of the family were finishing their lunch, so I knew that I was in trouble. My Mother's first comment was, "Richard, what on earth have you done to your clothes?"

Never quick to take a hint, I replied, "Nothing. Why, what's wrong with them?" The rest of the conversation does not bear repeating. Suffice to saying that I got a hiding, and missed out on lunch.

My parents believed in corporal punishment. This was frequently dished out to William and me, mostly to me, but never to Angus. In defence of what my parents did, whacking kids was an acceptable thing at the time. Moreover, I cannot think of a single occasion when I had a belting that was undeserved. The implement used by my parents to inflict this punishment was The Flex. We had a selection of Flexes hanging on a hook behind the kitchen door. These were normally used to supply power to a variety of electrical implements but, when punishment was threatened or actually applied, the words "get The Flex" struck palpable fear into my heart. Each Flex had bakelite plugs on the ends and I still recall the clicking sound of the plugs hitting together when The Flex was being removed prior to the administration of a hiding. In fact, I was often required to go and "get The Flex" myself and bring it to the place of punishment. Nice touch that, getting the victim to carry his own instrument of torture – a technique that I later learnt was applied to good effect at crucifixions by the Romans. My Mother gave us the choice of whether we would have it on the hands, or the bottom. With my Father, it was always on the bottom.

Sometimes the punishment was two or four strokes, occasionally as many as six. I remember one awful time, however, when I lost count. Afterwards I ran away from home. This was quite easy to do simply by heading down the block into the bush beyond. After an hour or so, I snuck back unnoticed and hid underneath the house. Our house had a large area under the floor that was completely unused, and that reduced to a very narrow height in the farthest corner from the access door. This remote spot could only be reached through a convoluted labyrinth that reflected the layout of the rooms above. It was into this space that I retreated, determined never to come out. When my parents realised that I was not around, they started calling and looking for me. As the afternoon wore on, they became quite concerned, and I can still recall crouching in this tiny space in the dark, sniggering to myself at the anguish they would suffer when they finally discovered my bones in a few years time. Finally my Father came under the house with a torch and found me cowering as far away from him as I could get. I was dragged out, expecting to get another belting, but I think he was so relieved to find me that he decided enough was enough.

To be fair to my parents, I am certain that they did not enjoy having to discipline me with physical force. My Mother, in particular, seemed continually to be in search of non-violent ways of ramming home the message that unreasonable behaviour would result in adverse consequences. One of her favourite non-impacting penalties was *100 onion weeds* (or any other number that came to her in the heat of outrage – always, however, multiples of 100 if I recall correctly). This was an exceptionally effective punishment to apply, for several reasons. Our garden contained a seemingly infinite supply of these noxious weeds, and my parents were always at war with them. To utilise one of your recalcitrant sons as forced labour in this never-ending struggle simply made good sense. Further, digging them out was a most unpleasant chore, and being compulsorily forced to do this for a long time was something that I disliked intensely. Obviously, it was hard for me to get into further strife when I was down on my hands and knees harvesting the little buggers because I could be viewed serving out my sentence from the kitchen. Finally, the penalty could be applied without all of our neighbours hearing my howls of pain from a belting and presumably thinking bad thoughts about my parents abusing one of their children – or maybe not, since most of them probably believed that I deserved whatever came to me. There was a significant disadvantage in this form of punishment from my Mother's point of view, however. She seldom had the time or inclination to check that the prescribed number of bulbs had indeed been dug, and I quickly learnt that a little license (let's face it, quite a lot) could be applied to the quantity of the harvest, resulting in a substantial mitigation in the severity of the punishment. In short, I lied to her, and quite frequently.

Lest there be any doubt about it, I hold no grudge against my parents for the punishments, both physical and non, that they inflicted upon me. It was a time when belting kids was a perfectly acceptable thing to do. Moreover, they never did it to me without good reason. I am sure that they did not enjoy it, and that there was nothing sadistic in their makeup. I think that they reasoned that it was the only language that I understood. Clearly, I didn't even understand this. I remember looking forward to when I would be bigger and stronger than my Father so that I could beat *him* up, but by the time that I got there, I had lost the urge. I loved my parents deeply, and I recognise that everything that they did was with the best of intentions. I am most sorry for the anguish that I caused then. I still cannot understand why I was so chronically disobedient. I seemed to be incapable of obeying simple instructions. (Marilyn tells me that nothing has changed over the years.)

Once my inability to act sensibly nearly had disastrous results. There was an older boy who lived in our street who had lost an eye in a game of bows and arrows. My Mother frequently used him as an object lesson that bows and arrows were dangerous things – we were expressly forbidden from having them. Of course this did not stop me, and I secretly constructed many, using them in my sorties into the bush. On one such occasion, I managed to hit Angus right in the middle of the forehead, just above his eyes. Blood immediately started to flow, and I knew that quick thinking was the only thing that would save me from a fate worse than death. I told Angus that we would *both* get into trouble if Mum found out that we had been playing with bows and arrows, and insisted that he tell her that he had walked into a branch. He obeyed me, the wound was treated, and that was the end of the matter. However, as a result of this experience, I finally got the message about bows and arrows, and never played with them again.

Angus often seemed to get the rough end of the pineapple from me. Since he was four years younger, he was still on a tricycle when I graduated to my two-wheeler bike. Of course he then could not go as fast as me, so I tried to fix this by towing his tricycle behind my bike. Instead of starting slowly to check what would happen, I set off full tilt first time. I did not know that a tricycle becomes unstable at high speed, and goes into a death wobble. Angus suffered a most fearful crash and was quite badly abraded by the experience.

I was very fond of my bike. I treated it with great care and often used to decorate it with streamers and ribbons. I learnt to take it apart to the last ball bearing and reassemble it, well oiled and greased. I even recall making little wooden propellers that rotated in a most satisfying way when I travelled fast. I developed many designs of these propellers that turned in either direction and at different speeds. The bike remained my principal mode of transport right up until the time that I was married.

From my earliest days, I had an intense interest in why the world behaved as it did. I can still recall my first scientific experiment, although of course I did not call it that at the time. I was curious to see if I could dry out the soap bubbles from my bath. I expected that they would become brittle, like fine china. I took a small tin can, filled it with bubbles, and placed it in the corner of the bathroom overnight. I was quite disappointed next morning when all that I found was some greasy grey water in the bottom of the can.

Perhaps the most clear early indicator of where I would go in my future life was evident when William and I played with our Meccano sets, which we did quite frequently. William always selected a plan from the book of instructions and built it piece by piece, bolt by bolt, exactly as it was described. I cannot recall a single occasion when I did this. I would always decide what I was going to make – a car, or a crane, or a machine to wind silk from the cocoons of silkworms – and I would start building it from scratch and then modify it until I got it to work. Needless to say, William's constructions looked like boats and cars and trains, and mine looked like nothing obvious, except that they worked, after a fashion. Later in life, William became an engineer, and I a scientist. Although we did not realise it at the time, we were both preprogrammed.

It was common in those days to ask kids what they wanted to be when they grew up – it probably still is. In contrast to William, who always knew that he wanted to become an engineer like our Father, I had no such idea. Much later in life, I formed the view that my position was not an unreasonable one. After all, how can you know what you want to do if you haven't done it yet? At the time, however, it was always implied that I *should* know what I wanted to be, and that not to know meant that there was something wrong with me. On one occasion when pressed by my Mother to express an opinion about my future vocation, it is perhaps telling that I said that I would like to become a train guard. She was appalled, and asked why. I replied, "It's the job that has the least responsibility that I can think of." My Mother vetoed this idea, and I did not pursue it. However, by the end of 1951 when I completed primary school, there were all sorts of signals that, had they been analysed, would have provided a clear indication about what the future held for me. I was single minded, and absent minded, to the point that I drove people to distraction. I was intensely curious about why things were the way they were. I had demonstrated an ability to generate ideas, and to test these ideas against observations that I made, either of the world as it was, or of the outcomes of specific things that I did to it. I cared little for authority, and was quite unable to take orders or advice, often to my own personal risk or detriment, and to that of others. I was a shocking show-off, and liked to be the centre of attention. (Indeed, my Mother often said that I should become an actor!) I had proven myself to be energetic to the point of hyperactivity. Over the next decade at high school and university, these somewhat antisocial traits developed further and, supplemented by the acquisition of a little knowledge, confirmed the direction that, even then, had unknowingly been defined for the rest of my life.

Class 2A, Eastwood Infants' School, 1947
Richard is in the back row, third from the left.
His future wife, Marilyn, is in the second row, extreme left.

Lessons for Life

In the 1950s, students who did well at Sydney primary schools had the option of attending a selective high school. The schools available were determined geographically – from Eastwood, we could choose to go either to Fort Street Boys' High School, or to Homebush Boys' High School. For reasons that are completely unclear to me, in 1951 my parents decided that William should go to Homebush. The following year, the decision about where I went was automatic. It turned out to be an inspired one.

The selective status of Homebush, and its Headmaster, Mr Robert (Bob) A Golding, made the school a highly desirable place for secondary education. Mr Golding, known universally as *The Boss*, was a great man. He had very high standards – academically, on the sporting field, and for our presentation as students. All boys were required to wear a full and complete uniform at school, and when travelling to and from school. As part of his efforts to emphasise the importance of appropriate dress, *The Boss* wore a black academic gown while at school. He struck a most impressive figure striding along the corridors with the gown flowing out behind him like a giant bat, or standing in front of a General Assembly of the school like a bald eagle.

The Boss was a strong disciplinarian. He did not hesitate to use the cane to enforce rules, and this responsibility was shared with only the Deputy Headmaster (*The Dep*), a dapper little man called Mr Myers (*Candy* Myers behind his back). As far as I can recall, the cane was not applied excessively, and I personally never received it at high school.

Throughout the entire five years of my time at high school, I was extraordinarily fortunate to have talented and dedicated teachers who were genuinely interested in the progress of their students. The subjects that I took in First Year were predetermined: English, Maths, Science, French, Geography, Music, and Manual Arts (Woodwork, Metalwork and Technical Drawing). In my Second Year, I dropped Music, Geography and Metalwork. However, I continued with Woodwork and Technical Drawing for my first three years at Homebush, and the benefits that I received from these subjects have lasted throughout my entire professional and handyman life.

Science and Maths were my main loves at high school. I can still recall my first ever Science lesson at the school. It was given by long craggy gentlemen called Mr Cullen – Mickey Cullen, as we young boys called him. Mickey was idiosyncratic in the extreme. As well as being an excellent teacher, he had a penchant for telling dirty jokes in class, while at the same time apparently being very religious. In our first Science lesson he told us the following two gems:

> **Question:** *If the Devil sat in a bag of flour, what well-known weed killer would that make?*
> **Answer:** *White arsenic.*

> *The chemical name for lead is plumbum.*

This last fact particularly delighted us prepubescent boys.

Mickey Cullen was responsible for one of the most compelling and effective pieces of learning that I ever experienced. We had been given for homework a relatively straightforward calculation that required the use of log tables – an essential skill in those pre-slide rule, pre-pocket calculator, pre-computer days. When our submissions were returned, we were all docked two marks, and Mickey had scrawled on every paper: *Insane accuracy!* He objected that we had given the result of the calculation to four significant figures – the number automatically generated by the log tables. The numbers in our answers were not incorrect – there were just too many of them. This action was not preceded by any discussion about significant figures or errors – it just came out of the blue. We argued bitterly with him. After all, what was wrong with the extra two figures? Mickey was completely unmoved, and simply kept repeating the two words: *Insane accuracy!* So we lost the two marks, but I have never since knowingly quoted a measurement, or the result of a calculation, to other than the correct number of significant figures. It is interesting that modern educational philosophy would argue that students should be taught by positive reinforcement. Mickey's lesson was anything but that, but it could not have been more effective – and I'm sure that it didn't do us any harm.

I had Mickey Cullen for science in my first three years at high school. His classes were spiced with demonstrations, enthusiasm, insights, religious homilies, and bad language. Although it generally seemed to me that the education of that time was centred on facts, much of the science in Mickey's classes was related to things with which we were familiar in our day-to-day life. I certainly did not articulate it then, but I believe that I subconsciously realised that Science was a tool that could be used to improve the quality of our life. There is no question in my mind that Mickey played an important part in developing my future attitudes about the benefits of applying science for the good of society.

Many years later, in 1996 to be specific, I returned to my high school for a reunion of Old Boys. For me, the most significant thing about that evening was that Mickey Cullen was there. He must have been in his nineties, and seemed to have difficulty in standing unaided. I also got the impression that his vision was very poor. It was touching to see the long line of middle-aged gentlemen waiting to pay their respects to him. When I finally got to the top, I introduced myself, but I am fairly sure that he did not remember me. However, I knew that Mickey had played a significant part in the preparation of the famous high school Science Bluebooks, edited by the former Head of the School of Physics at the University of Sydney, Professor Harry Messel, and his colleagues. In this process, Mickey had come to know Harry quite well. When I told him that I was shortly to become the next Head of the School of Physics, and would sit in the same office that Harry had once occupied, he shed tears of pride at this achievement by one of his former students. I know exactly how he felt. As a teacher myself for over two decades, I similarly get much satisfaction in the achievements of my former students, and I take great pride in the small part that I played in their development.

Another extraordinary teacher that I was fortunate to have was Mr Barter (*Baron Barter* as he was known), who taught us Mathematics. *The Baron* was a wiry little man who also ran the Air Cadets at the school. He was a strong disciplinarian – no one played up on *The Baron*. He knew his subject, and taught it well. I learnt a huge amount from him that reinforced the love that I already had for numbers, mathematical puzzles, and the like. *The Baron* also really cared about whether we learnt this stuff. He

21

used all sorts of techniques to ram home the information. I recall an occasion when one of my fellow students had given the incorrect answer to a question. *The Baron* picked him up by the scruff of the neck and seat of his pants, and held him out of an open second floor window until the correct answer was forthcoming.

My English teacher in First Year was oddly enough named Mr England. We called him *Society England* because of his penchant for saying to students who caused him displeasure, "Boy! You're a menace to Society!" I found it difficult to switch on to English, and was quite unable to grasp what he was getting at in his analysis of novels, poems and Shakespeare. In Second and Third Years, I had another English teacher called Mr Heffernan, a tall muscular gentlemen who was naturally nicknamed *Mr Heftyman*. He needed no help in maintaining discipline in the class. However, I was similarly unresponsive to, and uncomprehending about, what he was trying to explain to us in this subject.

I have already mentioned that *The Boss* was very keen on sport. At the weekly General Assemblies held after lunch every Thursday, boys who had done well at inter-school sport the previous afternoon were paraded before the school and lauded. I was never one of them. In modern-day parlance, I suppose that I would be termed a nerd. I would have liked to be good at sport, but such was not my lot. Although I don't recall feeling hardly done by because of my inability to excel at sports, I often wished that academic achievements would be afforded the same degree of public recognition and approval by *The Boss* as those in the sporting field.

There was one trait that I possessed in those days that troubled me a great deal – I was exceedingly nervous about standing up in front of people and talking – so much so, in fact, that I even hated to answer the telephone at home. I remember thinking about this and deciding that, unless I did something about it, I would be very limited in the options available to me later in life. I therefore joined the class debating team, specifically to confront my phobia. I always approached debates packing death. A week or so before each event, I would become extremely nervous and apprehensive, yet when the time came I performed quite well. Subsequently, standing up and speaking in front of people became my job. I'm quite happy to admit that I have never managed to eliminate completely my nervousness before each talk or lecture, although of course the intensity has diminished over the years. However, I have learnt to use such feelings to build up my adrenalin levels before each performance. In a classic case of overcompensation, I came to love the theatre of public speaking. Maybe my Mother was right all the time, and I *did* become an actor.

In my final two years at high school, I took a quite unbalanced selection of subjects: Mathematics 1, Mathematics 2 (both at honours level), Applied Mathematics, Physics, Chemistry, and the obligatory English. During these Fourth and Fifth years, my fellow students and I worked very hard, because one needed to matriculate in order to go to university, and it was a one shot process. Again I was extremely fortunate to have excellent Maths and Science teachers. Mr Durack (*Vince Durack* to us, both behind his back and occasionally to his face) taught us Maths, and both he and the syllabus were fantastic. We learnt calculus (integration and differentiation), series, trigonometry, algebra, coordinate geometry and a whole range of clever manipulative skills that I have found very useful throughout my professional life. My Mathematics honours classes included several other talented boys and we were very competitive. In a typical lesson, Vince would introduce us to a new mathematical procedure – perhaps a method of integration, or a technique for summing a series. We would then go to the textbook, and commence work on the set of problems based on this topic. We would do a few of these problems in class, and then compete with each other to come back the next day with the whole set finished. This went on throughout the two years – so much so that, when I finally finished Fifth Year, I felt that I could integrate anything that was integrable.

Applied Maths was taught to us by another fantastic teacher – Mr Leeder (descriptively known as *Tubby Leeder*). In this subject we learnt about statics, dynamics, oscillations and the like with similar rigour and application as in the other Mathematics topics.

Then there was science. For Chemistry we had Mr Macdonald – *Sleepy Macdonald* was his nickname because that's what he looked like, but he was anything but sleepy in his grasp of the subject and also in his extraordinary ability to do mental arithmetic. He taught us Chemistry as a series of facts with a small amount of overriding principles. I did well in Chemistry, because I seemed to be able to remember the facts without effort. It was not my favourite subject, however, because of the absence of understanding and interpretation that went along with the panoply of facts. I wanted to know not only *what* happened, but also *why* it occurred.

It was with Physics that I really struck gold. My Physics teacher in Fourth and Fifth Years was the Science Master of the school at the time – Mr Moss, or *Percy Moss* as we called him. *Percy* was in his last appointment before retirement, but he remained incredibly enthusiastic about his subject. Throughout his decades of teaching, he had acquired a veritable treasure trove of demonstrations for various physical principles, most of which he had built himself. His lessons etched themselves in my mind when he brought out these wonderful pieces of equipment and showed us how the theoretical principles of this subject were illustrated in the behavior of the hardware. I can still recall seeing him, a little sparrow of a man, standing *on the bench* at the front of our class after demonstrating some physical principle, his arms outstretched, shouting, "What a beautiful experiment, boys!"

"Yeah, *Percy*, yeah," we would mutter under our breath, as boys will when it is not cool to show excitement. Yet I was absolutely transfixed by the things that he told us, and showed us. It was like being in heaven.

Twice in my science class I demonstrated what seemed to me on later reflection to be quite impressive initiative. On one occasion, we had been learning about Cartesian Divers. A Cartesian Diver is a small cylindrical glass tube, open at the lower end and closed at the top. It is partly filled with water and partly with air, so that it just floats. It is put in a water-filled plastic bottle. When the bottle is squeezed, the water is pressurised, as is the air in the cylinder, and therefore the volume of air decreases. The cylinder thus becomes less buoyant, and sinks to the bottom of the bottle. I made a Cartesian Diver and in which the pressure was applied, not by squeezing the bottle by hand, but with a little mechanical gadget that I had designed and built. The bottle was located in a small wooden box with a moveable back, and it was compressed by turning a wheel that was attached to a screwed rod passing through the back. I took this to school and showed it to the teacher who was apoplectic with joy. In fact, he sent me to *The Boss* to demonstrate my modest invention. Another time, we had been learning about the stars, and the teacher told us that, because of the rotation of the earth, the stars appear to move in circles in the sky. This intrigued me, so one night I placed my primitive camera pointing upwards, and took a three-hour time exposure of the sky. I was rewarded with a tiny black and white print with faint circular star trails. I showed this to the teacher who was again beside himself. On both occasions, I believe I thought that the teachers were guilty of a bit of overacting. Years later as a teacher myself, however, I came to see why they responded as they did. My classmates were somewhat put off by the attention that I received, and I got called *crawler* more than once (read *brown nose* in modern parlance). I can honestly say, however, that I did not do these things to gain favour – I was genuinely interested in what I had learnt, and wanted to take it a bit further.

So it was that at the end of 1956 when I completed the Leaving Certificate, I decided to study Science at the University of Sydney. My expectation was that I would major in Mathematics because I had so much enjoyed the logic and challenge of this subject at school. However, as things turned out, my preferences shifted into a somewhat different direction.

Even before I attended my first lecture at University, it was made clear to us that the staff in this environment would be less concerned about our welfare and progress as students than our teachers at school. Indeed, during the 1957 Orientation Week, we were told explicitly that our lecturers didn't care whether or not we attended the lectures or passed our courses, that a large proportion of entering students would not survive the exams at the end of First Year, and that an even greater proportion would eventually fail to graduate. The remoteness of the lecturers themselves was consistent with the expectations raised by these statements. They came into the lecture theatres, gave their lectures, and then disappeared. Indeed, in my first three years at University, I do not recall having a single, meaningful, one-on-one conversation with any of my lecturers. Things these days could hardly be more different, and that is good.

In this unfriendly learning environment, idiosyncratic attitudes flourished. One of my better Maths lecturers was Dr Smith-White. He wore a tattered old black academic gown that continually slipped down from his shoulders as he was writing on the blackboard. His lectures were therefore interrupted by an ongoing set of callisthenics as he attempted to restore the gown to its correct position. For a couple of years, this gown appeared to get progressively more decrepit, but it managed to survive Smith-White's exercises. However, I was privileged to be in the memorable lecture when it finally met its demise. He had completed writing something on the blackboard, and took a large step backwards, catching the heel of his shoe in the bottom of the gown. This caused it to be ripped completely from one shoulder, accompanied by a most impressive tearing death cry. Smith-White stared disbelievingly at what he had done, and then without expression he ripped the remnants of the gown from his other shoulder and hurled them into a corner. He never wore a gown again.

The Head of the Pure Mathematics Department was Professor T G Room. Professor Room was a very organised person, but he was not a great teacher. In his meticulously prepared lectures, he conveyed all of the information in a droning monotone while simultaneously transcribing his words onto the blackboard in tiny letters and symbols. In his course on Tensors, the many small algebraic symbols were decorated with a much larger number of even smaller subscripts – for example a_{ijkl}. In a typical lecture, the blackboard would be covered many times by seemingly thousands of these symbols that we all slavishly copied into our lecture notes. One day in the middle of a lecture, a fellow student put up his hand and said, "Excuse me, Professor Room. Is that an i or a j that you have written there?"

Room looked at the piece of tiny script in question, thought for a while, chalked in the clarification, and then remarked, "You can tell my i's from my j's by the sign of the radius of curvature."

Professor Room is unique in my education, because he taught me the only course in which I learnt absolutely nothing. The course was Projective Geometry, and I later discovered that this subject was one of Room's research specialties. I remember being totally lost by the middle of the first lecture. I went to the remaining dozen or so lectures, and copied them into my notes while fighting to stay awake, but I understood not a word that was said or written. As the exams approached, I was worried about what to do with this material. It was completely incomprehensible and impenetrable to me. In the end, since Projective Geometry constituted only a fairly small proportion of the final mark, I decided to write it off. As luck would have it, the question in the exams could have been answered by studying only the material in the first lecture, and probably the first half of this lecture. If I had taken the time to review just this much, I could have had a pretty good shot at answering it. However, as I had not even done that, I got zero in Projective Geometry.

There was another Professor of Mathematics, Professor Bullen, who was Head of the Applied Mathematics Department. Bullen had written an excellent First Year textbook on Applied Mathematics, and his lectures were taken directly from this book. Every week or so, he would point out the exercises in his textbook that were relevant to the current topics. While we were encouraged to do these problems, I am certain that we were never told that they were compulsory. As it happened, however, I diligently solved them because of my experiences in Mathematics at high school, and anyway, I enjoyed doing them. Towards to end of the year, Bullen announced that he would be collecting the problems we had done in a couple of weeks. For most of the class, the following two weeks were a frenzy of late nights and cross-student copying, in order to meet the deadline imposed by this previously secret requirement.

There was an interesting corollary to the Bullen problem thing. The following year, it somehow became known to the next group of First Year students that I possessed a complete set of worked answers for the problems in Bullen's book. This made me much more an object of interest by one or two of the young ladies who were doing the course than a normal nerd would expect. Nothing extracurricular came from this, however, because by then I considered myself spoken for – to Marilyn, who had been in my infants' school classes.

The Mathematics lecturers did not have a mortgage on idiosyncratic behavior. One of our best Physics lecturers was Dr Geoffrey Builder. We thought very highly of him, because he really made an attempt to communicate effectively with us. However, there was one very odd part of his makeup – he had never accepted that Einstein's Theory of Relativity was correct, and had developed his own. That would normally have been fine, except that, when he taught us Relativity in Second Year, we got Builder's Theory of Relativity, rather than Einstein's. I remember reasoning that, while he might teach this weird stuff to us in the class, he would not be game to ask a question about it in the examination for fear of being ridiculed by his colleagues. I therefore made no attempt to learn this material. I was completely incorrect, and the exam questions were based on his peculiar ideas. Consequently I did quite poorly in this subject.

An even more bizarre thing happened in the following year when Marilyn did Second Year Physics, and was subjected to the idiosyncratic Builder Relativity stuff. Regrettably, after he had completed teaching the material, and before the final examinations at the end the year, Dr Builder died. Sad as this was, it presented the students with a peculiar dilemma. What would be in the exam? Since only Dr Builder believed in his theory of Relativity, no one else would ask the sort of questions that had been in my exam the previous year. And if the students answered *à la Builder* and someone else marked this stuff, would it be decided that they were wrong? In the end, Marilyn and some of her fellow students went to see one of the other lecturers and discussed the matter with him. He thought for a while and then said, "Don't worry about it." I think that I can work out what must have happened when the exam scripts were being marked, but nothing was ever said.

One of the worst Physics lecturers that we ever had was, in fact, a visitor to the department: Dr Paul Klemens. He taught us Thermodynamics and Statistical Mechanics, and his lectures were virtually incomprehensible. The following year, a new lecturer, Dr Mike Buckingham, took the course that followed on from Klemens' disaster. At the beginning of his first lecture, he attempted to find out what we had previously studied.

He asked us, "Do you know …?"

Negative response.

"Well, what about …?"

"No."

"And …?"

Sad shaking of heads.

"Who did you have for this subject last year?"

We informed him.

He said, "Ah, yes. Dr Klemens is not the acme of lucidity."

It is important to acknowledge that several of the staff did indeed try very hard to help the students with their learning. One of those was Phyllis Nichol, who had been there for many years and was quite elderly by the time that I knew her. She was a co-author of the well-known physics textbook – *Booth and Nichol*. Phyllis, or Miss Nichol as we knew her at the time, was quite eccentric, and had a very rough exterior. She was in charge of the Second Year Laboratory, and ran it like a work camp. Each session, before we were allowed to commence our experiments, we had to write a few lines in our lab books stating the physical *Principles* relating to what we were about to do. Miss Nichol was most insistent that we got our *Principles* correct, and would harangue us about their importance at high volume and great length. She had a peculiar way of saying the word, and the first syllable was usually accompanied by a fine spray that we took care to avoid by not standing too close. Despite her idiosyncratic behaviour, Phyllis was very dedicated to the students and concerned about their learning. As an Honours student in 1960, I demonstrated in the Second Year Laboratory. One of the students asked me to clarify some point of Physics that she had been having trouble with. After I had gone through the material with her, Phyllis, who had evidently been watching us, took me aside and thanked me for doing this, commenting that the students had been having problems with their lecturer on this topic. It was a warm and caring side of her that was not evident to most.

While still in my First Year at the University, I had started to form the view that Mathematics might not be for me. As much as I had loved this subject at school, I did not like the way that it was treated at the University. For me, there was too much emphasis on theorem and proof, and little attempt to solve specific problems. Virtually all of the things that I had enjoyed about Mathematics at school were absent from the subject as it was taught at the University. I thus drifted towards my other love – Physics. I believe that the course that finally convinced me that I could spend my life doing Physics was Kinetic Theory, taught to us in Second Year by Dr Freddie Hertz. Kinetic Theory is a most interesting part of Physics. It explains the properties of materials, usually gases, on the basis that they are made up of huge numbers of atoms or molecules. These molecules are assumed to have some specific properties, such as being perfectly elastic. One then develops an approximate model for the system by making simplifying assumptions – for example, the many gas molecules in a sample may be replaced by a very few molecules, perhaps only one. Relatively straightforward calculations are then performed to determine the macroscopic properties of the substance such as viscosity, compressibility, and the like. Kinetic Theory was one of the earliest examples of the effectiveness of using the molecular nature of materials to explain their macroscopic properties. This course split the class into two groups. The more mathematically minded of my colleagues hated it. I remember one of them saying, "The approach in this course is just a series of unjustified approximations. I will have nothing to do with this stuff."

My attitude was completely different. I realised that here was a way of thinking about very complex problems that would be intractable to exact analysis, but which could be understood, at least in part, by approximating them on the basis of physically reasonable arguments. The dissenters in our class went off and became mathematicians, statisticians, and other such things. I decided to become a physicist.

I recall one very interesting reaction to my decision. It occurred at a function held one evening at my old school. *The Boss* was there, and he asked me what I was going to do with my life. Proudly I said, "I am going to become a physicist."

He looked most displeased, and snorted, "Physicists! You made the bomb!"

It was my first exposure to the importance of consideration of the impact of Science on Society. Of course I went ahead with my plan, but I never forgot his reaction. Many years later, our daughter Kathryn, said almost exactly the same thing. There is no doubt that we scientists do have a responsibility for considering the social implications of the things that we do. More attention should be given to such matters in the education of scientists.

One of my good friends at University was Monty Newman. Monty was one of those people who really got into University life. He was extensively involved in many of the extra-curricular activities that were on offer. In addition, Monty had an extraordinarily wide circle of friends. It seemed that Monty knew everybody, and everybody knew Monty. One day, Monty informed us that his friend, Nicolas Chelonia, was standing in the election for the Students Representative Council. Monty told us that Nicolas was a good bloke, and asked us to vote for him. Although we had no interest whatsoever in the SRC, the mate of a mate is a mate, so we all duly fronted up and registered our vote. A couple of days later, Monty greeted us in high excitement informing us that his friend had been elected to the Council. We really couldn't see why this was such a big deal, until he told us that Nicolas Chelonia was, in fact, the Department of Zoology's pet tortoise. This achievement was actually reported in the newspapers in an article entitled: *Students Elect Tortoise*.

In 1960, I commenced my honours year in Physics, and finally started to develop something of a rapport with individual members of staff. Those days, the honours course in Physics was much more physical than it is now. Our first job as honours students was to carry several tons of lead bricks, two at a time, from the tower at one end of the Physics building, to the tower at the other. Gloves, and other protective clothing, were not supplied so that, by the end of this little operation, our hands were black, and our clothes were a mess. I remember my Mother going crook about this when I came home. A few years later, my hair started to fall out, but I'm sure that the lead brick job had nothing to do with this.

As part of our honours training, we were required to put in several hours soldering up circuits in the electronics laboratory of the School. The official rationale for this exercise was, I believe, that knowing how to solder properly is an important skill that all physicists should have. In reality, I think it is also relevant that we were a cheap (zero cost, in fact) way of building the large number of identical circuits required for the cosmic ray air shower experiment currently being set up by the School. The electronics laboratory had about ten soldering stations set up on a long bench that ran all the way down one wall. When the constant temperature irons were not actually melting solder, they hung from little hooks on the side of the bench. That would not normally have been a problem except that the genius that had designed this set up had arranged it so that, in the hanging position, the hot tips of the irons pointed upwards, and outwards. Our convivial soldering sessions were therefore quite frequently punctuated by short, sharp screams of pain as one of our number backed into a nearly red hot, pointed copper tip. Once again, this caused significant damage to our clothing, to my Mother's continuing displeasure. If you were ever to examine the bums of the University of Sydney Physics honours class of 1960 (and that is something that I most fervently hope you are never moved to do), I have often wondered whether you would find on most of us a few small arrow-shaped scars – mementos of those happy hours spent acquiring essential experimental physicist skills.

My supervisor in the Physics honours year was Dr Donald M Millar. Don, as I got to call him many years later, was a lovely man. He was gentle and kind, and spoke in a very precise way. When I returned to the University of Sydney in 1980, he became a valued colleague and a good friend. As part of our honours year, we had to undertake a major experimental project associated with one of the research programs of the School of Physics. Don gave me the task of refurbishing a small cloud chamber that he had brought with him to the University from the UK. As part of this process, he asked me to clean up the parts of the chamber before assembly. He gave me a thick walled glass cylinder, perhaps 40 centimeters diameter and 15 centimeters high, saying, "Be careful with this, Richard. It is very expensive."

I carried it out of his office, around the corner, and dropped it on the floor, causing it to smash into a million pieces. It was one of those moments when you wish that the ground would open and swallow you up. Trembling with fear and almost in tears, I returned to his office saying, "I'm terribly sorry, Dr Millar. I've broken it."

He stood there holding my future career in his hands. Then, with a look of infinite compassion, he opened a cupboard and handed me a replacement cylinder saying, "Never mind, I have several more."

It was not an auspicious start for me, and I will be eternally grateful to Don for his forbearance.

Shortly before our honours year, the School of Physics had acquired one of the first computers in Australia – a giant of a machine known by the acronym *Silliac* that occupied several rooms on the ground floor of the building. As part of our honours course, we were required to learn some elementary Fortran programming, and to do a specific exercise using this skill. The task was to get Silliac to plot the path of a satellite. I did not succeed in this endeavor. In fact, my simulated satellite followed a very odd path that took it through the centre of the earth. This commenced a long hate-hate relationship between computers and me. Indeed, I am slightly embarrassed to admit that I never really obtained even an elementary ability to program these monsters. As it subsequently turned out, there were often times when I absolutely needed to do some complex calculations for which a computer was the only option. Several times I started to learn to program, but every time someone would turn up who was much better at it than I was ever likely to be, and who seemed anxious to write the program for me. I eventually learnt that programming skills are quite widely distributed around the place, and that any programming that I needed to do could be readily performed by others. It therefore wasn't necessary for me to learn how to program, and I never did.

My relationship with computers illustrates a peculiar feature of my makeup that still surprises me – I am very conservative about the adoption of new technology. I remember being reluctant to make the transition from log tables to slide rule, and similarly from slide rule to pocket calculator. As I have said, I never effectively graduated from pocket calculator to computer. I'm similarly conservative about adopting new tools and techniques within my home workshop, and with the clothes that I wear and the food that I eat. I have no explanation for my reticence to modernise. It is quite inconsistent with my passion for developing new technologies that has occupied most of my professional life.

Shortly after the commencement of our honours year, we Fourth Year students were informed that we were required to attend the regular progress meetings of the School of Physics. These progress meetings were held about once a month, in the evening. The purpose of the meetings was for staff in the School to tell each other, and I believe specifically to inform Harry Messel, about the status of their various research activities. The meetings always had a very specific format. Harry sat at one end of a long table, puffing his ever-present cigar. Next to Harry on either side of the table sat the Professors, then the Associate Professors, the Senior Lecturers, Lecturers, and finally the graduate students. We lowly honours students sat in a second row of seats around the outside of this central group. We were never told why we were required to be there, although it was very clear that we were to be seen, and not heard. I suspect that the intention was to have us benefit from watching great minds shape the future of science. In fact, the meetings were incredibly boring. I can honestly say that I do not remember a single thing from any of these progress meetings, except the following incident.

A report was being given on the new Stellar Intensity Interferometer that was under construction at Narrabri in central New South Wales by the Astrophysics Department under the leadership of Professor Robert Hanbury-Brown. My colleagues and I have different recollections about who actually gave this report. I seem to recall that it was a rather elderly gentleman called Henry Rathgeber, but others think differently. For the purposes of this story, however, I will assume that it was indeed Henry. This interferometer consisted of two large mirror assemblies that were mounted on carriages. These carriages could be moved around a circular railway track, perhaps 100 metres in diameter, which passed through a huge building, or shed. When the system was not in use, or to protect the mirrors from the elements, the carriages would be moved into the building. Henry's presentation was concerned with progress in the construction of this building, and he went on and on about the numerous details of the work. He talked about the foundations, the frames, the cladding, the weatherproofing, and the doors – I recall a very long discussion about the doors. In the context of typical presentations at progress meetings, there was nothing exceptional about this one. It was boring, and seemingly irrelevant, beyond belief. In this case, however, there was an important difference. As Henry went on, we honours students became aware that his diatribe was making even Harry a bit tense. You could tell when Harry was getting up-tight – he would sit extremely still, the end of his cigar would glow red more frequently than usual, and he would emit even more smoke than we normally had to endure. So picture, if you will, the scene, as we lowly honours students watched in sick fascination from the outer row of seats as this drama unfolded, with Henry droning on oblivious to the growing clouds of cigar smoke at the far end of the table. We wondered if it would ever end. However, Harry resolved it, and he did this in the incisive way for which we had grown to know him, and to love him. Henry was in the middle of some excruciatingly boring bit – a discussion, if I recall correctly, about the priming of the bolt holes for the roof bracing brackets – when Harry finally cracked. He took an exceptionally deep draw on his cigar. Its end glowed fiery red – so bright in fact, that the lights in the room seemed momentarily to dim. He emitted an enormous mushroom-shaped cloud of black, evil smelling cigar smoke. With one huge fist, he reached up and dragged the cigar from his mouth. The other fist crashed down on the table and he screamed, "JESUS CHRIST, HENRY! IT'S JUST A FUCKIN' SHED!"

At the time, Harry Messel was a very high profile person, receiving extensive media exposure. We saw and smelt quite a lot of him and his ever-present cigar around the School in the four years that I was there. However, he did not teach us any lecture courses. In fact, as an undergraduate student, I received only one lecture from Harry. This occurred without warning one day in my Second Year. Instead of our regular lecturer, Harry walked into the lecture theatre and proceeded to harangue us at high volume and speed on many matters. The principal subject of his talk, however, or at least the bit that stuck in my mind, was *Enthusiasm*, which he spoke about with his characteristic Canadian accent. His message was very simple, and was well illustrated by his actions. He held a small piece of chalk between two fingers, and said, "Students, if your *entooosiasm* is this big, this is how far you will go." He then spread his arms out wide, and continued, "But if your *entooosiasm* is *this* big ..." and on and on.

There is no doubt that my academic experiences at the University were pivotal in the subsequent development of my professional career. However important these experiences might have been, they pale into insignificance compared with those that affected my personal life. In my First Year at the University, I once again met Marilyn with whom I had unknowingly been in the same classes at infants' school, although our paths had crossed briefly at a high school dance the previous year. I liked what I saw, and went for it. To my astonishment, Marilyn reciprocated, and in modern-day parlance, we became an item. This book is not about that relationship, other than to say that several of the decisions that have been highly beneficial to my career were a direct result of it. In addition, she has given me wonderful support during our lives together. I have no doubt that I would not have achieved to anywhere near the same extent without her.

By the end of my Fourth Year, Marilyn and I had decided to get married. We were both very young, and we had virtually nothing behind us financially. In fact, I didn't even have a job. I was therefore highly motivated to get out of the University, to start building a career and to earn some money. The decision to leave University was made easier by the fact that I was not particularly attracted by any of the research being undertaken at the School of Physics at that time. To be perfectly honest about it, I believe that I was also feeling jaded by study, and perhaps even a little disenchanted with Physics, or at least the perceived irrelevance of Physics, as it had been taught to us at the University, to the solution of practical problems. Our course had not been characterised by many considerations that related the Physics that we learnt to the real world. As an example, I had been taught a great deal about electromagnetic theory, but I did not have the faintest idea how a loudspeaker worked. Unlike most of my fellow students, I was one of only two of the 1960 Physics honours class of 22 who did not go on directly to higher degree studies, or at least stay within the academic environment. In my own words of the time, I went to industry to "do something useful."

Wheels of Industry

By the time that I completed my undergraduate degree in Physics, I had very little experience in the workplace. In fact, apart from quite a lot of one-on-one coaching of Science and Maths to school students, my only significant gainful employment had been at the end of my Second Year, in an eleven-week vacation job at the CSR Research Laboratory at Pyrmont. I enjoyed this work, because it combined some innovative laboratory techniques with, for the time, quite sophisticated data analysis. The most interesting aspect of this job, however, was that I took part in the formal induction program at CSR for new employees. This involved tours of several of the company's manufacturing facilities in Sydney. It was a real eye opener for me to see commercial production machines in operation, and I was impressed by their sophistication, and what was achievable with good engineering.

Perhaps because of this lack of experience, I really did not know what I wanted to do at the end of my honours year except that I was determined to get out of the university environment. I had a strong desire to use some of the things that I knew to help solve real life, practical problems. I applied for a position at the BHP Research Laboratory at Newcastle, and travelled there one day for a job interview. I'm pretty sure that I did not impress them at all, however, because no offer was ever forthcoming. I think that I scuttled my chances when I became very excited after I saw a fully equipped darkroom in the laboratory, and said that I would find this an excellent place to pursue my personal photographic interests. I considered a career in business administration with Ford, and I believe that I would have been accepted there had I not lost interest. I also remember going for another job interview with a company, and blowing it completely. When I was asked why I was seeking to work for this organisation, I replied that I really wasn't sure what I wanted to do with my life, and that a job with them for a few years might help to clarify the matter for me. They responded that they were only interested in employing people who were prepared to make a career commitment to their organisation, and they struck me from their list of hopefuls.

As it happened, I obtained a job as an electronics design engineer at Amalgamated Wireless (Australasia) Limited. I started there in January 1961, working in the Distance Measuring Equipment Group at the Ashfield plant of the company. This group, under the direction of a very nice man called Brian Johnson, was designing a system that measured the distance of an aircraft from specific ground beacons. The system worked by sending a pulse of electromagnetic radiation from the aircraft, and measuring the time taken to receive a reply pulse from the ground beacon. My job was to design the pulse-forming network in the ground beacons. The project was a commercial success, and the system, including my pulse-forming network, was ultimately installed throughout Australia. As an aside, before I left AWA towards the end of the 1970s, the entire system had become obsolete and was scrapped. The significance of one's achievements in life often tends to be rather transitory.

I believe that I made quite a good impression when I first started at Ashfield. Despite my highly bull-at-a-gate approach to most things, I felt very unsure of myself within this complex technical and commercial environment. On my first day there, in response to a question about my experience, I remarked that I had an honours degree in Physics and therefore knew practically nothing about anything. Because they had recently had some unsatisfactory experiences with new graduates who believed that they knew everything, this turned out to be a very sensible thing to say. I remember recounting this story to an old family friend, and he wisely remarked, "Yes, Richard, it's very good to start out knowing nothing, but you shouldn't remain like that for too long."

It is impossible to guess where my life would have led if I had stayed at the Ashfield plant of AWA, but this did not happen. I only found out the full story some time later. It turned out that the company had just formed a research laboratory at its subsidiary, Amalgamated Wireless Valve Company Limited, which was located at Rydalmere, just east of Parramatta. This factory manufactured radio valves (electron tubes), power valves, television picture tubes and transistors. AWA had appointed Dr Lou Davies as its Chief Physicist to head the AWV Physical Laboratory. Lou later told me that the then Chairman of AWA, Sir Lionel Hooke, had said to him that he had established the Physical Laboratory because he "wanted to put something back" into the science on which the company's business was based. Lou was starting to build up the Lab and was looking for physicists to staff it. At that time and, indeed, for the next decade or so, it was extremely difficult to persuade physicists to work in Australian industry. Lou called Dr R E B Makinson, one of the Senior Lecturers in the School of Physics at the University of Sydney, and asked him if any of the 1960 graduating Physics class might be interested in working in industry. Makinson replied that the only member of the honours class who had expressed such an interest was Richard Collins, and he was working for AWA! A couple of phone calls later, and Lou was talking to Brian Johnson. I'm very grateful that Brian took the big picture, and was prepared to disrupt his own project in the best interests of one of his staff (a philosophy that I have also scrupulously applied throughout my entire career). He asked me if I would be interested in transferring to Rydalmere to work with Lou doing Physics, rather than continuing to do circuit design with him. I was immediately attracted by the idea. Lou then called me and we arranged to meet.

Lou was a giant of a man, in many ways. Physically, he was very tall – at 1.96 metres (6 feet 5 inches) he was even a few centimetres taller than me. I became aware of this when he collected me from home on the morning of our first meeting. He pulled up in a tiny (borrowed) car and proceeded to unfold from it like an enormous stick insect. As we travelled to Rydalmere together, I was amused to see that he had to hold the steering wheel between his knees. Lou was also far ahead of his time in his views about the relation between science and industry in Australia, and he had backed his opinions with action. In those days, he was one of the very few scientists, and the only physicist that I knew, who had left the secure employment of CSIRO to work in industry. Lou became my boss, my mentor, and my very good friend. He, more than any other person, helped to shape my views about the role of science in society.

This first day with Lou at Rydalmere was memorable for me, in many ways. He spent most of the time with me, and took me on an extensive tour of the factory and his then tiny Laboratory. He explained to me the research that he proposed to do, and how I might participate in it. About one o'clock, he took me up to lunch at the Senior Staff table in the Staff Dining Room. My Mother had provided me with sandwiches, and I dutifully took them with me. For some reason, she had chosen this day to use a particularly large loaf of heavy brown bread, cut into very thick slices. Years later, Lou used to laugh about his astonishment at the daunting pile of sandwiches that I placed in front of me at my job interview lunch. Being quite nervous, I had extreme difficulty in consuming this mountain of food. After lunch, Lou took me to meet the Factory Manager, Doug Sutherland. Doug was a kind and gentle man, and widely respected within AWA. A few years later, he too played an important part in the development of my career. Doug asked me why I wanted to work in the Physical Laboratory, rather than continue doing circuit design. I remember replying that I found research in Physics more attractive because it was "what I had been trained to do." I don't think that this was a very impressive response.

I got the job. We negotiated a transfer date from Ashfield to Rydalmere, and it turned out that I ended up spending a total of eleven weeks at Ashfield. As this was exactly the same period as my vacation job at CSR, I wondered for a while if I would ever hold down a job for longer than eleven weeks. Fortunately, I soon managed to overcome this hurdle, and I ended up spending a total of 17 years within the AWA organisation, including a period of nearly three years on leave of absence during which I studied overseas.

In hindsight, many of the things that I observed during my first few years at AWV were quite bizarre. As a young graduate in my first significant job, however, the strangeness of much of this was totally lost on me, and I regarded most of what I saw as normal. Only much later did it start to dawn on me that AWV was, in many ways, a very peculiar place. Even the use of the word *Valve* in the title of the company was a little odd, although this had its roots in the British tradition of the Australian electronics industry. The word arises because radio valves, as they are called, can be used to modulate (turn on and off, or alter) a flow of electrons, just as a liquid valve can vary the rate of flow of water. In the United States, the word is not used, and the devices that we manufactured are referred to as *electron tubes*. At AWV, the different sections were all named according to the types of valves that they made: radio valves (RV), kinescope valves or television picture tubes (KV), power valves (PV) and, curiously, transistors or semiconductor valves (SV)!

More seriously, there was a very strong culture of class distinction within the factory. I had my morning tea and lunch with several other engineers in the Staff Dining Room, and we were required to sit in specific seats. This prearranged seating meant that people always sat with others from the same area, effectively eliminating casual interactions that might have broadened the perspectives of the staff, or otherwise been beneficial to the work of the company. The Senior Staff of the Company, including Lou Davies, also ate in this room, but at separate tables from us. A few years later, the top management of the factory withdrew from this room to have lunch in a separate private dining room, with tablecloths. The production workers were relegated to a much poorer eating area without a ceiling in the body of the factory. The Staff Dining Room was also segregated on the basis of sex. Women were not allowed to eat there. The one female staff engineer who worked at AWV at that time had to eat her lunch out with the workers, rather than with her fellow male engineers. There were also at least four levels of male toilets in the factory. Starting from the bottom, the general toilets could be used by anyone, including production workers. Within these toilets were some cubicles with locks that could only be accessed by charge hands and supervisors that had been issued with appropriate keys. Near the Staff Dining Room was a Staff toilet that was out of bounds to the production workers. There was also at least one private toilet next to the General Manager's office that was so exclusive that even I never got to use it.

Within this culture of, in hindsight, shocking discrimination, Lou Davies stood out as a shining beacon of exception. From my first day with him, I saw that he treated everybody equally. He greeted both cleaner and General Manager with undiscriminating friendliness and courtesy as he passed them in the corridor, and he was always willing to stop and exchange a few words. The way in which he related to people greatly influenced my own attitudes and, at least in this, I modelled myself on him. I soon learnt that, in addition to being the right thing to do, there was much to be gained from behaving in this way. I discovered that the process workers were a veritable fund of knowledge and information. They were usually the first to recognise when the production process was going off the rails and, while they might not have understood the technicalities or been able to articulate the reasons, they often had an intuitive gut feeling for the nature of the problem. I also greatly enjoyed talking with them, perhaps swapping a joke or two, usually obscene, before getting down to my business. I learnt that workers in even the most menial jobs possessed unique skills that were often of a very high-level. There was always something that they could do that I could not. Apart from the many things that he taught me, Lou showed me that everybody is equal, and is entitled to be treated that way. Throughout my career, I have always tried to interact with people in this manner, and I have never asked anybody to do anything that I was not prepared to do myself.

Over the years, I have learnt that all places have their fair share of characters, and AWV was particularly well stocked in this regard. One of these was a wiry little plumber that I only ever knew by the name of Buggsy. On one occasion, Buggsy was working up a ladder brazing together a copper piping system. Upon completion of the job, he descended, and started to remove the ladder, only to discover that one of the new copper pipes passed directly between its rungs. Those were the days long before email, fax, and other modern means of mass communication. The bush telegraph within the factory was so efficient, however, that within a very few minutes a large and admiring crowd, representative of all levels within the factory from cleaner to General Manager, had gathered around and was offering Buggsy helpful advice about how he might resolve his dilemma. Buggsy was completely unconcerned by all this attention. I have a picture of him in my mind's eye, standing at the foot of the ladder facing the crowd with his arms folded saying, "Youse can all get fucked."

The technical officer in the Physical Laboratory was an extraordinary fellow called Bill. Bill was one of the most unforgettable people that I ever met, but I wish that I could. Bill's sole redeeming feature was that he was an excellent tradesman. In every other way, he was a complete misery to have around. He had a particularly foul mouth, and he used bad language in a completely undiscriminating way, and in any company. He drank to excess, smoked continuously, was always late to work, argued with his neighbours and recounted these arguments at great length to us, and he winged incessantly. Bill lived in a Housing Commission place "at Seven Bloody Hills", and seemed to be painting it perpetually. He never got to the end of this task, principally, I believe, because he was always knocking off in disgust at lunchtime each weekend to "go down to the bloody pub." He also ate very poorly which ultimately resulted in all of his teeth being removed, causing the quality of his diet to decline even further. In short, he was the greatest pessimist and misery-guts that I ever met – the epitome of P J Hartigan's Hanrahan (as in "We'll all be rooned," said Hanrahan). It was through Bill that I learnt one of the immutable truths about any job – there is always at least one aspect of it that you wish was different. Bill's approach to life was perhaps best illustrated by the time when we had an incredible run of wet weather. Every day, Bill would slink into work about 9.15am, dripping wet, with a damp smoldering cigarette hanging from the corner of his mouth, and would proceed to spend the next hour or so complaining about the weather and all that it had done to him. After a couple of weeks, this was starting to get me down. Then one day it dawned fine and clear, crisp and cool – the sort of day that makes you glad to be alive. I thought, "At last, Bill will have nothing to winge about today." How wrong I was. When he finally arrived, late as usual but for once not dripping wet, I greeted him cheerily: "Great day, Bill!"

He replied, "Yeah. Too fuckin' good to be in this bloody place."

Our lunches were a particularly enjoyable and entertaining part of each day. Apart from Bill who usually didn't say much because he was preoccupied gumming his vegetable pies, we had a very convivial group at my table, mostly drawn from engineers in the transistor manufacturing section next to our Lab. The conversations at our table ranged far and wide and were often spiced by the exploits of a lovable old guy called Bob Rose who seemed to have done everything in his life. Amongst other things, he had built a fairly large oceangoing motor cruiser and his stories invariably seemed to gravitate towards graphic descriptions of how sick his fellow workmates had become when he took them out on one of his many fishing expeditions. With Bob's roguish personality, and our youthful exuberance, we usually became quite boisterous during our lunches and played practical jokes on each other – simple things like setting fire to lunch papers and then extinguishing them in the teapot, or deliberately causing someone to miss with the teapot while they were pouring a second cup of tea. In fact, we made so much mess that the long-suffering waitress in the Staff Dining Room finally placed newspaper all over the table to absorb the slops. One of my best friends in our group was a young engineer called Phil Kreveld. Phil was a chubby little guy who giggled a lot. He always finished his lunch with a banana, which he peeled half way down and ate into the skin. It made very good sport to try and squash Phil's banana into his face as he was attempting to consume it. I can still see him, hunched up like a little monkey with his half-eaten banana in his hand, looking nervously from side to side, and trying to take a quick bite from it before the predictable shove that would splat the whole thing into his face. They were great times.

We went to lunch at 12 noon every day and returned an hour later. Lou would then leave for his lunch, because the entrenched discrimination practices of the plant required that the Senior Staff should eat at different times from lesser mortals. The time in the Lab from 1 to 2pm used to be particularly interesting because, as they say, *when the cat is out* ... Our cleaner, Milton, would come in and he and Bill would attempt to outdo each other recounting tales of their sexual exploits. Milton used to refer to himself as *the Rydalmere Hereford*. Once he told us that the doctor had advised him to ease up a bit, not because he was getting too much sex, but because he was likely to have an accident or catch pneumonia getting out of bed at 3 o'clock each morning and riding his bicycle home.

On one occasion, I had set up a piece of equipment in the laboratory to measure very small electric currents. The shielding of the detection circuitry was not perfect and, whenever anybody walked by, the reading on the output meter would fluctuate. This equipment was located on a bench against a translucent glass wall, on the other side of which was a corridor. It was a very hot, dry summer day, and I noticed to my surprise that the movement of the meter was usually greater when a woman walked along the corridor than when it was a man. I presume that this had something to do with static electricity on nylon underwear, but I never carried the investigation far enough to prove this thesis. When Milton came in that day for his regular sexual exploit recounting session, I showed him my little discovery. He was most impressed. "Richard," he said, "That's bloody amazing. All you've got to do is get it to tell the difference between blondes, brunettes and redheads, and you'll sell millions."

It was at AWV that I had my first brush with foreigners. Before you read one more word, let me assure you that what follows has nothing to do with racism or discrimination. I needed to get some equipment made, and was taken up to meet the man in charge of the workshop. I started to describe my needs to him and, before I had got too far, he said to me, "Is this a foreign order?" I had absolutely no idea what he meant. He spelt it out. "Is it for you personally?"

I was completely shocked, and said, "Of course not. How could you think such a thing?"

I soon found out how. Foreign orders, also known as FO's, or foreigners, pose a peculiar dilemma for all organisations. From time to time, most employees need to have something made that requires equipment that they do not have at home, but that is readily available in the organisation's workshop. For obvious reasons, only qualified tradesmen can use workshop equipment. In order to get something built there, it is thus necessary to utilise the firm's equipment, and the time of its employees. How far should this process go? My experience is that it is completely futile to try and ban foreign orders. On the other hand, they have to be kept to within reasonable limits. I have seen workshops where the motto might as well be: *Never let work interfere with the smooth flow of foreign orders.* Over the years, I have commissioned my fair share of foreign orders. However, this does not trouble me because I genuinely believe that I have given back service over and above the call of duty that justifies what might otherwise be regarded as little more than stealing. Treated in this way, I believe that foreign orders are useful in maintaining morale and providing small perks to employees, particularly those that would not normally have access to such things during their work.

I loved visiting the workshop at AWV. The tradesmen there knew so much that I did not. I found out that they liked telling me about their machines, and describing the things that they could do with them. Although I consider myself to be a quite competent woodworker, I have done very little work with metal over the years. In fact, it is only since my retirement that I have actually operated a metal turning lathe myself. However, I came to understand in some detail what metalworking machines could do, how different machining operations were performed, and the capabilities and limitations in this important area of technology. I also found that many tradesmen were highly skilled in design matters, and could often suggest ways of constructing equipment that were better than I had thought of myself.

Despite the many quirky aspects of the Rydalmere plant, most of its production operations ran very smoothly. There were several reasons for this. In general, the engineers were dedicated to their jobs and very knowledgeable about the technical aspects of their product. I found it very interesting to talk with people who understood in practical terms many of the theoretical Physics concepts that I had learnt during my undergraduate studies. Another reason that things ran well was that, with few exceptions, the technology was quite old. Many of the people working in the different manufacturing sections had been around for some decades, so there had been plenty of time to iron out most of the production bugs. Moreover, some of the equipment was positively archaic. For example, in the grid winding part of the Radio Valve section, the *new* winding machines were the ones that had been installed *just after* the Second World War! At the time, I saw this failure to modernise as a little strange, but not, as it later transpired, the early signs of a company in its death throes.

There were some areas of my work in which I did particularly well. In the research that Lou had given me, I made extensive use of vacuum technology. I read widely on this subject, both from textbooks and, very beneficially, from manufacturers' catalogues. I also talked extensively to the many people in the factory who knew about such matters. It became known around the place that I was quite knowledgeable in this area, and I was often asked for advice.

I found that I really liked working with people in the production areas, and helping them solve their problems. While I recognised that deviating from my main job to provide this assistance would inevitably slow down my own work, no one ever seemed to object. Lou Davies, in particular, was always very supportive of me involving myself more widely within the company in this way. Although I do not remember discussing it with him, I'm sure that Lou understood the beneficial implications of the general support for the Physical Laboratory from people whom we had helped in other parts of the company. I am certain, however, that this was not my motivation for being interested in the problems of other people. It gave me a kick to see a tangible, practical and beneficial outcome from something that I had done.

I discovered that I had a talent for designing innovative ways of performing an experiment, or of making a measurement. When I look back over my career, I find it dotted with the creation of several such new methods or techniques which, in themselves, do not constitute new Physics, but which have been quite useful in generating scientific advances. As an example, I was performing some experiments on electron emission from thin film devices that we called tunnel cathodes. The electron emission data that I obtained were quite different from what we had expected, and I proposed a reason for this. I discussed my ideas with Lou and, while he could see what I was getting at, he could offer little guidance about showing whether I was correct or not. I then independently built an analogue simulation system that enabled me to demonstrate conclusively that my thoughts were, indeed, correct. This ultimately led to an innovative design configuration for the tunnel cathodes that we used in all our subsequent work. Lou was most impressed when he saw my simulation and asked me to go and talk to Doug Sutherland about it. (As I went to see him, I had a feeling of *déjà vu* because of my experience at high school taking my Cartesian Diver up to *The Boss*.) It turned out that Lou had discussed the problem with Doug who, being a bit of a buff on electron optics, had then been trying to solve it theoretically. When I showed him my results, he smiled to himself, ripped up the paper that he had been working on, and patted me on the back. A couple of years after this, Doug did something for me that was most helpful in the development of my career. I am sure that this little interaction was highly influential in causing him to support me in this way.

More than anything else, I benefited from my first few years at AWA/AWV because of the things that I learnt. When I joined the company, I felt that I had a pretty good base of knowledge in Physics and Maths. I recognised, however, that I was quite deficient in what I knew about practical things. I am absolutely certain that I learnt far more of relevance to my professional career in my first few years in industry than in my entire previous life. AWV was a particularly good place to learn about many different technologies. The electron tube and transistor manufacturing operations utilised an enormous range of techniques and equipment, many of which had quite a strong base in Physics. In later years when working in universities both in Australia and overseas, I often utilised specific knowledge and experience that I had obtained during my time in this fascinating environment.

As well as learning lots of facts, I also gained a much better understanding about interacting productively with people, including how to get them to do things for me, and to tell me what they knew. Most importantly, I learnt to understand and respect their point of view. The importance of this last matter became obvious to me near the beginning of my time with the AWA organisation, soon after I moved from Ashfield to Rydalmere. The engineers at Ashfield used transistors that were made at Rydalmere. Before I heft Ashfield, I had been struck with how critical they were about the quality of these transistors, and the incompetence of the people who had made them: "Those bastards at Rydalmere don't know the first thing about making transistors." When I got to Rydalmere, I discovered that identical attitudes existed there towards the people at Ashfield who used the product that they made: "Those idiots at Ashfield wouldn't know how to plug a transistor into a socket."

This denigration of others working within the same company astonished and disappointed me. Having worked closely with people from each group and knowing them all quite well, I had formed a healthy respect for their ability. I quickly realised that these attitudes arose mostly out of ignorance. I have observed that, in general, few people ever bother to try and learn about the constraints under which others work, that might cause them to behave in an apparently illogical or incomprehensible way. If someone is not prepared to take the trouble to understand another person's position, they will often then defend their own, vociferously, and without giving ground. I have always attempted to see a problem from everyone's perspective and to seek a compromise solution that not only is compatible with where others are coming from, but also gives consideration to their feelings and integrity. In short, I learnt to be tolerant.

Of great significance to my future career, my time working with Lou Davies taught me how to manage myself. Working for a boss requires one to be responsible and accountable. It is necessary to deliver things on time, and to the boss' satisfaction. The experience I gained in this regard was immensely useful during my subsequent graduate studies, because I was more able than most of my fellow graduate students to set priorities, organise my time, and deal with the often extraordinary workloads without succumbing to pressure. Although I did not specifically plan my career with this in mind, I know that my graduate studies were far more productive, and my participation in them much more effective, than otherwise would have been the case because of the time that I had spent outside the university environment since my first degree. I would commend this strategy to any young student contemplating higher degree studies.

During my early time at AWA, I had my first real venture into public speaking. The occasion was the 1963 Convention of the Australian Institution of Radio and Electronic Engineers, held in Melbourne. Lou decided that it would be a good idea if I gave a paper on my research, so I duly prepared one. I can still recall Lou's comments on my first handwritten draft. As if in anticipation of what I did many years later to the writing of my own students, it came back to me covered with red ink. Of particular significance was Lou's correction of the large number of split infinitives that I had put into the draft. Elimination of split infinitives became something of a *cause célèbre* for me over the years. The talk in Melbourne was to be my first public presentation of a scientific paper, and I had no experience in such matters. As part of the preparation, I gave a dry run of the talk in front of some of my colleagues at AWV. I particularly remember the penetrating questions that were asked at the completion of the talk by a new graduate engineer in the factory, David Money. David comes back into this story several times later on. The most important part of my preparation, however, was at home, where Marilyn insisted that I present the paper to her. We did this with her sitting up in bed, and me standing at the end of it. It was one of the most difficult things that I have ever done in my life. Apart from everything else, she was highly critical of many aspects of my presentation style, which she ripped to shreds. Although this was quite damaging to my ego, I was smart enough to realise that, as a trained teacher, she knew much more about public presentation that I did, and I took notice of what she said. In a very real sense, she taught me the art of public speaking. At the conference, my presentation went well, even though I found it quite distracting when a member of the audience in the front row fell asleep.

Of the many things that I learnt at AWV, the most important was that I came to understand how little I knew. I realised, of course, that I could never master all the technical information in any discipline or subject, but my appreciation of my ignorance became very acute. Moreover, I realised that I was completely dependent on Lou for guidance, and had a long way to go before I could work as an independent researcher capable of generating new ideas. In fact, I remember thinking that, if Lou left the company, I would not know what to do. I had formed the view that I could well spend my life doing research in Physics. I had come to love the combination of using hard facts and data, with the lateral thinking and speculation that goes with discovering why a particular system behaves in a seemingly illogical way. It is very much like detective work, spiced by the knowledge that, above everything else, the laws of Physics apply and ultimately there is always a logical explanation. Because I believed that my formal scientific training and experience in this area was inadequate in order to do such work well, I started to think about undertaking postgraduate study.

I was greatly influenced by a colleague who had recently completed his Ph.D. in the United States, and accepted his arguments about the benefits of undertaking more formal coursework, in addition to a research project, as part of my Ph.D. studies. At the time, it was only in the United States and Canada that such postgraduate coursework was offered in Physics, so it was there that I set my sights. By this time, Marilyn and I were married, we had bought a of block land, had built enough of our first house to live in, and Marilyn was pregnant. In short, we were exquisitely happy. It was therefore not a simple decision to leave all of this, to go to the other side of the world to live, and to drop our lifestyle back to that of a graduate student. For obvious reasons, our parents were not at all pleased about what I was proposing, particularly as the new baby was to be the first grandchild on both sides of the family. Also Marilyn could see much more clearly than me that going back to study would result in very substantial stresses for both of us, and that the whole thing would not be a picnic. Even though I was keen to undertake a Ph.D. in this way, thinking about it made me feel sick in the stomach.

I received several offers of Graduate Assistantships to undertake a Ph.D. in the United States, but none of these would have been sufficient to support Marilyn and our baby daughter Kathryn. Because of my visa status, Marilyn would not have been permitted to work there, whether she wanted to or not. In any case, having a young child to care for would have ruled out the possibility of any significant work for her during my time as a graduate student. It was through my colleague that I received an offer of a half-time Instructorship in the Department of Physics at New York University that paid enough to justify the issuing of an Exchange Visitor visa to me. The United States system works on personal contacts, and they were prepared to take me on in this capacity, sight unseen, on the basis of the recommendation of somebody that they knew. I put in my resignation to the company, proceeded to finalise my work there, and to organise our travel to New York. This turned out to be quite difficult, because we did not even have the money for the airfares. Then one of those things happened that warmed my heart, and changed my life. Apparently Lou Davies talked to Doug Sutherland, and said how sorry he was that I would leave the company shortly. Doug suggested to him that I might be prepared to enter into an agreement to return to the company after my Ph.D. studies if they paid the airfares of my family and myself to and from New York. Lou obtained approval to do this and I received such an offer. It was like manna from heaven, not only because it solved the problem of how to fund the travel, but it also provided me with employment at the completion of my Ph.D. So it was that in August 1965, I went on leave of absence from AWA to become a student again.

Back to School

The period leading up to our departure from Australia was frenetic and stressful. We had to pack up all our belongings and store them. We rented our house, and this was quite painful to do, as we had been in it for just over a year and we had enjoyed the luxury of living in our own place and starting a garden. We had also formed very close friendships with several of our neighbours. We came right down to the wire getting everything finished in time. The evening preceding our departure, we were up until midnight packing, and woke again at the crack of dawn on the big day finalising things. We left late in the afternoon of 28 August 1965, and drove to the airport in our Holden utility, dropping off furniture at both of our parents' places on the way. At the airport, I handed the keys of our vehicle to friends who sold it for us. (For several months before our departure, the battery in this vehicle had been on the way out, and I had nursed it through by charging it every night. The first thing that our friends did before attempting to sell it was to replace the battery! When I learnt this, I resolved never to muck around with an unreliable car battery again, and I haven't.) Both of our parents were there to see us off, as was Lou Davies, and our departure was a most emotional affair. Marilyn's Mother has often told me how dreadful she felt as she watched our plane fly away, taking with it her daughter and her only grandchild, with no certainty about when she might see them again. My recollection is that Marilyn and I were almost too exhausted to care.

Our trip to New York was exciting. It was the first experience for both of us travelling outside Australia, so everything was very new. We stopped briefly at Fiji, and then at Honolulu for two nights, staying at a hotel at Waikiki Beach. The first thing that I did in the United States was to block the toilet in our hotel room with one of Kathryn's disposable nappies.

Staying in Honolulu was great fun. We took a tour around the island, visited Sea Life Park, and swam in the tepid water at Waikiki Beach. After two days, we flew on to San Francisco, and then caught an overnight flight to New York. We were totally exhausted by the time that we got there. My supervisor, Professor

Ben Bederson, had arranged for us to be met at the airport, and we were driven to the apartment that they had rented on our behalf. We thought that New York City looked ugly and forbidding – not at all as we had naively expected. The secretary in Ben's department, Shirley Mallies and her husband Michael, were there to welcome us. I had arranged a bank transfer to New York to give us some money to live on before my salary started to come in. Shirley took me to the bank, only to discover that they couldn't find these funds. (They resurfaced several weeks later.) She was wonderful, and quickly arranged an advance on my salary so that we wouldn't starve. After I returned to the apartment, the significance of what we had done started to hit us. The place could have been worse, but compared with what we had left behind in Australia, it was just awful. Marilyn was in tears. We lay down and slept from exhaustion, to be wakened at noon by an air raid siren going off just outside our place. It was the middle of the cold war period, and we knew that there were sirens in United States cities to warn of an impending nuclear attack by Russia. We were so tired and upset that we decided to stay on the bed and die. We soon learnt that the siren regularly went off at noon as a test. Later that day, we met our neighbours upstairs, Mary and Charlie Brauchle, and their daughter Joan, and also our landlord, George Silage. They were friendly, and did their best to make us feel welcome. We had some dinner out of a tin, and then packed away a few clothes before finally getting to bed about midnight. However, Kathryn's time clock was completely inverted, and she cried for a few more hours. I think that we both remember the day of our arrival in New York as the worst of our lives.

The furnished apartment that we had rented was right on the edge of the Bronx, a few miles north of the tip of Manhattan Island. It was part of an old family house that had been divided into four units. George Silage lived on the same level as us, and the Brauchle family was upstairs. Below us was a very old Hungarian lady called Mrs Keller. The house backed onto a high hill, at the top of which was a very nice residential area called Riverdale. This hill was covered in trees that gave us a lot of greenery during the summer. The street in which we lived, Irwin Avenue, also had many nice trees along it that again softened the outlook from our apartment in summer, but exposed the stark ugliness of the Bronx in winter. The property actually had small lawns at the back and front, and there were some shrubs in the garden. George Silage used to refer to the place as his "estate", and he was completely unable to comprehend that we could have lived in a nicer place in Australia. There were two large supermarkets, and quite a few other shops, about ten minutes level walk from our house. The 238th Street station of the IRT subway was a short five-minute walk away. The University Heights uptown campus of New York University where I worked was about fifteen minutes from the subway station by bus. Despite our appallingly bad first impressions, we were exceedingly fortunate to have found such an apartment within the concrete jungle of New York.

Mary Brauchle took us under her wing, and gave Marilyn a lot of help in setting up our home, and finding her way around. We needed a washing machine urgently, and Mary knew that the lady across the road, Gertie, had an old one in her garage. Mary put in a word to Gertie about how poor we were, and she sold it to us for $15. We became quite attached to this washing machine. It was old fashioned, but it served our needs very well. We used to fill it manually by connecting long hoses to the taps in the kitchen sink. More than once, we forgot that the taps were on, and flooded Mrs Keller below, but she never complained. Marilyn dried the clothes on an outside line, even in the winter when they froze solid there, and she then thawed them out in our heated apartment. George was in the sewing machine repair business, and he obtained for Marilyn a very simple straight sewing machine for $10 with which she made some lovely clothes for Kathryn and herself. We only had the things in the suitcases that we had brought with us on the plane. We were therefore very limited until the arrival six weeks later of a large box containing clothes and baby stuff, including Kathryn's stroller, which we had sent off by ship before our departure from Australia. We bought a secondhand cot for Kathryn, and I painted it yellow and white. Marilyn decorated it with teddy bear transfers on the ends, and we were very proud of it.

Ben Bederson was very good in allowing me a couple of weeks to settle in to our house, but inevitably I had to start my consuming graduate studies. Right from the beginning, I developed a great liking and respect for Ben. Although he had done a lot of work to get me to NYU, he knew that my past research interests centred around solid-state physics, rather than his field, atomic physics. He therefore gave me the opportunity to work with someone else in the Physics Department whose research interests were much closer to my background. I declined this generous offer, because I had already formed the view that Ben was a very good scientist who looked after his students well, and was a person from whom I would learn a great deal. This indeed turned out to be the case. Over the years, my consistent advice to students contemplating graduate study has been to consider mainly the person with whom they will work, rather than the science that they will do.

Ben Bederson ran a very dynamic and successful research laboratory containing several large and complex pieces of equipment for performing experiments on individual atoms. Ben had quite a few graduate students who, by and large, were responsible for running the experiments and getting the data. I quickly got to know them quite well. I shared an apparatus, day-on and day-off, with Marvin Goldstein. This apparatus had been designed by one of Ben's former graduate students, Ken Rubin, who was also my co-supervisor. Ken was by then an academic at the City College of New York, and used to come and talk to us once or twice a week. This equipment had been in existence for over five years, but it had not generated a single scientific paper. I soon found out why.

The first time that I ate lunch with my new graduate student colleagues, I made one of those classic mistakes by an ignorant Australian in the United States environment. Most of the offerings in the University cafeteria were unfamiliar to me, but the tuna fish sandwich seemed to pose no hazards. Because I always had two sandwiches for my lunch in Australia, I naturally asked for two there. I did not realise that sandwiches in the US are not only very large in themselves, but they also come with substantial additional material – pickles, crisps, cole slaw and so on. It was just like my first lunch at AWV all over again. The other graduate students looked on in amazement as I placed these two mountains of food in front of me, and I felt really embarrassed about my blunder. However, I could not let Australia down, and I somehow managed to stuff it all in. I never made the same mistake again, however.

Our living conditions were such that we decided that the best thing would be for me to work as hard as I could so that we could get back to Australia as soon as possible. I gave myself the goal of getting out in three years – this was very ambitious, because in those days the normal time for a Ph.D. degree in Physics at NYU was five years. As soon as I started, I realised that I had set myself an enormous task. My work was divided into essentially three parts: formal coursework and the associated exams that went with them, my research project that would form the basis of the thesis that I would write, and the quite heavy teaching load of my half-time Instructorship position. As soon as I started, I also became aware of the challenge and significance of the so-called Preliminary Examinations. The Prelims, as they were known, were regarded as the biggest hurdle to overcome in order to get a Ph.D. degree. In the Physics Department at NYU, they consisted of three written papers, each five hours in length, covering a wide range of topics in Physics. Candidates who did sufficiently well in these papers were then given an oral examination that could deal with any aspect of Physics. Only about half of the students who attempted the Prelims passed in any given year. You only had two shots at them – if you failed the second time, you were out.

In the normal progression through a Ph.D. program in Physics at NYU, students would complete two years of graduate courses before sitting for the Prelims. All of the other students in Ben's lab were at least one year into their courses, so they planned to take the Prelims a year after I started. I had my honours year at the University of Sydney behind me, so Ben suggested that I should set myself the goal of doing these exams at the same time. In fact, I requested some credit for my honours work towards my overall Ph.D. course requirement, but this was refused, causing me some difficulty very late in my time at NYU. I selected a set of courses that were appropriate to my background, and relevant to the topics that would be addressed in the Prelims. I was only permitted to enrol in three courses, and this did not provide me with sufficient coverage for the Prelims. I therefore sat in on two other courses as well. Even with this extra course load, there was still one gaping hole in my preparation, so I studied this independently later on.

Although it had been nearly five years since I had sat for an exam, I had not anticipated problems in this area. I was therefore absolutely shattered when I did the first mid-term examination in one of my courses. I was unable to think clearly during the exam, and I was certain that I had failed it. As it turned out, I received an average sort of pass. The experience shook me up, however, and I worked very hard to relearn the examination technique that had stood me in good stead throughout my school and undergraduate studies.

The people in charge of the teaching program at NYU were very understanding about my lack of teaching experience, and eased me gently into the task. In the first semester that I was there, I only had recitations (tutorials) and laboratory classes, although I was also asked to do a few substitute lectures. There were two obvious reasons for this. Firstly, they wanted to see how I performed, and whether they had a lemon on their hands. Secondly, it gave me a chance to become more familiar with the material before actually having to stand up and lecture on it. For the rest of my subsequent teaching there, I was given specific courses of my own, with full responsibility for lecturing, recitations, and the exam, including setting and marking it. The structure of the courses at NYU was ideal for this purpose. Physics 1 was taught in First Semester, and Physics 2 in Second Semester, and the classes in these subjects were quite large. However, there were always some students who, for one reason or another, wanted to do the out-of-sequence course – they may have failed, or they could have come from another university. I was given the responsibility for teaching these students. It was an absolutely wonderful, and formative experience for me. These classes were quite small, usually no more than thirty or so, and I often got to know many of the students quite well. I also had to teach the full range of elementary Physics topics, and I therefore quickly got on top of many of the things that I had not understood fully when I left the University of Sydney. The fact I had to understand Physics well enough to teach it was also enormously beneficial to me in my preparation for the Prelims, and has stood me in good stead throughout the rest of my professional career.

The laboratory classes that I taught in my first semester at NYU were scheduled from 5pm to 9pm – hardly a user-friendly time, but I was at the bottom of the pecking order of the teaching staff at that time. A particularly intriguing thing happened during the class on the evening of 9 November 1965. The students were performing an experiment in which they investigated the period of oscillation of a pendulum as a function of its length. They did this by measuring the time taken for pendulums of different length to complete about 50 oscillations, and dividing to get the period of one oscillation for each case. Early in this class, one of the students said to me that he had lengthened his pendulum, but it was oscillating more quickly. Of course, the opposite should have happened, so I suggested that he had counted incorrectly, and told him to repeat the measurement. Just after this exchange, the lights went out. It was the great blackout that caused power to fail over 80,000 square miles of the eastern United States. I dismissed the class and managed to catch a bus home. There was a high level of concern amongst the locals, because this was not something that they had ever experienced before. Many believed that, at last, the Russians were coming. The power did not come on again in our apartment until about 4 o'clock the next morning.

Some time later, I recalled my interaction with the student and realised that I might unknowingly have been one of the first people in New York to see the blackout coming. This is what I think was happening. The student was measuring the period of the pendulum with a mains-operated electric clock that depended for its timing on the frequency of the alternating voltage. Just before the actual blackout, the electricity generators in the system had been under rapidly increasing load, and it seems reasonable to assume that they had therefore been slowing down, causing the mains frequency to decrease. (After extensive searching of the Web, I was able to locate only one reference to the fact that the mains frequency was decreasing as the blackout spread. I found this in a history of the Gas and Electric Department in Holyoke, Massachusetts. The document records that the operator on duty at the power station on that afternoon observed unusual variations in the mains frequency. He correctly attributed this to problems with the supply of power feeding into the town along the tie line from the New England distribution system, so he started the town's emergency generator. When he saw that the outside power was "pulling the frequency down", he cut the incoming feeder line, and averted the power failure in this local community. It seems that Holyoke was one of only two towns over the huge affected area that avoided the blackout. There must be many great stories about this blackout. For example, it is said that an abnormally large number of births occurred nine months later!) But I digress. A decreasing mains frequency would have caused my student's clock to run slow, so that less time elapsed *on his clock* during the 50 oscillations. His measurement of the period of the pendulum would therefore have been less than it should have been, so the pendulum would have seemed to be oscillating more rapidly. As I have often said over the years, in Physics there is always a logical explanation, no matter how improbable! Of course there is another much simpler explanation – that it was just one of those extraordinary coincidences – but I like my more complicated version better.

Ben defined my research topic as soon as I arrived at NYU – for the record, it was to measure the differential spin exchange scattering cross-section of electrons off potassium atoms. The experiments were performed in a large and complex apparatus that consisted of three interconnected high-vacuum chambers, each having its own separate pumping system. In this apparatus, a beam of potassium atoms was produced by vaporising metallic potassium in a hot oven located in the first vacuum chamber. The beam passed through a strong non-uniform magnetic field that selected atoms having one particular spin state. The spin-selected atoms entered the second vacuum chamber that contained an electron gun, and the actual scattering events took place in this chamber. The scattered potassium atoms were then analyzed for their spin state in a second magnet that combined both non-uniform electric and magnetic fields. Finally, the scattered atoms were detected in the third chamber by ionising them (removing an electron) on a hot platinum wire, and detecting the charged potassium ions with an electron multiplier. The parts of the system that produced the beam of atoms, or performed the spin analysis and detection, could be translated laterally by moving the relevant components, enabling the spatial distribution of the spin-analysed scattered atoms to be measured. The entire experimental concept was extraordinarily bold, and the equipment itself was complex and sophisticated. The actual detailed design and construction of the apparatus left much to be desired, however. For example, the systems that defined the positions of the various components were poorly designed, and we had to put lead bricks onto several parts in order to avoid backlash when they were traversed in different directions. This introduced uncertainties into our data, and made the interpretation difficult. In addition, some of the welding on the stainless steel vacuum components had been badly done, and this caused intermittent leaks and consequential poor vacuum for much of the time that I was there.

In order for the apparatus to work, it was necessary for the beam of potassium atoms to pass through several slits on its way from the oven to the detector. These slits were quite narrow, and their alignment was therefore critical. By making small adjustments to the position of each slit, the magnitude of the beam reaching the detector could be maximised – an essential requirement, because we were always fighting to have enough signal. However, if only one slit had been accidentally misaligned so that no beam reached the detector, and you did not know which slit to adjust in order to get the beam back, the equipment was essentially useless. Soon after I started work on the apparatus, precisely this happened, and the beam was lost. We worked for weeks trying get the beam back, without success. Ben eventually concluded that the only thing that we could do was to dismantle the apparatus in its entirety, and then reassemble the various components, stage by stage, adjusting the position of each slit after it had been put in place. This would have been a major undertaking, requiring a huge amount of work. Just before we were to start this, I had the opportunity to work for one afternoon on the apparatus, for the first time by myself. At my own initiative, I obtained a long straight steel bar from the workshop, and mounted it on the apparatus parallel to the path of the beam, and just outside the vacuum chambers. I then went through the drawings of the different pieces of equipment, read off the distances of each internal slit from the outside surface of the relevant piece and, by measuring from my straight steel bar, I then repositioned each slit into what I hoped would be a straight line. This process took several hours to complete. I then heated up the potassium oven and discovered to my great joy and amazement that a barely-detectable beam of potassium atoms was coming through all of the slits, and reaching the detector. From then on it was simple and I systematically adjusted the position of each slit sequentially to re-establish the beam at its normal level. Both Ben and Ken Rubin were very impressed, so I certainly started off my work in the laboratory on the right foot.

One of the greatest assets in the atomic beam laboratory was our technical officer, John DeSantis. John was a tremendously capable guy who was very widely experienced in electrical, electronic and mechanical techniques, and he had an intrinsic ability to get things done. John and I got on extremely well and, judging by the level of the insults that we continually directed at each other, there was a lot of mutual respect between us. One day, John came into my part of the lab chuckling to himself, and showed me a letter that he had just received from a company. It read like this:

> Dear Mr DeSantis
> The order that you have placed with us is so small that it would cost us money to process it. We are therefore mailing to you as a gift the things that you want, with our best wishes for success in your ongoing research work.
> In the future, all that we ask is that you spell the name of our company correctly.

John had this letter framed, and it hung on the wall above his desk.

As my first year at NYU progressed, the mountain of tasks that I had to complete in order to get my Ph.D. seemed to get bigger and bigger. There was a requirement to pass a specific number of graduate courses and, with the refusal to allow me credit for my honours courses in Australia, I simply could not see how I could achieve that number in the three-year target period that I had set myself. The experiment seemed to have a negative soul, and was always developing vacuum leaks, electronic failures, or otherwise breaking down. In addition, the noise level in the detector was so high that the quality of the data was quite poor, even with long measurement times. My teaching load was large, and there was no prospect of reducing it. At home, life in our apartment was difficult because of our very constrained finances and also due to tensions associated with living next to our landlord. In addition, Marilyn had been very unwell with severe abdominal pains, and had nearly been put in hospital. She only avoided this because she was still feeding Kathryn, and the doctor who attended her at home was very keen on breast-feeding – a rarity in the United States. It is also relevant to recall that Marilyn and I were both quite homesick. We regularly wrote home, and received letters back from our parents and many others. However, due to the cost, we did not make a single telephone call to Australia in all the time that we were in New York. We had very few friends in those early days, and little support base, so we were essentially dependent on each other for almost everything. In the middle of all this, I learnt that I had to pass quite searching examinations in two languages before I would be permitted to graduate. (Later on, this requirement was reduced to one language, which was a real bonus for me, because I had only studied French at school.) Then there were the looming Prelims. As a result of the stresses associated with all of these things, my health began to suffer. I came out in a most dreadful, itchy rash all over my body. The doctor at the student health service looked me over and then said, "Hmm. I don't think that it's syphilis. Have you had any extramarital sexual encounters lately?"

I vigorously responded in the negative. He gave me some cream that eased the itch, and the rash eventually went away. In my highly stressed state, my experience in industry was enormously beneficial to me. I remember likening the task before me to walking towards a mountain that, from a distance, looks too steep to climb. When you get closer, however, it tends to flatten out a lot. I organised my work into priorities, and concentrated solely on the urgent things. I specifically adopted the strategy, that I have subsequently used time and again over the years, of shutting from my mind things that I could not address right now. Step-by-step, task-by-task, I set out to climb the mountain.

There were also some very positive experiences in all of this. I did very well in the courses that I took during the first two semesters of my studies, receiving straight A's for them. The following year, I took an evening Plasma Physics course that was taught by Ben Bederson. This was a really outstanding set of lectures. Ben presented virtually all of the material in two ways. Firstly, he derived the various results conventionally from the appropriate equations with approximations where needed. After each derivation, he would then say something like, "Now let's imagine what an electron would see in this situation." He then developed physically insightful arguments that led to the same functional relationships between the various parameters that he had obtained from the more conventional approach. In short, he taught us about the Physics of the problems. Throughout my career, I have found this a very insightful and productive way of thinking.

During one of these evening lectures, Ben reached a point in a derivation where he needed to sum a series. He got stuck there, and could not see how to do it. I put up my hand and said, "I can sum that series for you." He handed me the chalk, and I proceeded to pull out one of the tricks that I remembered from my Mathematics classes at high school. When I had finished, I handed the chalk back to Ben, and sat down. He didn't say anything, but I firmly believe that this exchange considerably shortened the period of my Ph.D. studies.

With all of the University pressures on top of me, there was a strong temptation to give my work there too much time, and to ignore my family at home. I tried very hard not to do this, but inevitably it occurred far too frequently. With Kathryn starting to run around, it was difficult to find a quiet environment in which to study at home. Moreover my teaching and coursework often did not finish until 9pm, and she was usually in bed by the time that I came home. I developed the habit of waking very early in the morning and working solidly until around 8am when Kathryn and Marilyn would surface. Although I had never been able to do this as an undergraduate student, I found that I could now work very efficiently at this time. Throughout the rest of my career, and even in my retirement, I have continued the habit of getting up early and working for a couple of hours when everything is quiet.

As I have said, the apartment in which we lived fell far short of what we had been used to in Australia, but it could have been worse. The front room, in particular, was beautifully sunny in the morning, and had quite a nice outlook onto trees. Except during the winter months, Marilyn could take Kathryn outside to play. Kathryn was, in fact, a real icebreaker. She was an absolutely gorgeous child, and people were naturally attracted to her. The old lady downstairs, Mrs Keller, had very little English, but used to come out whenever Kathryn was playing nearby and make loving noises, like, "Oh, the doll! The beautiful doll!" Even our landlord George and his new wife Vicki loved her, and used to fill her hands with biscuits at every possible opportunity – something that Marilyn found quite hard to take.

Mary and Charlie Brauchle who lived upstairs were also very fond of Kathryn, and she loved visiting them. They had a huge black poodle named Maggie that had extremely bad breath, and her mouth was almost exactly level with Kathryn's face. Marilyn hated it when Maggie licked Kathryn, but Mary, who had grown up on a farm in Ireland, sought to dismiss her concerns. "Don't worry about it," she would say. "There are no germs in a dog's mouth." Mary had some very odd views about many things. Having said this, however, the Brauchles were really wonderful to us. Mary was incredibly well meaning and kind, and asked us up for Thanksgiving dinner and other similar celebrations. Their daughter Joan was about the same age as Marilyn, and the two of them got on very well together. We were very lucky to have such warmhearted and generous people living nearby. It was particularly fortunate that we could leave Kathryn with Mary on the rare occasions that we needed to, knowing that she would be in good hands and looked after well, even if she was full of cookies when we got her back.

Our apartment was incredibly dirty. Apart from the normal New York filth, the family next door had a coal-fired furnace, and it was impossible to stop the fine black dust that it produced from coating everything. After we had been in the apartment for a year or so, we rented a carpet-shampooing machine, and were astonished to discover a floral pattern on the lounge room rug. It disappeared again a few weeks later, however. The apartment itself was infested with roaches – New York bugs, as we called them. They lived everywhere, particularly in the gas oven. Whenever Marilyn lit it, they would come pouring out and disappear down cracks around the wall. If you switched on the kitchen light in the middle of the night, the floor would be covered with hundreds of these roaches that would scuttle for cover. I can still remember the night that I went to the bathroom for a drink of water, and the horror when I realised that I had a roach running around inside my mouth. Ever since, without fail, I rinse my cup before taking a drink in the dark, and I suspect that I will do this for the rest of my life. We also caught the occasional mouse and rat in our apartment, much to George's disbelief. I imagine that he thought that we had planted them there!

Soon after we reached New York, I discovered that I simply could not live in an apartment without some basic tools. I therefore visited the local hardware store, and purchased a screwdriver and a pair of bull-nosed pliers – enough to enable me to perform simple maintenance jobs around the place. This was the same store from which I had bought the paint for Kathryn's cot. At that time, I must have told the fellow there that we were from out of town. When I went back to get the tools, he looked me over and said, "I remember you. You're the guy from New Zealand."

"Almost," I said. "Actually I come from Australia."

"Of course," he said, "Australia. What a good memory you've got."

Just near the hardware store was a shop that did shoe repairs. It was cheaper to have my shoes resoled than to buy new ones, so I took them there to be done. The bloke in the shop told me to come back in a couple of days, but he did not give me a docket for the shoes. When I came to get them, he looked at me, walked over to a veritable mountain of shoes awaiting collection and correctly selected mine.

"That's amazing," I said. "How did you do that?"

He replied, "I never forget a pair of shoes." In New York, everybody is a comedian.

The back door of our apartment opened onto a little concrete area with four of five steps leading up to the lawn behind. George Silage's apartment also opened onto this area, and he used to feed his Siamese cat there. George was very fond of this cat, and no food was too good for it. He would therefore put out such delicacies as baby lamb chops that the cat often sniffed at, and then left. Meat of this quality was quite beyond our means, and I remember standing at our back window looking at a chop that the cat had spurned and wondering if I could steal it for myself.

We had some quite interesting experiences with the meat that we bought. We could often get boiling chickens for 27 cents a pound, and they went a long way for very little money. We were exceptionally fond of lamb, but mostly were forced to buy the cheapest cuts, such as breast of lamb, which had huge amounts of fat in it. One day, Marilyn bought some lovely looking steak called *chuck deckle*. This was a quite unfamiliar term to us, but it looked good, so she gave it a go. However, after grilling it turned out to be completely impossible to cut or chew, despite our strenuous efforts. It was our practice never to throw anything edible away, but we ended up having to consign this to the rubbish.

On Saturday mornings, we had a regular shopping ritual. We would set off with Kathryn in her Australian stroller, all rugged up in the winter, and also towing a shopping trolley that we had salvaged from somebody's junk pile. We walked the kilometre or so to Bohack's supermarket at the end of our street, and bought our weekly provisions. We had to be very careful with money, and were quite adept at sorting through the cans on the shelf to find lower priced ones from some previous special. We used to allow ourselves one little treat – a loaf of bread from a nearby Italian bakery. We would then haul this pile of stuff home and up the concrete ramp beside our apartment before stacking it away and then having our bread with lunch.

Occasionally, we spent some time on the weekends exploring New York City. We were not permitted to take our big stroller with us on the subway, so we bought a very small, collapsible one. We would set off to investigate the well-known areas of the city – Central Park, the Empire State Building, Fifth Avenue, Washington Square, South Ferry, Staten Island and the Statue of Liberty, the many museums, and so on. In fact, we became quite knowledgeable about where one could go in New York City at practically zero cost. We would also sometimes walk the kilometre or so to Van Cortland Park just north of 242nd Street, where there was a very nice playground, and lots of grass to run around.

The University Heights campus of NYU was quite an attractive place, with open spaces and many beautiful trees. Sometimes, when I was working there on the weekends, Marilyn and Kathryn would come in and meet me, and we would spend time playing on the lawns. Kathryn used to love coming into the laboratory and looking at my equipment, which she called *Daddy's mess*. She was very keen on turning the knobs of a large high voltage power supply (suitably disabled) that was mounted down at her level.

Winter tended to be quite a difficult time for Marilyn. Going out with Kathryn was a big deal, because of all the clothes that she had to put on. Our apartment was so hot that by the time they got outside they were usually sweating. Eventually I installed a fan in one of the windows, and we used to suck the overheated air out when the conditions became unbearable – a sort of inverse air conditioning system! In addition, each winter we all seemed to get sick, probably due to the fact that buildings were closed up allowing bugs to thrive. We both saw our first snow in New York – at the age of 25! We had a few big snowfalls, including one full-blown blizzard that stopped the city. Snow was great fun when it was new, but it soon turned grey and fouled by dogs. It also became treacherous after it melted and refroze. The second Christmas that we spent there was actually a white one, and it was a thrill to be able to tell this to our neighbours from Australia when they called us from their traditional Christmas morning get-together.

While I was studying at NYU, work commenced on a large new engineering building at the Heights campus. The first step in this operation was to fence off the construction site. This was done by putting up lines of wooden posts, and then nailing to them plywood panels, 8 feet by 4 feet in size. The temptation to graffiti artists was irresistible, and early one morning as I was coming in, I observed that they had been at work. In fact, you couldn't miss it. The following message was painted in enormous letters, one on each plywood panel:

ON THIS SITE THERE WILL BE
AN ERECTION ONE BLOCK LONG

Regrettably, I was probably one of the few people to appreciate this piece of art, because just after 9am as I headed out to give a class, painters were hard at work turning the panels uniform battleship grey. The precedent had been set, however, and these panels immediately became an irresistible object of interest for anyone with a paintbrush and the creative urge. After a couple of weeks of application of successive layers of art work followed by covering paint, the authorities gave up, and started to run graffiti competitions in order to channel the artists' energy into more productive, or at least more controllable, directions. I think that everybody was disappointed when the fence had to come down after the building was finally completed.

We had quite a few Australian friends to stay with us during the time that we were in New York, and we loved it when this happened. Sometimes we went sightseeing with them. On one occasion, a former colleague from AWA stopped by, and I took him to the south end of Manhattan from where we walked north to 34th Street and the Empire State Building to meet Marilyn in the evening. Somehow, I led him off the beaten track and we found ourselves in the Bowery, or Skid Row. I do not think that we were in any real danger, but a lot of dead beats came towards us. I imagine that they just wanted money, but we didn't wait to find out, and headed out of there at high speed.

One of our visitors was John Hooke whom I had known quite well at AWV. John invited us to dinner at *Top of the Sixes*, a restaurant on the top floor of 666 Fifth Avenue. We left Kathryn with the Brauchles, and took the subway downtown. It was a most memorable evening, and we ate food that we had only dreamed about for a long time – in fact, Marilyn had lamb chops, just like George Silage fed to his cat! It was a real come down, however, to leave these elegant surroundings and get back into the stinking hot, filthy subway carriage for the trip home! A few days later, I took John to the University Heights campus of NYU to show him my research work. At about 1pm, I called Marilyn to check that it was OK to bring him back to the apartment, but all was not well. The chicken and fried rice dish that she was preparing, an old but good standard, had somehow gone off the rails, and she needed more time. I filibustered at NYU for as long as I could, but eventually we had to front up for lunch. My recollection is that the meal wasn't too bad, given the dire earlier predictions. Years later, John told me that he didn't notice that anything was amiss.

A few days after John Hooke's visit, we received a phone call from a man who introduced himself as Lou Shotliff. Lou was Director of International Licensing of RCA, and AWA was one of their licensees. Apparently John had mentioned to him that there was this young fellow on leave of absence from AWA doing his Ph.D. in New York, and Lou very kindly called to make our acquaintance, and to ask Marilyn and me to dinner. We were delighted by this, and set a date. A couple hours before the appointed time, however, I became ill with a migraine headache, and we had to cancel. Lou was not deterred, and tried again, this time inviting all three of us to visit with him and his wife Barbara at their home. We met Lou and Barbara at the George Washington Bridge, and they drove us through the beautiful autumn colours of the Palisades on the western side of the Hudson River, and then to their lovely home in Haworth, New Jersey. From our first meeting, the four of us hit it off, and this was the start of a wonderful relationship between us. In fact, Lou and Barbara became our best friends in the United States. They were exceedingly thoughtful and generous to us, actions that were all the more meaningful because we had no way to repay them for their kindnesses. I particularly recall that Barbara lent us a rocking horse that was attached with springs to a wooden frame. Our daughter Kathryn just adored this horse, and she would bounce up and down on it on the bare floors of our apartment. Heaven knows what Mrs Keller who lived below thought, but she never complained. (I have often wondered if Kathryn's experience with this horse was influential in developing the love of horses that she has had throughout her whole life.)

Our friendship with the Shotliffs has endured and grown over the nearly 40 years since we first met. After our return to Australia, we regularly kept in touch and I tried to see them every time that I travelled to the United States. During a trip in 1975-6, we were able to visit them as a complete family. Before one of my later planned trips, I learnt that Lou had become very ill, but Barbara insisted that I stay with them. I was most upset to see how different Lou was from the man that I once knew. Even more distressingly, I could see the strain that Barbara was experiencing by looking after him at home. I was able to help her little in this regard and, with her agreement, I spoke about the difficulties that she was experiencing with her doctor, and with both of her children. Barbara later told me that these calls helped her family make the very difficult decision to have Lou transferred to a hospital immediately after my visit. I was always very grateful to have had the opportunity of doing something for Lou and Barbara in small repayment for the great kindnesses that they had given Marilyn and me many years earlier, although I wish that it could have been in another way.

Regrettably, Lou is no longer with us, but we have continued to visit Barbara, recently with her partner Chuck, and she and Chuck have stayed with us in Australia more than once. It warms my heart that what obviously started out as a simple act of business courtesy by Lou grew into such a strong and lasting friendship.

There was another very interesting outcome of John Hooke's visit with us. Shortly after his return to Australia, I received a letter from Lou Davies saying that AWA had allocated $200 for us to use to entertain people, such as from RCA, "on the company's behalf." The only people in this category that we knew were the Shotliffs, so we asked them out. In fact, this made them feel quite uncomfortable, because they did not think that we had money to do this. I explained to them about the windfall from AWA and they came, but I know that they felt bad about us picking up the tab. My recollection is that we blew virtually all of the money on one evening when we took them to dinner and a Broadway show – *Sweet Charity*.

My teaching and coursework responsibilities in my second semester at NYU finished up around May 1966. I then started to prepare in earnest for the Prelims. These exams were taken so seriously that Ben gave us essentially all of the summer off from our research work to study for them. Despite the intensive level of study, it was a very nice time for Marilyn, Kathryn and me. Typically, I would get up very early and study until about 8am. We would then have breakfast, and spend the morning together. After lunch, I studied again for a few hours. Sometimes, I would do another hour or two after dinner at night. The subjects that were to be covered in the written Prelim examinations were mostly those that I had studied in the courses that I had taken, or sat in on, in my first two semesters. The exception was Statistical Mechanics, which I had not been able to do, and for which my preparation was inadequate as a result of Dr Klemens' lectures some years before. I attempted to get on top this subject by reading textbooks, making copious notes as I went. I read five books from cover to cover before I finally felt comfortable about my grasp of the subject.

In fact, the summer of 1966 was not entirely given over to intensive study. In June, we went on a three day trip by bus to Washington DC. We greatly enjoyed this experience, and saw many of the sights there, even though we were entirely dependent on public transport. This trip occurred near the start of my period of preparation for the Prelims, and it was very beneficial in relaxing me before I got stuck into the study in earnest. About two weeks before the actual Preliminary Examinations, we had the opportunity to travel by car with friends to visit Expo in Montreal. Marilyn let me make the decision about whether we would go or not and, after lengthy thought, I eventually decided against it. As it turned out, we could have gone, but I was not to know that.

A week or so before the Prelims, I saw my fellow graduate students from the laboratory again. I was quite upset to learn that they had all been studying together over the summer in an office at NYU. Nobody had said anything about this to me, and I felt most disappointed that I had been left out of the group. Had I known about the joint studying, I am not sure whether I would have been part of it or not, but this hardly seemed to be the point. I still cannot imagine why they clearly decided to exclude me from their joint endeavors, because at work I got on with them all very well. We seldom mixed socially, however, because they were all very much better off than us financially and, without children, they did things that were not possible for us.

Finally, the day of the first exam arrived. I felt comfortable with my preparation, in the sense that there was nothing more that I could have done, given the time available to me. I had regained my examination technique, and I remember feeling good throughout the five hour period. The next two exams also went well. All of the exams tended to concentrate on the basic principles of the relevant parts of Physics, rather than the esoteric, more complex or mathematical aspects. As I had taught much of this fundamental stuff, I felt that they suited me very well.

The results came in very quickly, and to my astonishment and delight, I found that I had topped the 50 or so students who sat for the exams that year. I even obtained 100% in the section on Statistical Mechanics! Of course, we immediately wrote letters home telling our parents about this. I will never forget my Father's reply – he described himself has being "speechless with pride."

Following my success in the Prelims and my obvious ability to handle the teaching, coursework and research, I entered my second year at NYU full of confidence that a Ph.D. was now achievable, rather than an impossible dream. We had settled into a comfortable routine at home. Kathryn was about 18 months old, Marilyn was well established with some nice friends nearby and, apart from the fact that the demands on my time was still very great, we felt as though we were getting on top of things. Joan Brauchle from upstairs worked as a nurse at the Roosevelt Hospital at 59th Street in Manhattan, and through her, Marilyn had been introduced to the maternity and gynecological clinic there. She was told that she would be accepted into their maternity program, should she become pregnant. This excellent program provided good care for mothers who would otherwise not be able to afford it, at a cost that was defined before the event. On the basis of the knowledge that Marilyn would be well cared for, and that the cost was within our means, we decided to have a second child.

I believe that Marilyn's pregnancy was by far the nicest thing that happened to her during our stay in New York. Being from overseas, she was regarded as quite special at the Roosevelt Hospital clinic. Of course, being very intelligent didn't hurt either. Most of the doctors that looked after her also came from overseas, and were in the United States for training. She got to know several of them very well, and both she and the doctors enjoyed her regular visits to the clinics. I usually went downtown with her and, during Marilyn's appointment took Kathryn for a walk in Central Park, to chase the pigeons amongst other things. We would often have a bite of lunch there before heading home on the subway. It was a good time for us.

Our baby was due in July 1967. The months leading up to that time were extremely busy for me. I took an extra course over the summer, because I was still falling short of completing the specified number of courses for my Ph.D. within my target three-year period. I also taught a concentrated course to out-of-sequence students, mainly because it gave us some much-needed extra money. My highest priority at the University during this period, however, was the experiment. After much effort, we had it operating quite well and generating reasonable data. I worked extremely long hours in the laboratory, using all of my scheduled days, and most of the weekends as well. One weekend, I nearly had a nasty accident. The oven had run out of potassium at about 11am on the Saturday. Normally when this happened we would shut down the apparatus, and open the vacuum chamber next day when the oven had cooled in order to recharge it. This would have meant that I would not have been able to take data on the Sunday. I decided to try to speed up the process. I waited until about 3pm and then opened the vacuum chamber while the oven was still quite hot. In the high humidity of the New York summer, the potassium on the walls of the chamber immediately caught fire, and it was only through very quick action that I avoided a disaster.

I continued to work on weekends right up until the baby was born. In fact, on Sunday 9 July 1967, I had started in the lab at 6am as usual. The experiment was not operating well, and about 3pm I gave up in disgust. I shut down the apparatus and headed for home. At about the same time that I left the University, Marilyn went into labour. She tried to call me at the lab, but I was not there. When I arrived home she was preparing to go to the hospital by herself. I am not a person who often wishes that I had done things differently. However, I would really like to have the opportunity to relive the time leading up to my return home on that day. I can't imagine why I did not keep Marilyn informed of where I was. I greatly regret the anxiety that I caused her because she could not contact me when she needed me. Of course, it worked out all right in the end, but that was purely by good fortune.

We left Kathryn with the Brauchle's, and set off in a taxi to Roosevelt Hospital. The traffic was not heavy, and we arrived there in good time. They were expecting us, and immediately began preparing Marilyn for her caesarean operation. Jenelle was born at about 6pm that day, and both she and Marilyn were just fine.

I visited Marilyn most of the days while she was in hospital. Once I took Kathryn with me, but she was not permitted to visit her Mother, so Marilyn waved to us from a window. The welfare officer in the hospital interviewed me, and informed me that our income was such that we could get welfare support. I declined this offer. On 18 July, Charlie Brauchle drove Kathryn and me down to the hospital, and we all came home together.

The first couple of weeks with the baby at home were not straightforward. Jenelle was not feeding properly, and she was starting to become dehydrated. We had a set of baby scales, and so we weighed her before and after each feed. This allowed us to provide supplementary feeding to her, and we eventually got the problem straightened out. The doctor who had delivered her, Lily Chua, came to visit us one day and this was a very special moment. When Jenelle was nine weeks old, we had our second brief holiday during our time in the United States. We travelled by bus to Atlantic City, and spent four interesting days staying at a hotel on the boardwalk. It was very built up, and somewhat decrepit – not at all like the beach holidays that we had been used to!

Of course the arrival of the new baby stopped my frenetic efforts to acquire data on the apparatus but by then Ben told me that I had enough, at a pinch, to graduate. Soon afterwards, however, another group published some results that were so much better than ours that he was forced to reverse this decision, and I had to do much better. I am not critical of Ben for insisting on this. From my present perspective as an experienced supervisor, I would have done exactly the same thing. My results certainly would not have stacked up against those of others in the field. The only way that we could get better data was to rebuild the apparatus completely and remove the sources of noise that had limited its performance up to that time. This would take some months to do, and then the data acquisition would have to begin all over again. I had no way of estimating how long this might take, but it seemed that I would be unlikely to complete my Ph.D. within our three-year target period. Marilyn and I talked about the problems associated with her and the children living through another winter in New York with Kathryn suffering tonsillitis frequently, and we decided that it would be a much better option for them to return to the Australian summer. This would free me up to work full-time at the experiment and, hopefully, to finish up earlier.

The decision for Marilyn and the children to return home and leave me in New York was a really tough one to make. The worst aspect of it was that we had no idea how long we would be apart. All that we knew for certain was that I would be able to finish earlier with them at home in Australia, rather than with me New York. They left for Australia on 15 December 1967, our fifth wedding anniversary. Barbara Shotliff drove us all to the airport. I remember standing on the observation deck in the freezing cold with tears streaming down my face watching the plane take off. Later that night after I returned to the apartment, I wept uncontrollably.

Then I pulled myself together. I talked to Marilyn at the hotel where she stayed in San Francisco overnight, and busied myself getting things ready to pack up and ship back to Australia. Our faithful washing machine chose that evening to die. Well, actually, it wasn't quite a death, rather than a most serious injury – the main drive pulley cracked into three pieces. I had a big load of washing in progress, and I had to complete it by hand! A couple days later, I took the pieces of the pulley to the Physics workshop, and the technician there brazed them together (see how essential foreign orders are), enabling the washing machine to survive for the rest of my time in New York.

Marilyn's trip back Australia was very tiring for her, and she got essentially no sleep. On the leg from Fiji to Sydney, the Captain of the plane announced that the Australian Prime Minister, Harold Holt, had drowned. Our parents, and Lou Davies, met her and the children at the airport, and she stayed with her parents for a month before moving back into our home. Her early return to Australia certainly did avoid the New York winter and all the things that went with it. However, it was a very demanding and trying time for her, and she had to work extremely hard. Nevertheless she managed it really well and, by the time I returned Australia, she was well established back in our home, with a new (secondhand) car, and plans finalised for our house extensions!

In January 1968 when I enrolled in what turned out to be my final semester at NYU, I still needed five courses to complete the required number for my Ph.D. I selected three lecture courses, and then Ben gave me permission to take two seminar courses that involved no lectures, but required one or two presentations by me, and attendance at talks by other students. The Dean of Graduate Studies was reluctant to approve such a large number of courses, and tried to stop my enrollment. It turned out, however, that there was no rule limiting the number of courses that could be taken at any one time, and he was ultimately forced to agree. As a direct result of this, however, the rules were changed to prevent graduate students enrolling in more than three courses at once. This problem would not have arisen had I been granted credit for my honours courses in Australia. In hindsight, the decision to refuse credit was clearly wrong. I am really glad that I won this little battle, because otherwise I would have had to remain at NYU for another whole semester, just to meet this formality.

The rebuild of the experiment went well, and we obtained a beam without any problems. The performance of the apparatus had improved so much that, within the first couple of days of running, I had better data than I had extracted during the several months of intensive work before Jenelle's birth. From then on, it was only a matter of time. I knew what data were required, and how long it would take to get them, and I set out to do just that. On several occasions, I operated the apparatus right through the night. On one of these nights, the potassium oven ran out and so I had to shut the equipment down. It was long after the last bus, so I decided to sleep on the laboratory floor until morning. As luck would have it, one of the security officers came into the lab that night and found me there. He thought that I was a hobo who had wandered in off the street to get out of the cold, and he wanted to throw me out. I managed to produce enough documentation to dissuade him from doing this.

In addition to getting data from the apparatus, I commenced writing my thesis. I had given a lot of thought to this over the preceding few months, but it had been very difficult to get started. Ben advised me to begin with the bit that I knew the best, and so I commenced writing the chapter on the new electron gun which had been one of the major innovative features that we had introduced into the experiment. It was like clicking a switch, and the words started to pour out of the end of my pen. I also had to prepare a large number of diagrams, all laboriously drawn by hand with pen and ink, and labelled with a lettering guide, and this was also very time-consuming. However, the end was in sight.

Although mine was primarily an experimental thesis, there was also a certain amount of theory involved. I needed some help with this, so I went downtown to the Courant Institute at Washington Square to discuss my problems with Professor Larry Spruch, a theoretical physicist who was an expert on scattering theory. There are a lot of derogatory theoretician stories around, mostly apocryphal I'm sure, but this one is true. I was sitting in Larry's office discussing some aspect of my experiment, the winter sunshine was coming through the window, the heaters were going flat out, and I was sweating profusely. It was not uncommon for rooms to be overheated in the middle of winter, but Larry's office was absurd.

I said, "Larry, why don't you do something about the heat?"

He responded, "Yeah, it's awful, but I don't know how."

"It's easy," I said, pointing to the perforated box that covered the steam convection heaters. "See that little metal door on top of that box." I lifted up the door to reveal a valve. "You just turn that valve to cut off the heat."

Larry said, "I knew that valve was there, but I don't know which way to turn it."

I said, "I don't know which way to turn it either, but there will probably only be one way." So I turned it, and the heat cut off.

And then Larry slammed the metal door shut on my thumb.

Alongside the extraordinarily large amount of work that I had to do to complete my thesis, I actually found some time to relax, and enjoy myself a little. In order to reduce the cost, I looked for someone to share our apartment with me and was fortunate that Ben's new post doc, Tom Miller was seeking accommodation at the same time. Tom and I hit it off right from the start, and we enjoyed each other's company. Tom brought his car with him – a racy red MG convertible – so I enjoyed the luxury of being driven to University each day. Tom's Father was a senior executive in an airline and, through this, Tom often got tickets to Broadway shows that advertised in the airline magazine, so we had a few great afternoons mixing in circles that had previously been inaccessible to me.

Finally, my thesis was finished and typed. I was fortunate to receive the NYU Sigma Xi Graduate Award for Excellence in Research (courtesy of Ben, I have no doubt), which came with a nice cheque for about $80. This was almost exactly the cost of getting the thesis typed! I submitted it, and the examiners reports came in quite quickly, all positive. My thesis defence was a formality, and I had achieved my goal.

Was it all worth it? Although I could not answer that question then, over the years I have formed the very strong view that it was. However, it was not the Physics that I learnt during my

Ph.D. studies that has benefited me most over the rest of my career. Rather, it is what I learnt about myself. As I have tried to do for my own students, Ben stretched me to my limit, and taught me what I have inside. Many times over the subsequent years, I have faced formidable challenges that I have been able to tackle with confidence because of my knowledge of what I am capable of doing when I pull out all the stops. These days I can't work that way for as long as I did then, but some of it is still there, and this has always been an enormous asset to fall back on when the going gets tough.

Would we have done it if we had known how hard it was going to be? There is no doubt that we would not. Yes, things worked out well in the end, but they might not have, in so many ways. However, we didn't know what it was going to be like, and it was good that we didn't. Over the years, I have observed that young people do things that I would not because they are simply unaware of the potential difficulties. And that is one of the great strengths of youth. Taking the global view, our time in New York left us better for the experience. Certainly, we had a few wounds to patch up afterwards, but these things heal with time. For many years, I used to have this bad dream in which I was about to go into an exam that I could not possibly pass because I had not done any study for it. The dream doesn't happen any more.

The last couple of months of my time in New York were quite busy preparing to go home. I bequeathed to Tom Miller a lot of the things from our apartment, including our faithful washing machine. I was delighted that Kathryn's cot, which we had so lovingly and proudly painted and decorated after our arrival nearly three years earlier, was able to be put to good use by the DeSantis family. I needed to buy a bag of some sort to get my stuff home, but there was too much to fit into a suitcase of reasonable size. In my frequent correspondence with Marilyn, she had mentioned to me that she had seen an elephant soft toy in one of the shops, and she wished that she had taken it home with her. I went to look at it, and concluded that it was just too big to bring back with me. I wrote and told her this, and received a very quick reply: "I very much would like that elephant. If you really love me ..." So I bought it, but that exacerbated the problem of how to get it, and all my other stuff, back to

Australia. Then I had a brain wave. I went into an Army Disposal store near Times Square, and said to the guy there, "Duffel bags."

"Why not?" he replied. Another comedian.

A couple of minutes later, I was the proud owner of the biggest duffel bag that I had ever seen.

I still had to complete teaching my courses, and marking the exams, so it was about three weeks after my thesis defence before I could finally leave for Australia. I was most touched that Ben and his wife Betty gave a farewell party for me at their home a few days before my departure. Ben asked me if I would stay and carry the flag at the annual outdoor graduation ceremony that was to be held at the University Heights campus in a few weeks, but there was no way that I was prepared to delay my return to Australia for a moment longer than necessary. As it happened, this was an inspired decision for a quite unexpected reason. It seems that the heavens opened during this ceremony, and the beautiful and impressive purple colour of the NYU academic robes turned out to be water soluble, so the "violets", as they called themselves, were more aptly named than they would have liked. (I was later told that the graduation ceremony at which I did not carry the flag was the last that NYU ever held outdoors!)

On 21 May 1968, I flew to San Francisco where I stayed with friends for a day. I remember walking around that city in a state of sublime happiness. Finally, I set off across the Pacific, feeling almost capable of flying without the aircraft. I arrived at Sydney early on 24 May 1968. I had been away from Australia for two years and nine months. The first thing I did upon my return to Australia was to whack my head on the doorway of the aircraft as I came out of it. I could see Marilyn, my parents and Lou Davies waving to me in the morning sun. I had to wait for a long time for my duffel bag to appear, and most of the other passengers had disappeared when I finally dumped it in front of the Customs bloke. He said, "What have you been doing overseas?"

Proudly I replied, "I've been studying for my Ph.D. in New York."

He looked at my duffel bag, and said, "What have you got in there, then? Ph.D.'s?"

I didn't like the way this conversation was heading. "Just clothes and stuff," I said.

"Well, open it up."

I unzipped the bag and he pulled the flaps back to reveal the pink and grey elephant staring expressionlessly at him. He looked at the elephant, and at me, seemingly lost for words.

"A present for the kids," I mumbled weakly.

He zipped it up, and said, "Get out of here."

Shaking all over, I grabbed the bag, the elephant, and my Ph.D., hurried through the doors, and into Marilyn's arms. It was fantastic to be back in Australia.

Wheels Falling Off

We built our first house at Beecroft in several stages. The first, which was completed before we went to New York, had just one bedroom. We had always intended to extend it and so we had asked the bricklayer to construct the end wall using lime mortar so that it could be more readily taken down later. However, he was too much of a perfectionist to do this, and could not bring himself to use anything other than full strength cement mortar. So it was that the first significant job that I undertook with my brand-new Ph.D. was to demolish this uncooperatively strong wall, and to clean the highly adherent cement from the faces of a couple of thousand bricks.

For several months before my return to Australia, I had been in correspondence with Lou Davies about the work that I would commence upon my return to the AWA Physical Laboratory. He essentially let me choose my own topic. In hindsight, this was not wise thing. I made the mistake of commencing work in an area that had emerged out of my Ph.D. studies as being highly desirable for the extension of this research, but which was completely irrelevant to AWA. I set out to build a system to produce polarised electrons. The idea was to emit electrons from a magnetic material in a strong electric field (so-called field emission), and subsequently to perform a spin analysis on them. The ultra-high vacuum technology that I developed for the field emission work was in the same general area as some of the production technology at AWV, but the science that I was doing was not.

I constructed quite a lot of equipment, and actually managed to get the field emission part of the experiment working quite well. I wrote a couple of papers on aspects of the experimental design, and I also obtained a large Australian Government grant to support the work – indeed mine was the only such grant to a scientist in industry in Australia at that time. However, the project was far too ambitious to be undertaken by one person working in isolation, and I fell far short of the original target for the work.

Although I was not aware of it at the time, some people within the company were quite critical of the research that I was undertaking. I believe that they had every right to feel that way. However, Lou shielded me from this criticism. The first time that I became aware of it was after a group of visitors had come through the Laboratory, and the Deputy General Manager took me aside as they were leaving saying, "Some time you will have to tell me why we are doing this work at AWA." This made me feel quite uncomfortable.

After I had been back in the Lab for a year or so, Lou Davies mentioned to me that there was a need to develop a replacement for the telephone microphone. He suggested that electrets, or permanently charged insulators, might be useful as part of such a replacement. This interested me a great deal, and I started to work in this area. I was smart enough to realise that, while Lou might be able to protect my polarised electron work, I was really like a fish out of water doing it in the company. I therefore slowed down my efforts on this work, and it soon died. I was . very relieved to escape from the noose that I had started to put around my neck. Although he never said anything to me about it, I believe that Lou was, too.

I learnt a very important lesson from this experience. If research work is to be undertaken in a commercial environment, it is absolutely essential that it should be on a topic that is relevant to the operation of the company, and to the strategic direction that it has set itself. Quite apart from anything else, doing otherwise is simply wasting money. I am quite prepared to accept criticism for choosing to work in an area that was irrelevant to AWA. I actually believe, however, that it should never have got this far. Someone more senior than me in the company should have pointed out that, whatever the scientific merits of the research, it should not have been done at AWA.

Quite a few things were different in the Valve Company at Rydalmere after my return. For a start, I graduated to the Senior Staff so, whatever I thought about my enhanced participation in the class distinction that still flourished there, I had to exercise a higher level of decorum at lunch. More importantly, eating with the management gave me the opportunity to talk on a regular basis with several of the more influential people in the company. Doug Sutherland was no longer General Manager of AWV – he had been given an important new challenge – and the GM position was now occupied by Jack Niven. Jack was good with numbers, and ran the company very profitably. However, he spent virtually nothing on developing the business. Within the first few months after my return, I had concluded that AWV was not being managed with its long-term welfare in mind.

This backward-looking attitude towards innovation was not limited to the Valve Company part of AWA. I recall Doug Sutherland telling me that there was a belief within the management across AWA that the Government would always look after the company, because of the strategic importance to Australia of a local electronics industry. Perhaps the most pathetic illustration that I saw of this corporate philosophy occurred after the opening of a new AWA factory at North Ryde. The Government Minister who performed the opening ceremony said something in his speech which was regarded as so important by the company that his words were framed and hung in the entrance lobby for all to see:

AWA is a company that must succeed,
and the Government will ensure that it succeeds.

AWA had not always been this way. The company had a strong tradition of innovation that went back to its earliest days. During the Second World War, the company had made very significant contributions to the Australian war effort. In the decade or so following the war, there had been a worldwide shortage of electronics components and equipment, and AWA had established modern manufacturing facilities for a wide range of engineering and consumer products, and for the components that went into these products. Within the relevant Government departments, such as the PMG (Post Master General's Department, the telecommunications part of which is now Telstra) and Defence, many of the senior management had lived through this era when it was virtually impossible to acquire things from overseas, and had formed the view that a viable local electronics industry was essential for our commercial and strategic security. The problem was that, as the capacity of overseas production facilities increased and the price of their products fell, Australian industry became more and more uncompetitive. Because local manufacturing volumes were so low, Australian companies could not compete in overseas markets, and much of local industry therefore attempted to operate only in Australia behind a protective wall of tariffs.

To be fair to AWA, the company made some efforts to address these issues. The existence of a transistor manufacturing section in AWV was evidence of that. The company also established the first Australian facility to make integrated circuits, initially referred to as the Advanced Devices Development Laboratory, or ADDL for short. This laboratory prospered and grew, and eventually was called AWA Microelectronics.

The company's venture into making integrated circuits started during my time in New York. Initially, Doug Sutherland was in charge of the operation. It was very exciting for us to have this embryonic microelectronics production facility located right next to the Physical Laboratory. A close and productive relationship developed between the two sections. The first engineer that Doug took into ADDL was David Money, whom I had known before I left for New York, and who had impressed me with his creativity and extraordinarily sharp mind. Indeed, David is the best engineer that I have ever known. Even though more than two decades have passed since we both left AWA, and our subsequent careers developed in totally different directions, Marilyn and I regard David and his wife Renate as amongst our closest friends.

There is a wonderful story that came out of the early days of ADDL. Within the small facility, one special oven, used for baking photoresist, was kept as clean as possible in order to prevent contamination of the circuits by tiny particles of dust. One day, Doug Sutherland opened the door of this oven to discover that one of the technical staff was using it to heat his meat pie for lunch.

It is also relevant to note that there was a strong anti-intellectual streak in the many parts of the company, particularly by some of the senior management. In some ways, this was understandable. Many of these people had grown up at a time when it was unusual to undertake tertiary education. They had come up through the trades, and had achieved at a high level, earning their promotions by hard work. I had the greatest respect for them. They had an enormous amount of experience and knowledge about technical and business matters, and they taught me a great deal. Some of them, however, were very wary of smart young blokes with university degrees that thought they knew everything. More than once, I heard people in the senior management of the company say that the acquisition of an MBA was the end of a person's career advancement in AWA. Not that the company had anything like a career development program. With just one small exception, during the fourteen years that I spent there, I was never encouraged to undertake any training or development courses, and no one ever talked to me about how my career might evolve. I am sure that my experience was not exceptional. Having said all of this, however, it was very clear that Lou Davies was highly regarded throughout the company, and by people at all levels. Many years later at a reunion of former AWA staff, I heard him referred to as "the great Lou Davies." Also, I believe that I, too, became well respected for the contributions that I made in different parts of the company.

On the positive side, morale within the Rydalmere factory was very good. The Physical Laboratory was an exciting and dynamic place in which to work, and we had excellent interactions with people in the Microelectronics facility next door, and in other parts of the factory. The company did quite a lot of things to make the Valve Works a happy place to be, including fairly frequent after-work drinks sessions when a member of staff made an overseas trip. And then there was the annual Christmas party. There had been a long tradition of running a pretty spectacular Christmas bash on the lawn in front of the factory. The principal beneficiaries of this function were, of course, the children of the employees. However, it was also a very nice social occasion. The highlight of the afternoon was the entrance of Santa Claus, followed by the distribution of presents to the children. I recall one year when all this did not go quite according to plan. For this particular party, I believe that there had been some difficulty finding a person to be Santa. Eventually, one of the men in the workshop, Jack, had been prevailed upon to take the job. He was not at all happy about being volunteered for this role and, on the afternoon, it is my understanding that he needed quite a lot of last-minute liquid persuasion to go on with it. For this year's party, Santa made his entrance driving a horse and cart. The cart was one of those old-fashioned types that had been used in my youth by bakers and milkmen. The driver stood on a platform at the back, holding onto the horse's reins. At the appointed time, the horse, cart and Santa emerged from the side of the factory, and pulled up on the grass in front of a large, and excited throng of expectant kids. Jack had been briefed on his role, and when the cart came to a halt, he lifted a megaphone to his mouth with one hand, keeping a firm grip on the cart with the other, and shouted a tentative, "Ho! Ho! Ho! Merry Christmas!"

The response from the kids was enthusiastic and encouraging, and I noted that Jack appeared to grow visibly in confidence. Emboldened by his welcome, he tried again, megaphone in one hand, but this time with his other hand raised high in the air: "Merry Christmas! Merry Christmas, everybody!"

Unfortunately, at this exact moment, the horse that had been standing placidly, decided to take one extra step forward. Unrestrained, Jack fell flat on his back. My daughter Jenelle was absolutely appalled, saying, "Santa isn't supposed to fall down."

At this time of essentially zero expenditure on developmental activities at AWV, it is curious that I recall a course that was held there to improve the effectiveness of our technical writing. This course was attended by all of the senior staff of AWV, and I was also invited to participate. I can't imagine that Jack Niven would have regarded such a thing as appropriate expenditure. I therefore suspect that the sessions that I attended were replicated throughout the AWA organisation. Also, given the attitudes of several of the participants, I am pretty sure that attendance was compulsory, by order of a higher authority. The person who gave this course was a Mrs Lavin-Roberts – a nice, if rather brash American lady. (For the record, her message, stretched over the two days of the course, was actually very simple – effective technical writing uses short words and short sentences. This has helped me a lot over the years.)

At the opening session of the course, she went around the table asking us all to introduce ourselves.

"I'm Dick Collins."

"Hullo, Dick."

"I'm David Money."

"Hi, David."

And so on, until it was Jack Niven's turn.

"Niven," he said.

"Yes, but what's your first name?"

Uncomfortable pause. "Mumble Niven."

"Sorry, I didn't quite get that."

Finally, and with great reluctance, he squeezed it out: "Jack Niven."

"Ho, the old Jackeroo, eh?"

I nearly pissed myself. When she had got through the group, she said, "Thanks, guys. Nice to meet you all. You can call me Mrs Roberts."

I think that this time I did!

In 1973, I was fortunate to be appointed as the AWA representative on the year-long Industrial Mobilisation Course. The IMC had a long standing, and successful tradition. It was run by the Department of Defence, and its purpose was to give people in industry, Government and Defence an appreciation of the capabilities, challenges and problems in the other sectors should it be necessary to mobilise the nation in the event of an emergency. Approximately thirty representatives from all of these sectors undertook the course in New South Wales each year. They were drawn from middle management of the various organisations and, in the words of the course literature, were supposed to have "career potential." I was only 33 years old at the time, slightly less than the nominal lower age limit, and the second youngest member on our Course. Throughout most of the year we met for dinner each Monday evening at Victoria Barracks, followed by a lecture on a particular segment of Australian industry. The next day, we went on a visit to an organisation that was representative of that industry. During these visits, we were taken on in-depth tours of the facilities, and given a slap-up lunch. The visits always concluded with detailed discussions, including a searching question and answer session, with the senior management of the organisation. The Course began, and ended with week-long, live-in periods at defence establishments, and there were also several interstate trips during the year.

I will talk a bit more about the Industrial Mobilisation Course in a later chapter. At this stage, all that I need to say is that it was a wonderful and formative experience for me. I got to listen to, and talk with, very capable senior people from diverse fields. I walked through factories and saw machinery, processes, and techniques that impressed and amazed me. And I made some extraordinarily good friends, both with other participants in the Course, and from the organisations that we visited. The things that I learnt during the Course reinforced my growing feeling that all was not well at AWA.

During that year, the electronics industry, and indeed much of Australian industry, was in turmoil. The Whitlam Government had been elected at the end of 1972, and one of its first actions was to introduce a 25% across-the-board cut in tariffs. For the Australian electronics industry, this action effectively made the local manufacture of most components uneconomic, and many operations went out of business, including virtually all of the Valve Company. The factory building itself was required anyway for the establishment of a manufacturing plant for colour television sets, so the timing was quite good from that point of view. Our Physical Laboratory was moved to the relatively new North Ryde plant of AWA. Lou Davies became Chief Scientist of the company, with responsibility for the Physical Laboratory, and the venerable AWA Research Laboratory that undertook research on the design of aerials and the propagation of radio signals. I was appointed Chief Physicist, and became Head of the Physical Laboratory.

North Ryde was much closer to the centre of action in AWA than Rydalmere, and the work of the Laboratory quickly became known to a much wider group of people than before. We were a regular stop on factory tours by the large number of visitors who came through, and I got to know many of the people within the North Ryde plant quite well. The word got around that I was interested in talking to people about their problems, and I was often able to make useful contributions towards solving them. These interactions ranged from short, one-off discussions, through to quite comprehensive and detailed studies on particular issues. If I look back over my entire time within the AWA organisation, my most significant beneficial contributions to the company were to the production and operating parts of the organisation through these usually informal interactions, rather than from the outcome of the research that we undertook in the Lab.

In fact, the research programs in the Lab should have been far more successful commercially than they were. With the exception of my ill-guided foray into polarised electrons, all of the research that we undertook was directly relevant to the business of the company, and should have provided a vehicle for innovation within the organisation. At Lou Davies' initiative, the Physical Laboratory undertook a very creative effort on optical fibres. This work emerged out of some early advances on optical fibre technology at CSIRO, and quickly evolved to be quite close to the cutting edge of international optical fibre research. It was unlikely that this research, by itself, would ever have formed the basis for a comprehensive optical fibre manufacturing industry, or indeed would have enabled the company to become a leader in optical fibre communication systems. However, it should have helped the company to position itself to take advantage of the rapid overseas developments in this important emerging field, but it did not.

My own area of research, electrets, also did very well. We had a small, but active group of people working on the production of electrets, and methods of characterising their stability. One of my own contributions was the invention of a new technique for measuring the distribution of stored charge through the thickness of the thin polymer foils from which we made the electrets. I published a number of papers on this technique, and it ultimately became quite widely used overseas to study these materials. I also obtained an Australian Government grant to support the work. The electret work formed the basis of a most interesting and rewarding period in 1975-6 when I worked for several months at the National Bureau of Standards (now NIST) in Gaithersburg, Maryland. My entire family joined me for the time that I was there, and it was a most enjoyable trip.

The purpose of our electret research was to support the development of a new microphone for the telephone handset. In those days, telephones still used microphones that worked on a principle that had been developed by Alexander Graham Bell. This microphone was the most unreliable part of the entire telephone system. The Australian Government telecommunication authority, the PMG, had therefore indicated its desire to replace it with an active microphone consisting of a transducer to convert the sound wave into an electrical signal, and an integrated circuit to amplify the electrical signal and convert it into a form suitable for sending down the telephone line. I did a lot of the fundamental work on the design of the microphone.

My friend and colleague, David Money, designed the integrated circuit. Together, we performed the basic work on what I believe to be the world's first active telephone microphone.

This work attracted the interest of others in the company, including the people at the Ashfield plant who made telephones for the PMG. We set up a working group, including people from this plant, and David and myself, to engineer the electret microphone/integrated circuit assembly into a company product. The working group met regularly, and we actually produced a few hundred prototype electret microphones. Many of these microphones were installed into telephone handsets around the place, including our own at home, and people often used to comment on the clarity of our telephone line. It was a very promising development, potentially having great commercial significance.

Having said this, however, the whole experience with the electret microphone at AWA was also enormously frustrating. David and I would travel to the Ashfield plant every few weeks, and almost always come away quite confused, frustrated, and even angry about the lack progress that had occurred since the previous meeting. We eventually worked out what was going on. The people with whom we were interacting at Ashfield were very well meaning, and extremely competent, but their principal responsibility was to the production process. That was entirely appropriate. In industry, production always takes precedence over long-term developments. It is absolutely essential to keep products moving out the door, because it is on this that the company's cash flow depends. Even with the best will in the world, the Ashfield people could not devote sufficient time to the electret microphone development to enable it to move forward satisfactorily, and the company would not commit additional resources to enable this to occur.

We were also extremely disappointed by the response to our work from the PMG. Although the development had been stimulated by their stated need to replace the carbon microphone, it was virtually impossible even to extract from them a set of design specifications that any replacement active microphone would have to meet. As time progressed, it became clear that the problem was twofold. Firstly, we were well ahead of our time in the development of the microphone, and they had no overseas experience to guide them. Secondly, as a result of a number of quite unfortunate experiences, the PMG was quite averse to being an innovation leader. We therefore constituted a problem for them, because they did not want to commit to any microphone before the technology had been established and proven overseas.

David and I also observed similarly discouraging attitudes coming out of parts of AWA. The existing carbon telephone microphone business was a nice little earner for AWA. Each year, they made hundreds of thousands of these devices for the PMG on fully depreciated plant, and at a good profit. There were very powerful voices within the company that argued against doing anything that might disturb this business. Our exciting technical development was going nowhere commercially.

While all this was happening, we in the Physical Laboratory had settled in well into our new environment. Our group now contained a dozen or more scientists and technical staff. Morale in the Lab was high, and we all got on very well together. The usual practice at North Ryde was for people to have morning tea at their desks. We used our morning tea breaks to interact. We would down tools and get together in a corner of the Lab, telling jokes, having fun, and occasionally talking shop. They were happy, often riotous times, and our laughter would drift out into other parts of the factory environment, sometimes generating mild disapproval. We also interacted socially, and some strong and enduring friendships emerged.

Three of our number in the Lab, including myself, had sailing dinghys, and our conversations at morning tea quite frequently got around to related matters. On one occasion, someone raised the possibility of designing a boat that would sail directly into the wind. I argued categorically, and on the basis of no evidence whatsoever, that such a thing was quite impossible. One of my mates, Jim Harvey, said that that he had read about a boat of this kind in a book, and he even recalled the design – a windmill on the top coupled to a propeller in the water below. Words led to words, and a bet emerged. The stakes were a dozen bottles of beer, and to win them, Jim had to construct a boat that would achieve what was, in my view, an obviously impossible feat. Over the next few weeks, the tempo of our morning teas picked up quite a bit as Jim recounted his unsuccessful efforts to build an into-the-wind sailing boat, and we abused him. Then one morning, he claimed that he had done it. Since he was an engineer, I did not believe him. In fact, I was so confident that he was bluffing that I arranged a barbeque at our home for all the people in the Lab, and their families. It was a really great day. After lunch, we filled our little wading pool with water, and Jim produced his model that he had kept locked away in his car because, as he put it, you can't trust scientists. Jim's boat was a most elegant thing to behold. It consisted of a tetrahedron made from six thin steel rods, each about 0.5 metres long. The bottom three rods were fixed to styrofoam floats. Another steel rod ran through two bearings, one fixed near the apex of the tetrahedron, and the other attached to the bottom of the frame. On the top end of this rod was a windmill, and on the other end, under the water, was a propeller. To add insult to injury, Jim had even painted the thing – in two colours!

There was no wind that day, so we simulated it with a fan. Jim placed his model in the wading pool with the crowd gathered around, and we turned on the fan. The model was immediately pushed backwards by the air stream, and I thought that I had called his bluff. Then slowly the windmill began to rotate and the boat inexorably clawed its way forward, directly into the wind. You could have heard the cheer miles away. Jim had won his bet, and I had lost my beer.

There was a sequel to this happening a year or so later. At morning tea, we were discussing an upcoming Australian challenge for the America's Cup. Someone said that we would win a race or two – I reckoned that we wouldn't win a thing. A bet was struck with the stakes again a dozen bottles of beer. As it happened, I was correct this time and, in due course, a Saturday picnic was arranged for the presentation ceremony. Unfortunately, due to illness, my family and I could not attend. On the following Monday morning, I was expecting to have my winning stakes presented to me, and I did, or at least what was left of them. Those bastards, my friends, had drunk the lot, except for a bit of stale beer in the bottom of the last bottle. As has been demonstrated to me many times over my long career, there is no justice in life.

As I have mentioned, we had a lot of people coming through the Lab as part of more extensive tours of the factory. Most of these visits were routine, but some were quite memorable. I recall one occasion when a Commonwealth Government Cabinet Minister came through. For reasons that have completely escaped me, we decided to show him the beginning of the process to draw an optical fibre. The operation was performed by our very capable technical officer, Charles Storey. With the Minister and all his hangers-on watching, Charles heated the end of a quartz rod in an oxy-acetylene flame, touched the molten end with another small piece of quartz, walked along the length of the drawing apparatus pulling out a fine thread of quartz as he went, attached the end of the thread to a rotating drum, at which point the fibre broke. The fibre also broke the second time, and the third time, and on and on. Finally, the visitors ran out of time and the party had to leave. The Minister was most understanding, and patted Charles on the shoulder saying, "Don't worry, son. You'll get the hang of it one day."

On another occasion, we had a visit from an Admiral in the United States Navy. I was showing him our work on surface acoustic waves. These are high frequency mechanical oscillations that are launched and detected on the surface of a small crystal of piezoelectric material, such as quartz. The Admiral was looking a bit glazed, from over exposure I suppose, and didn't seem to be getting the hang of what I was saying, so I tried to illustrate it with something familiar. I recalled something that one of my colleagues and a former sub-mariner, Doug Edwards, had once told me. I said to the Admiral, "All of the motion in the surface acoustic wave is very close to the surface, rather like a water wave. That's why submarines always go under the water at lunchtime – so that their lunch doesn't get spoiled because of the motion of the waves."

The Admiral immediately brightened up. "You're partly correct, my boy," he said. "It's certainly true that submarines go underwater for lunch, but that's not to cut out the motion of the waves. It's so those bastards in the Pentagon can't interrupt our meal."

Towards the end of the 1970s, I had become very disillusioned with AWA. I had been around long enough to be sure that the company was thinking far too little about its future, and was not doing enough work that would result in the evolution of its product lines, and the development of completely new initiatives. I was sufficiently senior in the company by that time that I felt I could do something about it. I discussed my concerns with many people in management, who should have been influential enough to change things. All I ever got was excuses. I even managed to get myself into the position of producing the first draft of submissions that the company made to various Government enquiries relating to industry policy and the like. I would write into these documents all sorts of good stuff about research and development, innovation, strategic planning, international competitiveness, and so on. My drafts would go into Head Office, and the actual submission would emerge with all of this material taken out, and replaced with words about tariff protection.

I found it quite difficult to deal with my failure to have any impact on these attitudes within the company, and with my inability to interest people in the rest of AWA in the outcomes of our research work. I started to become very stressed at work. In fact, I remember going through entire days when I felt that my pulse rate was higher than it should have been. I had already figured out that achievement is one of the principal things that I need in order to be satisfied with what I am doing, in any activity. I felt that I was not achieving anything at AWA, and this made me very tense. In short, for the first time in all my years within the company, I was not enjoying my job.

Finally, I formed the view that I should start looking for alternative employment. Marilyn saw an advertisement for the position of Principal Lecturer and Head of the Department of Applied Physics at the New South Wales Institute of Technology (now the University of Technology, Sydney.) She encouraged me to apply and, despite having some reservations about going back into academia, I did. I made one last attempt to get the company to think about its attitude towards innovation and planning for the future. I went into Head Office one morning to see Jack Niven who, by this time, was General Manager of the whole AWA organisation. I recall sitting in his office and arguing my case. At one point, I was going on about the fact that we were having little success in getting people in the company to be interested in taking up the things that we did in the Lab. I said, "Jack, I really don't understand why you even bother having a Research Laboratory in the company. We come up with all sorts of good things and there is absolutely no mechanism for taking them out of the Laboratory and moving them towards commercialisation."

Jack replied, "You're absolutely right, Dick. I am completely disinterested in the things that you do in the Research Laboratory. As far as I'm concerned, you're just part of my advertising budget. All I want you for is to put on a good show when I bring visitors around."

I was completely stunned. It was as if scales had fallen from my eyes and, for the first time, I saw the company as it actually was. As it happened, a couple of days later I received an offer for the job at NSWIT. Jack Niven made the decision to leave AWA very easy for me.

As a footnote to this part of my story, over the decade or more after I left AWA, the fortunes of the company declined steadily. Gradually it withdrew from manufacturing in both consumer and engineering electronics, and it sold many of its service operations, such as its radio stations. Some of these changes occurred following shifts in the controlling shareholdings. Now, although the name survives (as AWA Limited), the company only provides technical and computer services into the gaming industry. In fairness to the people who oversaw the decline of AWA as I knew it, many much larger and better-resourced organisations that operated in the same general field, such as RCA in the United States and Marconi in the United Kingdom, went the same way. As fundamental and rapid changes occurred in the industry, it became very difficult for companies with large existing infrastructure commitments to redirect their resources into new directions. In addition, as the world electronics industry became progressively and rapidly more internationalised, it is hard to see how relatively small and independent operations like AWA could ever have survived. Upon reflection, I have to accept that it is actually possible that the management attitudes that so frustrated me over the last few years that I was there, and that I have criticised as being so backward-looking, were the best that could be done within the very difficult commercial environment in which the company operated. My decision to leave the company was certainly not made with any insights about what the future held for it. In the light of what subsequently occurred, however, the timing of my departure was probably optimal, both in terms of what I could have achieved had I stayed, and for the development of my subsequent career. Overall I have much to thank AWA for.

Ivory Towers

I was just 37 years old when I rejoined academia. I was pretty disillusioned by my experiences at AWA, and remember thinking that I would withdraw from the highly intensive type of life that I had lived in industry, and take it easy. In fact, I even felt that I might become a dropout. In hindsight, I'm astonished that I could have been so self-indulgent as to think in this way. I was clearly affected much more than I had been prepared to admit to myself by the stresses in my last couple of years at AWA. Dropping out is not my style.

My first day of work at the New South Wales Institute of Technology was appalling. I was asked to substitute for someone at a meeting of a committee dealing with matters relating to graduate students. The meeting went on for over three hours, and achieved almost nothing. I was staggered by how much my new colleagues could find to talk about on matters that seemed to me to be worthy of only a few minutes of deliberation. In short, I was astonished at the extraordinary waste of time. I felt quite down about this, and wondered what I had got myself into. However, things soon picked up.

NSWIT was a very interesting organisation. It was not a university at that time, although several of the senior academics would have liked to believe otherwise, and even gave themselves the title of Professor, which they weren't. NSWIT was one of the Colleges of Advanced Education within the tertiary education sector in Australia. The courses taught there were supposed to be more applied than those in a university, and it was expected that the staff would have more interaction with industry. Both of these things were very close to my heart. NSWIT did not have a strong culture of research, but they were very keen to develop this. They were therefore delighted when I brought with me from AWA my research work on the distribution of charge in electrets, including the Australian Government grant that I had to support it. I was very grateful to Lou Davies and AWA that they generously made available to me all of the equipment that I had built up over the years for this research.

I ended up enjoying my time at NSWIT immensely. There were significant challenges in the Department of Applied Physics that I headed, and I believe that I helped my colleagues there to think about these in a positive and productive way. I know that one very beneficial outcome of this was that some previously inactive members of the staff in my Department became motivated to get back into fully productive academic life. I also continued my electret research, with some quite useful outcomes. Perhaps most importantly, I developed a number of stimulating interactions with industry that were mutually beneficial, both technically, and because they generated some much-needed money for the relatively impoverished Department.

I cannot pretend that I worked as hard at NSWIT as I had before I went there. During my time at AWA, my good friend Jim Harvey had often been at me to take the odd afternoon off and go sailing with him. I could never bring myself to do this when I worked for a company whose bottom line depended directly on the efforts of its employees. At NSWIT, however, I had no such compunction and we had perhaps a dozen or so idyllic Wednesday afternoons together, playing truant. The format of these expeditions was fairly standard. We would get Jim's dinghy into the water near Meadowbank at about 1 o'clock, and sail from there towards the city. Our only cargo was an unused six-pack of beer. The prevailing afternoon breeze was normally a north-easter, and this was initially against us, so the outbound trip was fairly busy with regular tacking. Our goal was to get to the Harbour Bridge, but we never made it. On several occasions, however, we did circumnavigate Cockatoo Island. The run back to Meadowbank was straightforward with the wind behind us, and we had nothing to do in the late afternoon sun but sit back with one foot on the tiller, finish the six-pack, and tell each other what a lousy life we led.

A couple of these sailing afternoons were particularly memorable. Once we were near the beginning of our series of tacks towards the city when we noticed a large pleasure cruiser moored in the river, full of suits, all eating and drinking. We were outraged that they were doing this on a weekday afternoon, and decided to sail over and abuse them. When we had closed in to within about 20 metres, however, we noticed the familiar AWA logo on the side of the boat. Jim, who still worked for this erstwhile organisation, went for the bottom of the dinghy, and I did a hasty ready about and headed for the opposite bank. It was a very near thing.

On another occasion, we were sailing in my own Mirror dinghy, and we became fouled up with a trawling line behind a fishing boat. We were loudly abused by the indignant skipper. After we had got ourselves disentangled, we noticed a sharp bank of black clouds coming up rapidly from the south, and blocking out the previously clear blue sky. This did not look good, so we turned for home. Our run back was exhilarating and unforgettable. My little Mirror dinghy is not built for speed, but when the squall hit us she got up on the plane and the bow wave was higher than the gunwales. Jim is pretty heavy bloke, and we needed all of his ballast to stabilise the dinghy in the howling gale and driving rain. The force from the wind was so great that we broke part of the centreboard. Our final manoeuvre was a jibe to get into shore. It was purely by good luck that we managed to complete this without capsizing. Soaking wet, we packed up the boat, and finished the six-pack in front of Jim's fire. It was a great afternoon.

During my time at NSWIT, I completely recovered from the negative attitudes that had developed during my last few years at AWA, and began firing on all cylinders again. In fact, I was quite content there. I was therefore very surprised when I was approached by the University of Sydney and asked to apply for a new Chair of Physics that they were advertising. One of the responsibilities of the appointee was to lead a small and very productive group of researchers that had made significant advances in the field of solar energy. The University was keen to see the scientific developments from this group make the transition into industry. Even though I had essentially no experience in the solar energy field, I felt that I knew quite a bit about how, and how not, to take a technology from research to commercialisation. The position was therefore of great interest to me, and I applied.

Prior to the job interview, I was invited to the School of Physics by Harry Messel to have a chat with him and some of his senior staff. In hindsight, I think that this was probably a more important meeting than my actual job interview, but I didn't realise that at the time. Harry asked me why I had left the

University of Sydney in the first place. I replied that I had not been interested in any of the research that had been going on in the School of Physics during my honours year. Harry looked quite put out by this.

My official job interview was just before Christmas 1979. I met the Vice-Chancellor of the University, Professor Bruce (later Sir Bruce) Williams in his office, and he talked with me for a while before he took me to the interview. I was very touched by this courtesy. The room in which the interview was held contained what seemed to me to be a very large number of people – in fact there were probably only about twelve. My old friend and mentor, Lou Davies, was on the committee. The job interview was very searching, with some quite tough questions, particularly from Lou. I had thought that the committee would ask me about my lack of experience in the solar energy field, but they were much more interested in hearing my views on interactions between the academic sector and industry. I was also asked about my specialities in Physics, and whether I would see them as being reflected in the courses that I would like to teach. I replied that I did not see myself as carrying a torch for any particular area in Physics. Given the opportunity, I said that I would to like to teach Physics in the context of the *application* of the subject. I also said that I wanted to teach First Year students. This came as quite a surprise to some people on the Committee, because it had been over a decade since any Professor in the School of Physics had taught a First Year course. It is worth recording that the Committee took a very positive view of the fact that I had a couple of years of academic experience at NSWIT. They could see that my teaching at a tertiary level was satisfactory, and that I was able to function within the academic environment. I have no doubt that my time at NSWIT made me academically respectable in the eyes of the University of Sydney. I can only speculate about whether the University would have been prepared to take a chance on me if I had not had this prior academic experience.

Later that day, I was told informally that I would be offered the job. I came home that evening feeling as if I was walking on air. I joined the University of Sydney in July 1980. I remember having a very strong belief at the time that I would not see my career out at the University, or within the academic sector in general. I thought that I would end up back in industry. However, while I had many productive and rewarding interactions with industry during my time at the University, the next twenty years seemed to pass like a flash, and I found myself still there when I retired at the end of 2000.

Following the announcement early in 1980 of my appointment as a Professor at the University of Sydney, many people contacted me to offer their congratulations. I was most touched by this, and I still have all of the cards and letters that were sent to me. I also had some very heartwarming conversations with old friends. One of these had a most beneficial outcome for me. The significance of the story goes back to the time, more than a decade before, after I had completed my Ph.D. degree at New York University. The staff and students in Ben Bederson's Lab gave me a farewell present – a book on advanced quantum mechanics. After I had received it, one of my colleagues told me that they had discussed whether to choose this book, or another entitled *Handbook of Electron Tube and Vacuum Techniques* by Fred Rosebury. The book by Rosebury was published in 1965, and is a veritable encyclopedia of information of relevance to the field of its topic. My colleagues and I at NYU regularly used it in our day-to-day work. Of course, I was delighted to receive the quantum mechanics book, but my preference would very much have been for Rosebury. When I returned to AWA, I arranged for the company's Library to buy a copy of Rosebury, and it sat for the next decade in my office on permanent loan, being used extensively. People in other areas of the company found out about the book, and also arranged for the AWA Library to buy copies for their use. When I left AWA in 1978, I returned my copy of Rosebury to the Library. At the beginning of 1980, when I knew that I would again become involved in vacuum science and technology, I attempted to obtain a copy of Rosebury for myself. However, it was out of print, and my colleagues in the United States were unable to find a copy for me. In June 1980, a former AWA colleague, Bernie Simpson, who had taken over the management of the AWA Library, called me to offer his congratulations on my appointment. During our conversation, I must have remarked to him that I was going back into work involving vacuum technology, and that I was very sorry that I would not have a copy of Rosebury, as it was such an excellent reference source. A couple of days later, a package arrived in the mail containing a copy of the book, and the following note:

Richard
We have two copies of Rosebury, and as we are reducing duplicates where possible, please make good use of this discarded copy.
Bernie

I was most touched by Bernie's action. The copy of Rosebury that he gave me became one of the most valuable books that I own, and it is now falling apart from use. Recently, I bequeathed it to my former student and now colleague at the University of Sydney, Nelson Ng, on "permanent" loan.

Initially it felt very strange to be back at my alma mater as a staff member, rather than as a student. However, I quickly settled into the place. My former honours year supervisor, Don Millar, was now Deputy Head of School, and it was a delight to renew my association with him, and to work closely with him once again, albeit in a completely different capacity. It was also very interesting to work with Harry Messel. Amongst his many attributes and idiosyncrasies, Harry is a remarkably methodical man. He was able to retrieve the files from my honours year in 1960, and to see that he had put the following notation next to my name:

—> *to industry*

Harry claims that he did this following a discussion with me about my future. I have absolutely no recollection of such a discussion. Indeed, I don't believe that I ever spoke personally to Harry during my time as a student at the University of Sydney. On balance, I am inclined to think that my recollection of this matter is more accurate than Harry's, although it really doesn't matter.

Harry made much of the fact that one of his former students had gone the full circle and returned to academia. There was an article about my appointment in The Sydney Morning Herald with the headline: *After two decades, an arrow is reversed.* It carried a large photograph of me, and I had the slightly weird experience of travelling to work in the train one morning and seeing my face looking at me from the paper being read by the bloke sitting in the seat in front!

When I joined the University, I had to make a decision about whether to continue with my research work on the distribution of charge in electrets. The work was proceeding well, and my Australian Government grant that supported it still had some time to run. I dearly wanted to take this work further but, when I discussed the matter with Harry, his advice was unequivocal. He said that I had many new things to learn, and that continuation of my previous research would only act as a distraction from what should be my main game. As things transpired, he was absolutely correct. I therefore packed up the equipment, put it in a cupboard and, except for looking wistfully at it every five years or so, forgot all about it. In 2002, nearly two years after my retirement, the work experienced a very pleasant, if brief, resuscitation. I was contacted by a former colleague in the field from Monash University, Bob Fleming, who was organising the 11th International Symposium on Electrets in Melbourne. As part of the Symposium, Bob planned to run a one-day workshop on techniques for measuring the distribution of charge in electrets, and he asked if I would like to give the first presentation. I was delighted with the idea, and agreed. I pulled out my old papers, and made a few overheads from the figures that summarised the state of my research when I had left the field. Marilyn and I went to Melbourne for a week's holiday, and we took a day off for me to attend the workshop. I enjoyed giving the presentation, but the greatest thrill for me was to meet up with many of my former colleagues in the field, and to renew some friendships that had been dormant for over two decades. It was stated that the work that I did in the 1970s had served as a trigger for the development of several other methods to perform measurements of charge distribution in electrets, and that I was, in a very real sense, the originator of a significant area of activity. All in all, it was a most enjoyable and fulfilling experience.

During my time at the University, I had countless discussions with Harry Messel. Two early ones that stay in my memory are worth recounting here for what they reveal about how things were at the time. The first concerned the title of my Chair. This had not been specified in the advertisement for the position, presumably to give more flexibility in the selection process and to attract a broader field of candidates. As Head of School, Harry was required to make a recommendation on this matter to the Vice-Chancellor for approval by Senate, and he asked me for my opinion. I obviously could not call myself *Professor of Solar Energy*, because I demonstrably knew virtually nothing about this field. Even though much of my research had been in Solid State Physics, I felt that, given my general background, *Professor of Solid State Physics* would have been almost as inappropriate. I gave some thought to this matter, and rationalised that the thing that turned me on most, and the area in which I had the most experience, was seeing Physics *applied* for the practical benefit of society. I therefore suggested the title of *Professor of Applied Physics*. Some of my academic colleagues thought that this was not a good idea. In their view, and this was reinforced many times by my experiences in subsequent years, the words *Applied Physics* somehow equated to *Second-rate Physics*. I disagree strongly with this thesis, and I even wrote a paper on the subject a couple of years later. However Harry's response was quite different. "I think that would be a very sensible thing to do politically," he said. So *Professor of Applied Physics* I became.

On another occasion, Harry and I were discussing the evacuated tubular solar collectors that had been developed by my group before my arrival, and how this technology might make the transition to industry. I asked him, "What are the markets for these tubes – where will they be used?"

Harry's response was interesting, and revealing. "Markets!" he snorted. "Who cares about markets? This is the best technology in the world. People will beat a path to our door to get their hands on our tubes!"

Some years earlier, I had heard Harry describe the development of these solar collectors as "like finding barrels of oil in the desert." This description astonished me at the time, and I had tucked it away for future reference. Neither Harry, nor anybody else that I knew at the University of Sydney in those days, had any idea about the issues involved in taking a technology from the research stage to commercialisation. There were completely unrealistic expectations about how difficult it was to do this, and how long it might take. I do not make these observations in a critical away. It is a fact, however, that for many years I was the only member of the academic staff of the School of Physics at the

University of Sydney who had *any* experience in industry. This did not make me any better than my colleagues – far from it. But it did make me different. I was often able to use perspectives from my broader background to make contributions that were useful in resolving specific issues. Over the years, I learnt that the University of Sydney is staffed by some extraordinarily intelligent and talented individuals. With very few exceptions at that time, however, they had never been out of school, and their view of the world was therefore often very narrow.

I saw two examples of this at the first Academic Board meeting that I attended. I found meetings of the Academic Board quite difficult to take, in general. There were a few individuals on the board who appeared to approach every issue with an open mouth, and the debates were often long, tedious, repetitive, and with little point. I spoke only very infrequently at Academic Board meetings, and many of my colleagues also adopted this strategy, specifically so that the meetings would end in a finite time. At my first meeting, I recall two discussions. The first concerned academic salaries – a perpetually hot issue in any university environment. Someone argued that we academics at the University of Sydney should be paid more than other Australian academics, simply because we worked at *this* University. This was my first exposure to a quite widespread weakness that pervades the University of Sydney, or at least that did in those days. The University of Sydney is a great institution, with a long history of impressive achievement. However, that does not make it better than other universities. It is only better if it *continues* to achieve a higher level than its competitors. All too often, I saw academics within the University of Sydney content to depend for their status on the history of the University, rather than on their current achievements.

The second matter discussed at this Academic Board meeting was perhaps even more revealing. The subject being debated concerned textbooks. The issue seemed to be that the Co-operative Book Shop within the University was often not notified early enough about the textbooks that were to be assigned for courses that would be taught in the following year, so that these books were not on the shelves when students wanted to buy them. During the debate, someone said that we should be very cautious about telling the Co-operative Book

Shop too soon which textbooks we would be setting, because we should not be giving them an advantage over their competitors outside the University. This seemed to me to an absolutely astonishing and outrageous thing to say, but it did not evoke any response from the rest of the people there. Another exchange in this debate, however, did lead to uproarious laughter. One of the board members was commenting about the frequency with which textbooks were changed, and said something like, "Of course, we all change our textbooks every year."

Quick as a flash, the Chairman of the board came back with, "Except for the Board of Studies in Divinity."

Shortly after I joined the University I received a letter from the Acting Registrar that contained the following:

Dear Professor Collins

The Vice-Chancellor and Principal invites you to give the occasional address at the ceremony of conferring of degrees to be held on Saturday 14 March 1991 at 9:30 am in the Great Hall at the University. At this ceremony, degrees in the Faculty of Science will be conferred. Addresses at these ceremonies are usually about 10 minutes in length.

The Vice-Chancellor has asked me to say that he very much hopes that you will be able to accept this invitation.

As a relatively new academic, I was a little bemused by this letter. The brief second paragraph certainly made it obvious to me that, whatever the term *academic freedom* might mean, it did not extend to refusing a request from the Vice-Chancellor to give the occasional address at a graduation ceremony. More importantly, the first paragraph left some important things up in the air. I therefore sought some more information from the bloke in the Registrar's office who had sent the letter. Specifically, I asked him what I was supposed to talk about. He told me that the subject of my address was completely immaterial – I could talk about anything that I wanted. The only important thing, he said, was that I should not talk for more than ten minutes, because graduation ceremonies operated to a very tight schedule and this must not be disrupted by the speaker going over time. He added that all new Professors were asked to give an occasional address, the implication being that it was a kind of sophisticated initiation ceremony.

When the appointed day arrived, I put on borrowed academic robes because I had none of my own in those days, and joined the Academic Procession into the Great Hall. After the degrees had been conferred, the Chancellor, Sir Hermann Black, welcomed me as a "distinguished alumnus" of the University, and invited me to speak. I stepped up to the lectern, everything shaking but my voice if I recall correctly, and proceeded to talk about the relationship between the University and the rest of society. Drawing on my experiences in industry, I argued that all universities should give more attention to the problems of society that provided the money for their work. I said that the time would come when the Government, which provided virtually all of the funding for the universities, would start to ask questions about the return that they were getting for their investment. I even foreshadowed that universities might see reductions in the money given to them if they did not more effectively justify the things that they did to the community at large. When I had finished, the organ played Aida or something similar, and the Academic Procession marched out of the Great Hall. Sir Hermann was a traditionalist, a strong believer in autonomy for the universities, and of the right for academics to undertake curiosity-motivated research. I therefore wondered whether the things that I had said might have offended him. I need not have worried, however. As we walked down the front steps of the Great Hall into the morning sunlight, he turned to me and, with the gentle courtesy for which we all knew him and loved him, he said, "Thank you very much, Professor Collins, for that occasional address. It was exactly ... the right ... length."

My use of borrowed academic robes at this graduation ceremony deserves further comment. For many years after joining the University of Sydney, I did not go to the graduation ceremonies of my students simply because I did not possess academic robes, and hiring them was a real hassle. Eventually, I decided to invest the very significant amount of money necessary to acquire the robes for my Ph.D. degree from New York University. My daughter, Kathryn, who lived in the United States at the time, organised to get them for me. In common with many North American universities, the NYU Ph.D. robes are very grand – a long gown, deep purple and black in colour, with a black and gold hood and a nifty floppy hat. When I put them on I feel how I imagine a woman does when she is all dolled up for a dance. I am usually the best dressed, or at least the most impressively dressed, person in the academic procession. In the quadrangle after graduation ceremonies, it is not uncommon for women that I do not know to come up to me and stroke my arm, and for students to ask to have their photo taken with me. I have a theory that the robes are designed to make you feel so good that, whenever you put them on, you want to reach for your cheque book and send off a donation to your alma mater. The main benefit from having my own robes, however, is not that they make me look and feel grand, but that I get to go to my students' graduations. I get a real thrill from sitting on the stage in the Great Hall, and seeing the looks on the faces of the students as they come up to receive their testamurs from the Chancellor. Acquiring my NYU robes was one of the best investments that I ever made.

Sir Hermann Black was succeeded as Chancellor of the University by Emeritus Professor Dame Leonie Kramer, who is internationally famous as a scholar of Australian literature. Like Sir Herman, Leonie was a wonderful servant of the University, and provided outstanding leadership in the way that she championed academic values. Leonie was a very strong supporter of the School of Physics (and still is), and she could always be relied on to come to our functions, particularly those of the Science Foundation for Physics. For many years, Leonie welcomed the Scholars at the first lecture of our Professor Harry Messel International Science Schools, which are held every two years, and are attended by some 140 Scholars – talented senior high school students from around the world. On one occasion, I gave this lecture, and Leonie stayed on to hear it. The lecture was a rapid tour through the energy field, with many demonstrations, mostly involving the Scholars themselves. The finale was a simulated nuclear explosion. Before the lecture, all the Scholars had been given a dozen or so sheets of scrap paper that they had rolled up into little balls – these were the neutrons. The demonstration started with me throwing a neutron into the crowd. Depending on how close it came to a student, they then threw one or more of their neutrons high into the air. As controller of the reaction, I shouted instructions to them defining how close a neutron had to come before more were released, and how many should be released each time. I devised this variant of the old mousetrap and ping-pong ball demonstration myself, and ran it live for the first time at an earlier Science School. It offers much more flexibility than the mouse trap demonstration, since it is possible to simulate the behavior of an unsustainable reaction, a stable reaction, and a nuclear explosion. Moreover, it has that intrinsic feature of all effective learning experiences – involvement. It was a great icebreaker with which to begin the Science School. The Scholars loved it, particularly those who came from countries where such uninhibited behaviour would have been frowned upon. At the end of the demonstration, the lecture theatre was littered with thousands of paper balls, so I ran a nuclear waste clean-up operation. I got the big shots present, including the Chancellor, the Dean of Science, Harry Messel, and anybody else that I could lay my hands on, to stand in front of the group holding plastic garbage bins. I then instructed the Scholars to throw the paper balls into the garbage bins. Of course, kids being what they are, they shied many of them at the individuals, rather than the bins. I have a lot of time for Leonie Kramer – there must be very few people at such an elevated level who would come up afterwards and say how much they enjoyed being pelted with paper balls by a mob of excited teenagers.

Another person with whom I enjoyed working, and whom I respected a great deal, was Professor John Ward, who succeeded Bruce Williams as Vice-Chancellor of the University. Tragically, John and his wife were killed in a train accident a couple of years after his retirement. His death was an enormous loss to the University. John was a reluctant Vice-Chancellor, who took on the job because he felt that he was the best person around to do it. He led the University with great distinction, and championed the cause of academic excellence through his leadership by example. I was a member of an Appointment Committee for a Professor of Chemistry that he chaired. This was a most enlightening experience, if at times somewhat frustrating. From a group of very good candidates, two stood out as being exceptional. One of these was already an Associate Professor within the School of Chemistry – the other was from overseas. They both interviewed very well, and both had academic credentials that made them difficult to separate. There was, however, a very significant distinction between them. The internal candidate already had an active and productive research program within the University.

The external candidate would have required perhaps one million dollars to get his research started at the University. At its deliberative meeting, the Committee could not make a decision. The problem seemed to be that the Professors of Chemistry who were on the Committee had a great deal to say about both candidates, but they never made their point entirely clear. They certainly did not speak with one voice. When a decision was not forthcoming, John Ward adjourned the meeting to a later date. When we met again, however, exactly the same thing happened. An awful lot of talking took place, but we could not get to a decision. Another adjournment, another meeting. At this third get-together, I said something along the lines that we had two essentially indistinguishable candidates, one was for free, and the other would cost a lot of money, and that we should make the most cost-effective choice. This seemed to crystallise the decision, and the internal guy got the job. John Ward concluded the meeting by thanking all the members of the Committee saying, "It's been a most interesting experience for me. I don't know any more Chemistry, but I've learnt a great deal about chemists."

One of my favourite people within the University was Professor Robert Hanbury-Brown, universally known as Hanbury, who was Head of the Department of Astronomy within the School of Physics. Hanbury had been responsible for the conception and building of the Stellar Intensity Interferometer that was housed in the shed of my memorable 1960 honours Progress Meeting. For many years, he and his colleague John Davis had been building a new interferometer that would take the science further than had been possible with the original one. Hanbury was a remarkable man in many ways. He was very highly regarded internationally as a scientist, being a Fellow of the Royal Society, amongst many other things. He was quiet and unassuming yet, in front of a crowd, he was one of the most brilliant speakers that I ever saw. He was also a very religious man, and had written books on the relation between religion and science, but he did not thrust his beliefs in your face. I once attended a lunchtime lecture by him on this subject and was enormously impressed with the way that he presented his arguments. During the discussion session at the conclusion of his lecture, someone asked a question that was prefaced along the following lines: "Professor Hanbury Brown, you're an expert on both science and religion, so ..."

Before he responded to the question, Hanbury thought for a while, and then said, "You know, I've never considered myself an expert on anything – except perhaps the Professorial Superannuation Scheme."

Hanbury and I shared a passion – we were both dedicated do-it-yourselfers around the house. We had many long and fascinating conversations about the design of household equipment, and how to fix it. In fact, we even talked about jointly writing a book on this subject entitled *Domestic Engineering*. It turned out that we were both the not-too-proud owners of the same sort of gravity-fed, off-peak hot water system – a Joseph Auto-Hot – that was distinguished by having an exceedingly complex control mechanism. The system would heat up overnight, leaving it full of hot water in the morning. As hot water was used during the day, cold water flowed into the system keeping the water level constant. This caused the temperature of the water in the tank to decrease gradually. When the hot water in the tank had cooled below a specified temperature, the flow of cold water ceased, and further use of hot water caused the water level in the tank to fall. The components that controlled the water inlet, and the water temperature, were very poorly designed and unreliable, so that the operation of the system would vary depending on dimensional changes of the galvanised tank that enclosed the system. Both Hanbury and I developed independent solutions to these design flaws that enabled our systems to work tolerably well.

Another very unattractive quirk of the Joseph Auto-Hot system was that it could completely run out of hot water without warning. On many occasions, our house was penetrated by an anguished shriek from someone in the shower: "There's no more hot water!" I discovered that, when this happened, there was still a bit more hot water in the storage tank below the level of the outlet pipe. I developed a method of getting some extra cold water to flow back into the tank, raising the water level slightly above the outlet pipe, and thus providing an additional few minutes of warm shower water. This technique involved removing the rose from the shower, blocking the outlet with my thumb, and then opening the hot and cold water taps in a specific sequence so that cold water was forced backwards past the normally non-return hot water tap, and up into the tank. I recall doing this often, with some naked, soapy, shivering kid in the corner of the shower recess pleading, "Hurry up! Hurry up!" This complex procedure provided enough extra warm water to rinse and reheat the victim before she got out. It's a great pity that Hanbury and I never got around to writing *Domestic Engineering*. This technique would have been an important addition to the do-it-yourself literature. Come to think about it, however, it might have had only historical significance because, for obvious reasons, the Joseph Auto-Hot Company went out of business.

The School of Physics was also blessed with some extraordinary characters in their support staff. One of these was Wally Gill, who ran the Store. Wally was an extremely helpful bloke who had been around the School forever, and who was very happy in his job. On one occasion, I was attempting to develop a method of mounting my sailing dinghy onto a box trailer. When I did this, the boat protruded too far forward, so that it would have damaged the rear of the car if I turned sharply. I therefore had to extend the tow bar mounting attachment on the box trailer. In order to do this, I needed some material, and I also had to replace completely the electrical cabling in the trailer. I went down to see Wally, and asked him if he had a piece of steel bar of a particular size.

"Sure," said Wally. "I've got tons of it. Help yourself."

I then asked for a couple of heavy steel bolts.

"No problem," said Wally. "There's boxes of them."

Finally, I said to Wally, "I don't suppose that you've got any four-core electrical cable?"

Wally said, "Oh, so you're doing a box trailer, eh?"

I later recounted this conversation to one of my academic colleagues and he remarked, "Wally has got something on everyone in the School."

The School of Physics in those days was a very sexist place. My recollection is that there were no female members of academic staff at that time. As I mentioned in the second chapter, Phyllis Nichol, one of the co-authors of the famous Physics textbook, and the dedicated Head of the Second Year Laboratory, had been a Tutor many years before when I was a student in the School, but I don't think that she was ever promoted to the full academic staff. Perhaps the most obvious indication of the sexist attitudes in the School at the time of my return was the sign on the male Staff toilet. (Yes, we did have a male *Staff* toilet in those days – shades of AWV!) This toilet was simply identified by the word STAFF. After a decade or so, I finally managed to get the sign changed to something more appropriate, and eventually the class distinction disappeared so that it became available for use by all males. Before this happened, however, one of the female secretaries in the School insisted on taking the sign literally, and would often come into the room to wash her hands. This was a bit of off-putting if you were having a pee at the time and I, for one, never quite got used to it.

In the late 1980s, computers started to enter our lives. I took a very dim view of this at the time and, while I now use these things regularly and recognise the enormous benefits that they have brought to our work, I still feel generally negative about them. One of the problems with computers is that you can never have enough of them, because the machine that you bought a couple of years ago is now essentially useless. They now represent a major budget item, with no end in sight to the increasingly rapid and costly cycle of engineered obsolescence. My principal objection to computers, however, is that they often stand in the way of understanding the Physics of a problem, and cause people to avoid thinking, and therefore developing insights into it.

The obsession with personal computers in the School of Physics during the 1980s was initially limited to a few enthusiasts, but the disease rapidly spread. Although I stayed right away from them for as long as possible, I recognised that we needed some within the Department of Applied Physics, and so I bought a couple for the Lab. They were very heavily used and continually in need of upgrading and replacement. Uncharacteristically, I started to wonder whether the absence of a computer in my office was presenting the wrong image to my students, so I had one installed on my desk. I never used it, but many other people did. Eventually, the students decided that their needs were greater than mine (which was evidently the case) and, without asking, they relocated my computer to their own room. About three weeks passed before I noticed that it had gone. Before this happened, however, the following occurred.

One of the academics in the Department of Applied Physics, Bernard Pailthorpe, was a big gun on computers and subsequently developed an international reputation in numerically intensive computing. Bernard led the development in Australia of methods and facilities for the visualisation of computer data. On this occasion, he came bustling into my office in a somewhat agitated state, informing me that he was running late for a deadline, that the students were occupying all of the other computers, and that he had to use mine. "Sure, Bernard," I said. "Feel free."

Bernard settled himself down while I returned to whatever had been occupying me previously. In the corner of my mind, however, I soon noticed some heavy breathing, and I then observed Bernard gathering up his papers and heading at high speed for the door. I asked what was wrong, and he said, "There's something wrong with your bloody computer. It won't boot up."

I reached over behind the computer and jiggled the plug in the power point, whereupon the computer made a most satisfying noise and started to come to life. Bernard stood there, eyes and mouth wide-open in astonishment and disbelief. Rubbing salt into the wound, I said, "I don't know much about computers, Bernard, but I'm very good on plugs."

Of course, as the years progressed, I also started to use computers. However, I kept pretty quiet about this, and maintained my public image of a computerphobe. I found it useful to do this, because it helped me bring back to earth those misguided individuals who thought that computers were an alternative to experimentation, and even thinking. Many years before, I had observed that several of my graduate student colleagues added years to their Ph.D.'s by becoming addicted to the game of bridge. Their lunchtime bridge games often extended right through to afternoon tea, and sometimes longer. These days, surfing the Web is the modern equivalent of these bridge games. I saw many students fritter away enormous amounts of time in this way, and I was very critical of this. I therefore refused to have anything to do with the establishment of the School's website, because I couldn't see how this was anything but a waste of time. Of course, I was wrong, but that didn't become obvious to me until much later. Before that happened, one of my graduate students, Tom Simko, discovered that someone had put my picture on the School's home page. He photocopied it, and sent it to me with the notation, "You're right, Dick. There certainly *is* a lot of junk on the Web."

One of the very attractive features of academia is that it is quite forgiving of idiosyncrasies. Many people in this environment behave in a way that would not be tolerated in the outside world, or would at least be regarded as pretty odd. Within universities, however, such behaviour usually scarcely raises an eyebrow. Some may say that this is simply because academia is a sheltered workshop, and that everyone there is a misfit who can't hack it in the real world. I disagree. With only a handful of exceptions, everybody that I knew within the University of Sydney worked very hard and effectively, and had a high level of commitment and dedication to their chosen field of activity. The fact that they may have some peculiar or unusual characteristics seems to me to be quite irrelevant to the main game. Indeed it adds to the spice of academic life.

One of my favourite unusual people at the University of Sydney, and a very good friend, is Manfred Lenzen. I first met Manfred when he visited Australia towards the end of his Ph.D. degree in Germany. His visit had several purposes, one of which was to find a place to work after he had finished his graduate studies. He planned to apply for a German postdoctoral fellowship that would permit him to work at an overseas university of his choosing. I have only vague recollections of our first meeting – visits to my office from such people were a common occurrence in those days. However, Manfred tells me that I spent a considerable amount of time with him, gave him a detailed tour of the laboratory, discussed with him possible projects on which he might work should his fellowship application be successful, and took him to lunch. In due course, he did indeed obtain the fellowship, and came to work with us for three years, at no cost. Having somebody who is as talented as Manfred working with you for free is like manna from heaven. As we got to know one another better, I asked him why he chose to work with us, rather than with one of the many other groups in Australia that were researching environmentally-related issues. He replied that I had showed him more courtesy, friendship and consideration than he had received at any other place that he had visited. This astonished me, because I am certain that I would not have treated Manfred differently from any other person who had come in off the street.

In addition to being a very good scientist, Manfred is by far the most dedicated conservationist and environmentalist that I have ever met. He attempts to lead his life in a way that will leave as little adverse impact as possible on the environment of the planet. As far as I can tell, he hardly ever buys anything new. This is not because he is tight with his money. He genuinely believes that most of the things that people throw away are still useful. I understand that he supported himself through his Ph.D. study by collecting bicycles that had been thrown out for rubbish collection, and refurbishing them. Manfred was responsible for introducing the practice within the School of Physics of printing draft material on the back of previously used paper. He doesn't own a car – indeed he hardly owns anything. On one occasion he showed me five milk crates in his office that were full of old clothes, and told me that these contained his entire worldly possessions. Another time, Manfred came to visit us on the Central Coast sporting a nifty pair of new swimming pants, and saying that he had found them on the beach the previous day.

Since most of his clothes are second hand or castaways, one could never describe Manfred as being a snappy dresser. His typical garb is a threadbare T-shirt, holey jeans and sandals. This once caused him problems at the graduation ceremony of one of my Ph.D. students, Christopher Dey, which Manfred attended. At the conclusion of the ceremony, along with the rest of the gathering, he joined the new graduates for morning tea on the lawns in the quadrangle. He was then approached by a security officer who tried to move him on, saying that the morning tea was not for students. Being a man of principle, Manfred refused to say that he was a guest of someone who had graduated, and instead started to lecture the man about the wrongs of stereotyping individuals on the basis of how they are dressed.

"See that man over there," he said, pointing to a well-dressed gentleman in a suit. "How come you are not asking *him* to move on because he is a student?" Fortunately, Christopher came to the rescue at this point, and Manfred was allowed to stay.

Another of the characters who added spice to life at the University of Sydney was Professor Julius Sumner Miller. Julius had been around for many years before I rejoined University. He was, and still is, quite famous in Australia for his television lectures and his provocative *Why is it so?* In front of a class, Julius was perhaps the best presenter of Physics that I ever saw. His technique was to provoke, embarrass and stimulate, rather than to encourage and explain. In keeping with this, Julius was an irascible old pedant, and I have to say that I never heard him laugh. He also took himself very seriously. On one occasion, I came into his room to find him speaking on the telephone to the switch girl at the Sydney Morning Herald newspaper.

"I am Professor Julius Sumner Miller," he said, "And I take great exception to the statement in your newspaper that today is the first day of autumn. Today is the first day of March. Autumn does not begin until the equinox which is on the 21st or the 22nd of March."

Clearly the girl on the switchboard didn't know what to do with this caller and, more seriously, she evidently had never heard of Professor Julius Sumner Miller. It was a very tense encounter.

My fondest recollection of Julius was the last time that I ever saw him lecture. He was well over 70 years old, could stand unaided only with difficulty, and had lost much of his sight. Nevertheless, I watched spellbound as he held a packed lecture theatre in his hand, presenting conundrums in Physics, provoking responses, and insulting us all. The finale of his performance was the collapse of a 200 litre (44 gallon) drum that had been boiling away on a primus stove in the corner throughout the lecture. (This dramatic demonstration of the magnitude of atmospheric pressure is now banned, because of the danger of the drum exploding.) Julius directed the lecture demonstration staff to seal the drum and then pour cold water over it, resulting in a spectacular and impressive collapse. This prompted a prolonged standing ovation from the staff and students who had been fortunate enough to witness the whole performance. I can still see Julius propped up against the lecture bench at the front of the theatre, tears pouring down his cheeks, in gratitude for this acknowledgment of his extraordinary talent. In hindsight, I think that he probably knew that this was the last lecture that he would ever give. He was very unwell at the time, and died soon afterwards. The whole experience is one that I treasure.

Another of the great characters that I was fortunate to know at the University, and who has already featured in this book, is Harry Messel. There are many great stories about Harry, and I hope that they will eventually be written down in one place.

Here I content myself with just a few. Harry continued to run his progress meetings during the twenty or so years that I was away from the University so that upon my return, I found myself as a presenter, rather than an uncomprehending member of the audience. I don't think that the meetings ever reached great heights in interest or intelligibility but, Harry being what he is, we had to endure them. The exception was Harry's last Progress Meeting ever, which occurred just before his retirement from the University at the end of 1987. Quite on the spur of the moment, we presenters decided that, instead of giving our regular reports, we would simply table them, and then tell our favourite Harry story. What followed was a memorable evening full of hilarity and pathos, and enlightening in what the stories revealed about the extraordinary complexities of this remarkable man. Of course, I told my *shed* story, but there are couple of others that need to be included here.

Don Melrose spoke about the time that Harry returned to the School of Physics following a meeting in which he unsuccessfully attempted to persuade the Vice-Chancellor to accept an argument that he was putting. We were all having morning tea together when Harry burst in, his face black with rage. It is not often that Harry is lost for words, but on this occasion he had difficulty getting them out.

"That Vice-Chancellor," he screamed. "He's a bloody fuckin' … a bloody fuckin' …"

He had the adjectives, but he could not get the noun. Finally it came to him.

"He's a bloody fuckin' PSYCHOPATH!"

The Vice-Chancellor at the time was Professor Sir Bruce Williams, and many years later, I persuaded him to tell the story of the preceding encounter with Harry that had prompted this outburst. Bruce did this at a black tie function to honour Harry and, given the vernacular involved and Bruce's correctness, I consider it no mean feat that I got him to tell it. It seems that when Harry's arguments left the Vice-Chancellor unmoved, Harry adopted his normal technique of increasing the volume and pitch. However, none of these entreaties swayed the Vice-Chancellor from his negative position. Finally, as Bruce tells it, Harry stormed out of the office, pausing at the door to deliver his parting shot: "Jesus Christ, Vice-Chancellor! If you were arguing with the Viet Cong, I'd feel sorry for the fuckin' Viet Cong."

For most of the time that I was at the University of Sydney, I kept my nose reasonably clean. Of course I had a few disagreements with Heads of School, particularly Harry Messel, but generally I managed to attract very little adverse attention from those in more elevated positions. On one occasion when I was Head of School, however, I came very close to receiving a formal reprimand from the University. The initiative that prompted this was the refurbishment of one of our lecture theatres. Before I became Head, we had conducted an extensive refurbishment of our main lecture theatre, with very good outcomes. We turned a dingy, old-fashioned room into a modern one, with excellent acoustics, sophisticated computer support capabilities, and good lighting. It was an environment in which very effective teaching could, and did, occur. At one stage, I believe that this was one of the best lecture theatres within the University. As Head, I oversaw a program of progressive refurbishment of the remaining four lecture theatres in the School of Physics. We managed this process entirely within the School – my colleague Rod Cross interacted with a builder, and we did all of the design work, the choice of equipment and facilities, and the project supervision. The results were spectacularly good.

My problems occurred when we attempted to apply this procedure to our last remaining lecture theatre. We were well into the project, and had done a lot of the demolition of the interior of the theatre when I received a blistering letter from the Deputy Vice-Chancellor, Professor Ken Eltis. He pointed out that we had no authority or approval to do this work, that we had not given appropriate consideration to safety or industrial issues and, perhaps most importantly, that we were ignoring heritage aspects of the School of Physics building. All of this was undoubtedly true although, given that we had done similar refurbishments several times before, it seemed a bit late in the day to raise such matters. The letter arrived just before Christmas, and I called Ken, with whom I had a good relationship, and asked him whether he required us to stop work on the project. I pointed out that, if he insisted that we do this, we would have significant problems when classes resumed the following year. Ken was very reasonable, and said that he did not want us to stop work, but that he needed a response to the matters raised in his letter. I told Rod to get on with the job, and to make sure that the demolition was complete before it was necessary for me to respond to Ken towards the end of January. He did this, and I wrote a few pages of waffle that got me off the hook, and evidently allowed Ken to placate the individuals in his staff who had raised these concerns. In due course, the lecture theatre was completed, and it sits alongside our others as an excellent teaching area. Later in the year, I invited Ken Eltis to visit the School of Physics and took him on a tour of our teaching facilities. He was very impressed. He then acknowledged that, if we had followed the correct practices, our very limited budget would not have permitted us to do the refurbishment. It was a nice example of practice triumphing over theory. I hold no grudge towards Ken for giving me a hard time over something that we were clearly doing incorrectly – and we remain good friends.

I retired from the University of Sydney at the end of 2000. I was only 60 years old at time, but I didn't want to find myself in the position where people were wishing that I would leave – I preferred to be farewelled with regret, rather than with relief. I have to say that I enjoyed my twenty years as a Professor at the University enormously. I joined the University soon after I left industry, where I had been very frustrated with my inability to achieve satisfaction in my job. A university is one of the few environments that allow you to define your own goals, and then give you the freedom to go out and achieve them. I found that very satisfying. The ability to choose what one does is a great privilege. In my opinion, it also comes with significant responsibilities to consider matters other than personal interest in deciding the areas in which to undertake research. My observation is that most academics do not believe that they work for the University. Rather, they think that, and act as if, they work for themselves. This is an excellent attitude for achieving significant outcomes. It poses real challenges, however, when it is necessary to move the University, as a corporate body, in particular directions.

Very soon after my arrival at the University, I understood the dilemma about management within this environment, and the difficulties in doing it effectively. Academics are very clever people, but they are also often very clever, unreasonable people. The concept of management within a university environment is something of an oxymoron. As someone else once said, it's a bit like herding cats. Within a year or two of my appointment at the University of Sydney, I had made up my mind that I did not want to climb the academic administration ladder. I never considered seeking to become a Dean, or a Pro-Vice-Chancellor, or whatever. I was very happy doing what I did, and I think that I did it quite well. I never even wanted to become Head of the School of Physics until I formed that view that I was the best person available for the job. Then I wanted it very badly, and I was delighted to be appointed. I enjoyed my four years as Head immensely. Of course the job had significant challenges, and there were times when I worked under great stress. However, I had learnt by then that one feeds on the positive things in a job, and uses the satisfaction and energy derived from these positives to cope with the negative times. All this, of course, begs the question about whether I might have similarly enjoyed working at a higher level within the University. I will never know, but I have no regrets about the choices that I made.

The secretary's job is to keep the OUT tray empty;
the boss' job is to keep the IN tray empty

123

Extracurricular Activities

Throughout my working life, I have been fortunate to participate in many professional activities outside the normal responsibilities associated with my regular job. In the main, these extracurricular activities have been highly enjoyable and interesting, if at times perhaps a little memorable. They also significantly aided the development of my professional career, and helped to broaden my perspectives.

In 1973 I was nominated by AWA as their representative on the Industrial Mobilisation Course. During the meetings and visits associated with this Course, we met with people at all levels, right up to chief executives of companies, and senior staff in Government and Defence organisations. I was therefore exposed to a broad range of ideas, and had many in-depth discussions with very interesting individuals. In addition, the visits to the diverse establishments during the course provided me with wonderful insights into the operation of manufacturing facilities, and the technologies that were used in many industries. I was also able to learn at first hand about both appropriate, and inappropriate philosophies for running successful organisations. Along the way, I developed close friendships with many of the course participants. For many years after we completed the course, several of us continued to meet regularly on a social basis, reliving the great times that we had experienced together, and maintaining the friendships that we had developed. My participation in the 1973 IMC was one of the most informative, enjoyable and developmental experiences of my professional life.

One of the very attractive features of the course was that we were fed like kings wherever we went. Without exception, the food provided to us during our daytime visits, and when we lived in at various places, was absolutely outstanding, both in quality and quantity. I was then, and still am, something of a tooth man and, being quite young at the time, I did not put on weight. I therefore got to eat all this fantastic stuff without any adverse side effects. Many of the other participants in the course were quite a bit older than me, however, and had a tendency to be slightly on the rotund side. I think that I was almost the only person whose girth did not noticeably increase during this year.

One of the things that greatly impressed me during my visits to Defence establishments was the amount of training that this organisation provides for their employees. I learnt that Defence takes a very strategic view about developmental activities that its personnel must undertake in order to keep up-to-date with modern technology and thinking. I was particularly struck by the contrast between this, and total lack of career development programs in my own organisation. On one of our visits, a very intense warrant officer described a system that had recently been introduced for examining the students who participated in their training courses. It was actually just a simple multiple-choice paper. However, he was very proud of fact that the paper could be marked rapidly by placing a template over it that contained little holes in the positions that corresponded to the correct boxes. "To evaluate the student," he said, "all that we have to do is count the number of marks that show in these holes."

I thought about this and then said, "That wouldn't work. If a student put a mark in every box, he would get 100%."

The WO looked at me with disdain and, even though his superior officer was standing nearby, said, "There's one in every crowd."

I also formed a very positive view of the work ethic of virtually all of the Defence personnel that I met during the year. In general, they were highly motivated and dedicated to their jobs, and enthusiastic about what they did. I was also impressed by the respect that they showed for their superiors (not that they had any alternative). This insight had a very positive benefit for me. The year after I did the course, I received an enquiry for a job from Doug Edwards, who had recently resigned from the Australian Navy as a Chief Petty Officer in submarines. As it happened, a vacancy had just occurred for a technical officer to support my research program and, my view of Defence people being so positive, I put him on without question. He was a fantastic person to have on the team. He was almost manic in his dedication to his work, and showed great initiative and creativity in all that he did. His contributions were far above the call of duty. Doug had an enormously positive impact on my research program, and I will be forever grateful to him for the things that he did for me, and to the IMC for making me aware of the talent that was available in Defence personnel.

Occasionally, the IMC provided us with insights into some industries that reflected on them negatively, rather than positively. One of our visits was to an oil refinery. During the question-and-answer session that followed our tour, we asked how the industry would react if the supply of oil from overseas were to be restricted due to security problems or political action. This question provoked surprise, and perhaps a little scorn.

"We have never considered such a possibility," was the answer. "We think that this scenario is highly unlikely."

The oil shocks of 1973 followed a few months later.

One of the very enjoyable features of the course, for me, was the practice in many of the presentations, and amongst the participants, of telling jokes. Many of these were rather splendid and, although I can remember many of them to this day, I regret that I did not systematically record them all for posterity. Some of the most amusing things, however, were not retold jokes, but spontaneous happenings. Perhaps the funniest thing that I can recall from the course, and certainly the best vote of thanks that I have ever heard, occurred during our visit to a company that produced aluminium. The person who thanked the company for hosting our visit was Merv Chapman, who worked for a firm that manufactured stainless steel products. Merv's thank you speech was brief and memorable:

"I have had an absolutely appalling day," he said. "I trudged around this site for hours seeing nothing but aluminium. Huge lumps of aluminium, cauldrons of molten aluminium, rolls of aluminium, aluminium being extruded, bent, straightened, hardened, and softened. Nothing but bloody aluminium. All day I kept looking for some stainless steel. And finally when I found a bit, what were you doing? Pissing on it!"

I was asked to give the vote of thanks after our visit to the Australian Atomic Energy Commission at Lucas Heights, presumably because I was one of the few scientists on the course. I am sure that nobody there could possibly have predicted that fourteen years later I would be Chairman of that organisation.

My research interests during my twenty years stay at the University of Sydney covered many diverse fields of science. A continuing theme of the *application* of this work, however, was energy. It was no surprise, therefore, that I was asked to participate in several energy-related activities outside the University. One of these was as a Member of the National Energy Research, Development and Demonstration Council, known more commonly by the hard-to-pronounce acronym NERDDC. NERDDC made recommendations to the Australian Government about the provision of financial support to researchers in the energy field. The Council consisted of about ten people, all but one from outside Government. All of these Members were active in, or representative of, significant energy-related fields – coal, oil, gas, conservation and, in my case, a potpourri including solar energy, wind energy, wave energy, geothermal energy, fission and fusion. Recommendations for support of projects by NERDDC came to the Council through its seven Technical Standing Committees, or TSCs, as they were known. Each TSC was chaired by a Member of the Council, and the membership of each one included researchers and others with interests and experience in that particular energy field. The recommendations that came from my committee, TSC 5, seemed to give the other Members of the Council more trouble than most of the rest put together.

During my time on NERDDC, the Chairman was Jan Kolm who had recently retired from the position of Executive Director of ICI Australia. Jan is one of my heroes in Australian science. His Chairmanship of NERDDC was just one of many contributions that Jan made to science, technology and education after his retirement. I loved working with Jan on NERDDC. I have the highest regard for the unselfish way in which he used his vast wisdom for the benefit of our country. He provided very perceptive insights that guided the deliberations of the Council. He was also a highly cultured person, and extraordinarily knowledgeable about many other things. Although English was not his first language, Jan spoke it like a native, and knew more about this language that anybody else that I have ever met. It is my understanding that in earlier days he had actually lectured on linguistics. I once participated with him in writing a NERDDC document, and he astonished me by quoting rules of English grammar that had been previously unknown to me.

Several of the members of the NERDDC Council came from

industry, and were pretty hard-bitten and down-to-earth. Some of them often had real problems with projects that were recommended from my Technical Standing Committee, and this provoked debates on these matters that were lively and frank, without being destructive or vindictive. At such times, Jan Kolm's superb Chairmanship usually managed to guide the Council to a position that, if not unreservedly supported by everyone, was at least acceptable to them, allowing us to move forward. I learnt a great deal about chairing meetings from Jan.

Each Technical Standing Committee on NERDDC was supported by a member of the Public Service who undertook the very significant administrative tasks associated with the management of the research portfolio in the corresponding technical area. This person was referred to as the Executive Member, Secretary of the Committee, or EMS for short. Inevitably, a close relationship developed between the EMS and the Committee, and with the Chairman of the Committee in particular. The EMS's were normally relatively junior officers in the Public Service, but they had significant responsibilities. They were often required to walk a very fine line between accommodating the views of Members of the Technical Standing Committee, and those of more senior Government bureaucrats.

One of the EMS's of my Technical Standing Committee was Bernard Pailthorpe, and we hit it off right from when we first met. A few years later, I lured Bernard from the Public Service to come and work with me at the University of Sydney. He went on to great things in computers, and is now the Professor of Computational Science at the University of Queensland. Bernard was so on top of his job as EMS of my Committee that he seemed to have lots of time to indulge in other activities, one of which appeared to be to bait his superiors. On one occasion, TSC 5 decided to hold a workshop on solar ponds. Solar ponds are bodies of water, a few hundred square metres or more in area, which heat up in the sun. The loss of heat from these ponds is reduced by various techniques, most involving suppression of the internal convection that normally occurs when water is exposed to sunlight. One way of doing this is to make the bottom of the pond saltier than the top, so that the more dense saline water at the bottom does not rise to the surface as it heats up. At that time, perhaps three Australian research groups were interested in solar ponds. One of these ponds had been built in Melbourne, but its temperature had stayed quite low due to the relatively small amount of sunlight at that latitude. Another was at Alice Springs and, indeed, this was the only successfully operating Australian solar pond at that time. Because of this, TCS 5 decided that the most appropriate place to hold its proposed solar pond workshop was Alice Springs. Bernard Pailthorpe took this recommendation to his boss, who immediately hit it on the head stating that such a Government-funded activity in a place like Alice Springs would simply be a boondoggle. He insisted that the solar pond workshop would be in Melbourne. Encouraged by Bernard, I decided that this was a battle worth fighting, both in principle, and because I genuinely believed that it would be better to meet where the action was occurring, rather than where the technology had not worked very effectively. So we made our arguments and injected them into the system at a slightly higher level. A decision was made to shift the workshop to Alice Springs. However, Bernard's boss was not finished yet and escalated the conflict even further. The workshop was moved back to Melbourne. Bernard and I were determined that this was an argument that we would win, so we raised the stakes to the top. The workshop ended up in Alice Springs. Bernard's boss was absolutely livid and Bernard told me that he ranted through the Department screaming, "I'll get TSC 5 and Dick Collins for this!" Surprisingly, however, he and I remained good friends. Our solar pond workshop was highly successful, even if it *did* turn out to be a bit of a boondoggle.

I believe that NERDDC did a really good job in accommodating the diverse views of the large number of researchers in many different energy fields, and making balanced decisions about which projects to recommend for support. I'm certain that part of this success was directly attributable to the wisdom of Jan Kolm as Chairman. Amongst other things, he set up meetings to inform people about the type of work that we wanted to fund, and the competing demands on NERDDC's resources. One of these meetings was held in Canberra, and many energy researchers from around Australia attended. The meeting was opened by the then Minister responsible for matters relating to energy, Senator Peter Walsh. At morning tea after his opening address, Jan Kolm took the Minister around to meet the

Members of the Council. When I was introduced to him, I remarked that he probably wouldn't remember meeting me a few years earlier when he had visited the School of Physics at the University of Sydney. He looked at me intently for a moment, and then said, "Yes, I remember meeting you. You had a beard at the time." He was correct, and I was astonished.

At this particular meeting, I was asked to give one of the early presentations. My task was to discuss some of the dilemmas between the desire by researchers to advance the science in their work, and the wish by NERDDC that the projects that it supported should have useful practical outcomes, and make a significant impact in the energy field. I began my talk by recounting the story about the Meccano sets that my brother William and I had played with as children – how he always built models from the book, and I built from my head, and that he eventually became an engineer, and I ended up as a scientist. I then linked this story to the difference between engineering and science, and developed my message. It must have struck a chord, because virtually every subsequent speaker on the program incorporated the Meccano theme into his or her presentation. It was nice object lesson to me about methods that will grab the attention of the audience, and help get your message across.

I have used this technique of introducing a subject through a seemingly orthogonal discussion on several occasions. Once I gave a talk on evacuated solar collectors at an international conference on solar energy in Perth. I began by remarking that we had many visitors from overseas and, as a public service to them, I proposed to present a lecture on the platypus. I then talked for a few minutes about this extraordinary creature highlighting its many unusual features. Every person in a lecture theatre was hanging on to my words. Having concluded that the platypus is a weird and wonderful animal, I then remarked that evacuated solar collectors are a similarly weird and wonderful way of collecting solar energy, and started in on my main theme, to the relief of most people present. At the end of the talk, I discussed the prospects for the commercial success of this type of solar collector and remarked that, if they did not succeed they, like the platypus, would be in danger of becoming extinct. The talk was well received, and the message stuck. For many years afterwards, I would meet the occasional person who said to me,

"I remember you – you gave the platypus talk." The only advice that I offer to others considering this strategy is that you need to tough out a period at the beginning of the talk during which the audience is not with you, and this can be quiet stressful. Never lose your nerve.

I served four enjoyable years on NERDDC, but all good things have to come to an end, and my appointment ceased in 1987. I was particularly attracted to the philosophy of funding research that was oriented towards achieving practical, quantifiable outcomes in a reasonable time. In those days, NERDDC was one of the few Australian Government funding organisations in the physical sciences and engineering field that articulated such a philosophy. A couple of years after my departure, a review of NERDDC was held that applauded this approach, but noted that even so there had been inadequate tangible benefits to the energy field from the projects that NERDDC had funded. The review concluded that the close involvement of Government in the management of the research projects tended to act as a barrier for the outcomes from the research being applied in practice. The review went on to recommend that the management of Government energy research funding initiatives should be separated further from the bureaucracy of the Public Service. It was therefore decided to establish the Energy Research and Development Corporation to manage all Government-funded energy research in Australia (except for work relating to coal). ERDC would have their funds provided by Government, but would operate essentially outside of the Public Service, and be managed by an independent board consisting of people with relevant expertise from industry and the research community. As with all such bodies, however, the board would include a Government representative to provide advice on policy and the like. I was surprised, and delighted to be asked to be the inaugural Chairman of ERDC.

There were many positives during my time as Chairman of ERDC. We set up an organisation that was generally regarded as being very well managed, and efficiently run, and which supported a wide range of energy research programs that were targeted towards achieving quantifiable practical outcomes. I also became good friends with quite a few people on the board and in the management of ERDC. On balance, however, I cannot say that I enjoyed my time as Chairman as much has I had expected. One of the problems was that many of the people within Government who had previously been involved in such work remained where they had been, and set about developing their own programs, some of which were quite similar to those offered by ERDC. In a very real sense, we in ERDC often seemed to find ourselves in competition with parallel Government initiatives. A direct outcome of this was that we sometimes competed with them for money, and when this occurred we were at a distinct disadvantage because they were within the process that determined where the Government funding would go, and we were outside it.

Another very unpleasant aspect of this Chairmanship was that I personally found myself the subject of much criticism from various parts of the energy research community. Because of our insistence that research projects should have practical outcomes, and should also receive matching funding from industry, many of the proposals that we received were rejected. Researchers in the field often objected to this, and some of these objections ended up transforming into abuse and vilification of me. At the time, I was also Chairing the Australian Nuclear Science and Technology Organisation, and occasionally my critics sought to draw links between these two responsibilities, alleging that my nuclear-related responsibilities represented a conflict of interest that resulted in me having a bias against non-nuclear research. Those who knew me well could see that such allegations were rubbish, and some of them argued on my behalf against these criticisms, but inevitably some of the mud stuck.

My term of appointment as Chairman was for three years and, as that time neared, I felt that I had had enough. I was requested by the Government to accept a second three-year appointment as Chairman, but this was not attractive to me. I agreed to stay on, but only for one more year while a new Chairman was found. When I finally left, it was with mixed feelings since I realised that my interactions with many interesting people and good friends would diminish. However, I really wanted to be relieved of a lot of stress that I didn't need, and that I believed I did not deserve. As it turned out, ERDC ran into considerably more trouble after my departure. The bureaucrats finally won the day, and ERDC was abolished. I believe that this was a dreadful decision. ERDC had done all that was asked of it by Government, and more. The industry that it served was highly supportive of ERDC, and regarded the way that it managed research as a natural and positive evolution of the philosophy that NERDDC had pioneered. Nevertheless, the arguments from within Government prevailed, and ERDC no longer exists. Sometimes it is hard to avoid becoming cynical in life.

Another outside organisation with which I had a close involvement, if only for a couple of years, was the National Standards Commission. I was initially approached to join the governing board of NSC (referred to as the Commission) by the then Chairman, and a good friend, Bill Blevin. Bill was right upfront when he approached me, saying that he had in mind that I should assume the Chairmanship of the Commission in a year or so after he stepped down, and that indeed is what happened. NSC is the Government statutory authority with responsibility for the system of weights and measures within Australia. It had been formed many years earlier to provide a framework in which standards of weights and measures could be coordinated throughout the nation, in order to help address incompatibilities between dimensions in goods produced in the different States. These existed at that time because the States used to trace their weights and measures back to international standards in several different ways. Over the years, NSC had assumed a range of other responsibilities, including testing the accuracy of various types of equipment used in commercial trade. In addition, NSC was given the overall responsibility for the management of Metrication in Australia, although this activity had largely been completed by the time I became involved.

I really enjoyed my time at NSC, particularly after I became Chairman. I got into the job with enthusiasm, and developed productive relationships with many people from the diverse industries with whom we interacted. Again, I found it meaningful to participate in activities that aimed to achieve useful practical outcomes. It was also very interesting to obtain insights into the complexities of Commonwealth-State relationships, and to observe how difficult it is to achieve change in a system in which responsibilities are spread all over the nation. However, the fun was not to last, because I was asked to take on a much more challenging task – the Chairmanship of ANSTO. I felt that I simply could not do justice to the two jobs, on top of my normal responsibilities at the University of Sydney. In 1987, after just two years with the organisation, I therefore resigned from the National Standards Commission. I was sad to leave it.

Throughout my entire career as a physicist, I had been well aware of the existence of the Australian Atomic Energy Commission (AAEC) at Lucas Heights in the south of Sydney. Indeed, I knew quite a few people from the AAEC through my involvement with the Australian Institute of Physics, and because of a couple of previous interactions on specific topics. Despite these few involvements, my interactions with the AAEC before 1986 can best be described as desultory. How things were to change! Around this time, I received a phone call out of the blue from a senior bureaucrat in Canberra. He told me that the Government had decided that the Australian Atomic Energy Commission would shortly cease to exist, and be metamorphosed into the Australian Nuclear Science and Technology Organisation, or ANSTO. Prior to this change, the Government wanted a review of the AAEC to be undertaken, looking at its organisation, programs, management and staffing. The purpose of this review was to generate a document, including aims for its future and recommendations to enable it to achieve these aims, which would be placed before the new board of ANSTO when it first met. The idea was to give the board a running start at the challenges of redirecting the organisation in ways that might be considered more relevant to the future than in the past. I was asked if I would chair the review committee.

To say that I was surprised would be an understatement. The AAEC was a very high profile organisation and, as for virtually all nuclear organisations around the world, it attracted a lot of publicity, mostly bad. I am not a nuclear scientist and, as I have said, my past interactions with the AAEC had not been close. I never really understood why I was asked to do this job. I speculate that it may have been because of my strong views, that I had made known publicly, about the importance of Australian science being more relevant to the needs of this country. It was certainly the case that the Government wanted ANSTO to be of more practical and direct benefit to Australia than had the AAEC in the past. I didn't need much persuading. Here was a golden opportunity to make an impact on the direction of a significant part of Australian Government science.

The work of my review committee commenced right in the middle of a very busy teaching period for me. Because we were required to complete the review and submit our report within twelve weeks, it was a pretty frenetic period. The Committee met at Lucas Heights for two days every fortnight. There were several highly experienced, and interesting people on the Committee, including Russ Fynmore who was an Executive General Manager at BHP, and Henri Meyer, a former employee of the AAEC, who was the obligatory representative of the Australian Council of Trade Unions. Russ was very widely experienced in business. Henri, too, had a very interesting background, having come to Australia as a migrant, and worked his way up to a position of significant influence. His experience was also invaluable to the work of the Committee. Henri made his views very clear at the start of the first meeting of our Committee when I asked members to introduce themselves and speak briefly about their background. Henri stated unequivocally that he would not be party to any recommendations that led to the loss of jobs of people currently within the AAEC. "If that's the way the recommendations go," he said, "I won't sign the report."

I am proud to say that nearly 20 years later, I count both Russ and Henri amongst my very good friends. Interestingly, although Russ and Henri are about as different as two people can be, in background, political views, and way of life, they also became good friends.

At the first meeting of the Committee, we decided that we did not want to spend all of our time in a room listening to submissions. We were keen to get out on site, to see what it was like for ourselves, and to meet some of the people. Our first visit was to the central workshop, and it was very memorable, at least for me. In many ways, it was like going into a time warp. Much of the machinery, while extremely well maintained, was 1950s vintage. I love workshops, and I broke away from the group to look at some of this gear. I then spotted something that made my eyes light up – a fully equipped woodworking shop. I made a beeline for it to discover things that made my mouth water. There was a young lad in there working away and I struck up a conversation with him.

"What are you making?" I said.

"I'm building a desk," he replied, and showed me. It was a beautiful piece of workmanship – well fitting joints, even dovetailed drawers.

I complimented him on his skills. "A special, is it?"

"No," he said. "That's what I do. I make desks."

It struck me as a bit odd.

You can imagine what happened after I left. The other blokes in the shop would have descended on this lad, and asked him what we had talked about. They would have been appalled by his admission that there was someone in the workshop of the Australian Atomic Energy Commission whose job it was just to make desks. A fortnight later, we had a meeting with the Unions, and I was just getting into my opening spiel when one of the men stood up and let me have it with both barrels. He complained bitterly that we were sniffing around the site, talking to people unofficially, and getting information from behind their (the unions') back. He even implied that it was a bad thing that we were finding out what was going on. I stood there dumbfounded, not knowing what to say. After a few minutes, his diatribe was cut short by Russ Fynmore's stentorian voice. I cannot remember exactly what Russ said, but it was measured, considered, and served to placate this excited individual.

After we returned to our meeting room, Russ complimented me on how I had handled the incident. "You did very well, Dick, not coming back at him and escalating the argument," he said.

I accepted the compliment, but frankly it was not deserved, because I simply didn't know what to say.

Our review of the AAEC was most stimulating and interesting. We found ourselves looking at an organisation that had lost its way. There were good reasons for this. The AAEC had been set up in the 1950s to manage the introduction of nuclear power into Australia. They even went as far as selecting the site for Australia's first nuclear power plant. In the early 1970s, the Government decided that this was not an option that they wanted to pursue. Since that time, virtually every new initiative that the AAEC had commenced had been subsequently terminated by the Government of the day. The organisation had therefore developed a defensive mentality, anxious not to put its head up in case it was shot off. Having said this, there was excellent science going on, and a large number of very talented people within the organisation.

Another feature of the AAEC that was completely out of step with the 1980s was the survival of the philosophy of the early days for the Commission to be self-contained. In addition to the woodworking shop, they had plumbers, painters, gardeners, a well-equipped print shop, a bus, even a garage – all non-essential overheads that had originally been justified by security arguments, but were no longer appropriate. It was hard to see how our review could do other than recommend extensive rationalisations of the workforce.

In order to meet the twelve week deadline for our report, we needed to have a fairly clear idea of what was going to be in it by the half way point. At this stage, the writing commenced. We had two public servants allocated to the Committee who did much of the administrative work. Their job was also to undertake the bulk of the writing. It very quickly became clear that they were not going to get the words down soon enough to meet our deadline. I therefore undertook to write much of it myself, using my dictation machine, and my secretary at the University of Sydney. Those were days before electronic communication, but the School of Physics had just acquired its first fax machine. I would fax my drafts to Canberra, and they would retype them into their computer and then fax this material around to the Committee. Without fax machines, we could not have completed our task in the allocated time. That being said, we still had to work extremely hard to meet our goal. It was almost like being a graduate student again.

Our report made 31 recommendations. The essential philosophy that we proposed for ANSTO, however, could be simply stated: the organisation needed to know where it was going, and it needed to be loved – that is, there had to be people outside ANSTO who supported what it did, and were prepared to stand up and say so. We also recommended very significant rationalisations of the internal infrastructure of the organisation, with substantial associated staff reductions. At the final meeting of my Committee, we reviewed our entire report. We then had to sign a covering letter to the Minister that was to be included in it. This was the moment of truth for Henri Meyer, and I watched with bated breath as one by one the Members of the Committee signed. Finally, when the letter got to him, it was a great relief for me to see him put his name on it. Our final task was to decide on the cover for the report. In good bureaucratic style, our support staff tabled six or seven covers for our consideration. For the first time, the Committee could not agree. I liked one, Russ Fynmore liked another, and so on. Finally someone said, "Let's have the one that Henri likes. After all, he didn't get his way on anything else."

Shortly before the Committee completed its work, I was asked to meet with the Secretary of the relevant Department in Canberra. I had no idea what this meeting was about, but he quickly let me know. "We like the recommendations that your Committee is developing," he said. "We think that they will form a very good basis for the new board to begin reshaping the organisation. The Minister would like you to chair the board."

I was absolutely astonished. "You don't want me," I said. "You want somebody who is much more high-profile than me."

"No," he said. "We want you."

I thought about it for a while, and then said, "OK. I'll give it a go, but I would like Russ Fynmore on the board as well."

They approached BHP and this was agreed. As it happened, I was also delighted that Henri Meyer was appointed as the ACTU representative, so three members of the Committee that recommended the future directions for ANSTO were on the board for the first few years of its operation. Upon reflection, I think that what the Department and Minister did was very smart. They asked some people to make recommendations without prejudice and, when these looked sensible, they gave them the responsibility to implement those recommendations. It is a very good managerial strategy.

I was Chairman of ANSTO for nearly seven years. During that time, the organisation changed dramatically. We made significant rationalisations in the activities that took place within the organisation and this inevitably led to substantial job losses. However, I believe that most of the people who left were ultimately glad to be gone. This is perhaps well illustrated by the first decision that I made as Chairman. Previous Chairmen had enjoyed access to a car and driver to transport them on AAEC business. Given that ANSTO was facing significant financial constraints, it seemed to me that such a luxury was inappropriate. I therefore said that I did not want the car. The former Chairman's driver was one of those who left the organisation. I often wondered how he took this, but later I met him and he told me that it was the best thing that had ever happened to him. It has been my experience that most people who are forced to leave organisations fall on their feet, often sooner rather than later. In this particular case, my decision not to use a car and driver reverberated around ANSTO, and set the tone for the change that was so desperately needed.

To tell the story of my time as Chairman would be a book in itself, and that is not what this one is all about. Suffice to say that I'm very proud of what we achieved while I was there. One thing that gave me particular satisfaction was the way that the ANSTO staff met the challenge of coming out from behind the fence, and establishing effective interactions with industry. In the past, one of the inhibiting factors that had discouraged such interactions was that any money that was earned through external consulting work reverted straight to Consolidated Revenue, and was not accessed by the organisation itself. As I have said on several occasions, it would be hard to design a system that more effectively discouraged an organisation from developing outside interactions. We argued to the Government that ANSTO should be able to retain revenue earned from external work, because this would encourage us to develop programs that were directly relevant to industry. The Government accepted these arguments and went further, requiring ANSTO and CSIRO to earn a specific proportion of their total budget from outside work. It was a complete reversal of the previous policy. I believe that this approach has been a very effective and sensible way of ensuring that Australia's Government scientific efforts are more directed towards the needs of the country.

Most of the meetings of the ANSTO board were held at Lucas Heights. However, the board decided that it should have one meeting each year away from there, preferably near a relevant industry. We therefore had some splendid trips to interesting places, including the Ranger uranium mine in the Northern Territory, Olympic Dam in South Australia, and Western Australia. The Territory trip was particularly memorable. One day, we flew south from Ranger to Coronation Hill, the site of a large uranium deposit. We were picked up by the site manager and his aboriginal assistant, and driven out to the deposit in a couple of four-wheel-drive vehicles. About half way there, one of the vehicles speared a tyre, and there was no spare. It was a stinking hot day, and we had to wait while the aboriginal driver went back for help. It was quite some time coming, and I still have this vivid image of the entire ANSTO board wilting in the extraordinary heat, and hoping that we would be rescued before we made more unfortunate nuclear-related headlines. Obviously the driver returned before anything untoward happened, but it was pretty trying couple of hours.

For much of my time as Chairman of ANSTO, I used to travel from home to Lucas Heights in my own vehicle – an elderly Ford Courier diesel truck. This contraption displayed a lot of character in the noise that it made as it bounced along the road. I formed the view that it would be unseemly for the Chairman of the organisation to drive in through the gates in such a beat up wreck, so I used to leave the thing in the external car park, and walk through the gates to my office. Nobody ever commented on my mode of transport but, given the effectiveness of the bush telegraph in the organisation, I'm sure that it was noted.

As the review committee had proposed, there were significant rationalisations of the internal support functions of ANSTO. One of the things that went was the woodworking shop that I had discovered on the first memorable day on site of the review committee. All of the equipment in the shop was offered for sale by tender. I thought long and hard about putting in an offer for the magnificent woodturning lathe. In the end, I decided against it because, had my bid been successful, some people would inevitably have believed that I had used my position to work the system. Pity about that – I would have loved to get my hands on that lathe.

During my time as Chairman of ANSTO, I reported to several Government Ministers. The relationship between the board of a quasi-autonomous Government organisation and a Minister is very important. We therefore adopted the practice of inviting every new Minister to meet with us as a board so we could explain to him what we were about, and to give him the opportunity of raising matters with us. In general, we developed exceptionally good relationships with our Ministers even though at times there were disagreements and arguments. However, we never hit it off with my last Minister, Chris Schott. Right from the beginning of our relationship, he found fault in the things that ANSTO was doing. For some time, I couldn't figure out what was going on. In hindsight, I have concluded that he was seeking to discredit ANSTO as part of a plan to merge the organisation with CSIRO. We at ANSTO thought that this was a lousy idea, as did CSIRO and, as far as I can tell, virtually all of the scientific community. After exhausting all of the normal methods of persuading him to change his mind, I resolved to fight him publicly. I argued strongly against his proposal in the media, including on live television. CSIRO also opposed the proposal, but they made their arguments using their unions, and past senior officers, as their spokesmen. I was frankly very disappointed that the senior management of CSIRO were not prepared to come out publicly and argue the case themselves. Eventually, Cabinet rejected the proposal. However, in an effort to save the Minister's face, it was decided that the ANSTO board should go. On the evening of this Cabinet meeting, I received a telephone call at home to tell me this. Specifically, I was asked whether I would resign if requested. I wanted to discuss this with my board, but was not given the opportunity. Eventually, I reasoned that if the majority shareholder, in this case the Government, wanted the board to go, there was no alternative, and so I agreed. For me, it didn't matter too much, because my time as Chairman was due to end in a few months anyway. Some Members of my board were particularly upset by this action, however.

I cannot be other than proud of what I did in opposing the Minister. I fought for something that I believed in very strongly, and won. I carry the scars of being fired as Chairman of ANSTO with considerable pride.

There are a few interesting corollaries that emerged from my ANSTO experience. The first occurred a few months after the conclusion of the work of the review committee, when I became very ill. I suffered an allergic reaction to some leech bites that caused pericarditis, or fluid buildup around my heart. I am here today because of the quick action of my daughters who were with me at the time, and alerted the doctor on duty in the Intensive Care Ward of the Cardiac Unit of Royal Prince Alfred

Hospital. The illness was so unusual that the doctors who looked after me subsequently wrote a paper about it. It is the only scientific paper in which I have featured as the subject rather than as an author. One of the doctors commented that I might have been more susceptible to this problem because I was run down after the extraordinarily tiring effort associated with the work of the review. In fact, I do recall being absolutely exhausted in the few months after the AAEC review, being unable to think clearly, or to work effectively. The message was that I am not as young as I used to be, and I can no longer work as hard as I did when I was a graduate student.

A second outcome of the ANSTO experience is that I have never again been asked to do anything for the Government. I had always thought that I would like to have the opportunity to make some more contributions to Government science, particularly after my retirement, in much the same way as Jan Kolm had done. However, I am clearly off the Government's list. Upon reflection, I can see why. I must now be regarded as a very high-risk option for appointment to a Government body. Any Chairman who publicly argues with his Minister would automatically rule himself out from similar appointments in the future. Frankly, I am not too unhappy with this. I find myself with more than enough to do in my retirement!

Since the termination in 1993 of my appointment as Chairman of ANSTO, I have never returned to the site, and I have thought very little about the organisation. I gave one interview that was published on the day after my appointment ended. Since then, until very recently I scrupulously kept my views to myself. Apart from ethical considerations, I had to adopt this approach for self-preservation. Having been deeply committed to the success of ANSTO, and proud of what we had achieved during my seven years of association, I felt that any ongoing involvement would be just too painful. Regrettably, most of the friendships that I had formed while I was there have also been casualties of the events that occurred. Perhaps at some time in the future I will go back, but I am not holding my breath.

(Recently, on two occasions I have failed to live up to my previous determination not to make further public comment on my experiences at ANSTO. Obviously, one of these is with the publication of this book. The other was when I agreed to be interviewed by a fellow physicist, Anna Binnie, who was undertaking a Ph.D. at Macquarie University on the history of the Australian Atomic Energy Commission. Anna wanted to conclude her thesis with a chapter about ANSTO, and so she asked me to talk to her about my experiences there. I had the pleasure of being one of the examiners of her excellent and beautifully written thesis. Anna has performed a very insightful and useful analysis of the way in which the scientific and technological aspects of the work of the AAEC impacted on the political decisions that affected the organisation and, through this, on how it evolved. I was surprised, although not disappointed or offended, when I found in the thesis a transcript of much of what I had said to her about my time at ANSTO, particularly relating to my last few months with the organisation. Anna's thesis has been accepted, so all of this is now on the public record, whether I like it or not. After so many years, however, it almost certainly doesn't matter any more – we have all moved on.)

Broadening the Mind

I had never been overseas until 1965 when I commenced my Ph.D. studies in New York. Subsequently my overseas trips became progressively more frequent, reaching a peak in the 1990s when, at one stage, I made six trips to Japan alone in each of two successive years. Before my first departure from Australia, I had this peculiar feeling that I would somehow be irreversibly changed when I set foot in another country. It didn't happen – at least not immediately. In fact, it was a mild surprise for me to see in other places so much in common with Australia. However, they are also different in many ways, some subtle, and some very obvious. Often my overseas experiences have been quite stressful, and I used to quip that the best thing about going away was looking at the slides of the trip in the comfort of our living room at home after it was all over. Nevertheless, my experiences while travelling have greatly enriched my life, and have changed me, hopefully mostly for the better.

Most of my early overseas travel was to the United States – not surprising, I suppose, given that I had undertaken my graduate studies there. It was not until the mid 1980s that I finally got to Europe, and still I did not make it to England for some years after that. In actual fact, I tell a lie – I did transit through Heathrow airport on this first European trip, but I don't think that really counts. Eventually, and inevitably, I made it to England. On the morning of my first visit, I struck up a conversation with an English lady at breakfast in my hotel in London. I remarked that I had done a lot of travelling, but that today was to be my very first day in London. She looked at me in surprise and said, "My, how I envy you!"

I soon found out what she meant, and I have since enjoyed many wonderful days soaking up the atmosphere of this very special city. I'm not sure that our son, Steven, shares my positive feelings about London, however. When he was 12 years old, Marilyn and I took him with us on a six-week overseas trip, during which we spent a week in the UK, starting with two days in London. We had come in on an overnight flight from the United States, so we were all very short of sleep. However, we had only limited time, so we checked into our hotel, and then set off to show him the sights. Every time we stopped, he just wanted to go to sleep. Around noon, we were near Buckingham Palace trying to watch the Changing of the Guard. I lifted him up so that he could get a better view and, in the process, gave his hip a severe bump on an adjacent stone ledge, causing him to dissolve into tears. We continued to drag him around all through the afternoon. Finally, about 5 o'clock we decided to have a meal and call it a day. We went to a Garfunkles restaurant and ordered. Steven's milk shake came in a tall glass balanced precariously on a saucer. He leant his elbow on the table and tipped most of it onto the evening dress of the lady sitting next to us. It was the last straw, and he slid under the table in the depths of despair. I got up to pay the bill, tripped, and sent my chair flying. We escaped from the restaurant and caught a bus to go back to our hotel. When I tried to pay our fare, the conductor said, "Hey, man. You' goin' de wrong way!" Correct bus number, opposite direction. We got out, crossed the street, took another bus back to our hotel, and slept around the clock. I think that Steven would probably regard his first day in London as one of the worst of his life.

In 1975-76, I spent several months in the United States, mostly working at the National Bureau of Standards (now the National Institute of Standards and Technology) in Gaithersburg, Maryland, just north of Washington DC. This was a wonderful trip, because we were there as a whole family for most of the time. Towards the end of our stay, we drove north from Washington, stopping off at New York City to visit friends from our time there in the 1960s, and then up through New York State, to Niagara Falls, returning through Pennsylvania. On the way, I had made arrangements to visit a scientist working in a similar field at the Army Materials and Mechanics Research Center at a place called Watertown. I spoke with this bloke by telephone before we left Washington, and set up the meeting for the afternoon of a particular day. Our travel was slower than we had expected due to very heavy snow, so it was about mid-afternoon when we finally arrived at Watertown. We checked into our hotel, and I called my colleague to seek directions. He asked me where I was staying.

"At the Holiday Inn," I replied.

"That's funny," he said. "I didn't know that we had one. Anyway you go down to the town square and drive out Arsenal Street. It's not far. You can't miss us."

I left the family behind in the secure comfort of the warm hotel room, found the town square, had a cop show me Arsenal Street, and headed off. Arsenal Street led to a trackless frozen wasteland. Nothing along it resembled a large research establishment. I turned around and drove back along the street again, all the way to the town square. I had not been mistaken. Back out along Arsenal Street once more until I found a phone box and called my colleague. An operator came on the line and said that I needed to put more money into the telephone, because I was making a long distance call. By this time, I was pretty tense, and said, "Lady, Watertown is a tiny little place in the middle of a huge frozen wilderness! How could this possibly be a long distance call?"

She said, "You are in Watertown, New York. The number you are calling is in Watertown, Massachusetts."

I had done all of the arranging for the trip by telephone, and had never bothered to check which State I had to get to. I missed my target by about 600 miles. I am still surprised at how long it took for the penny to drop. I never did get to meet that fellow.

My first visit to Japan was in 1973, at the end of a long overseas business trip for AWA. Before I left Australia, several people within the company had offered me useful advice about protocol, gifts and the like. I also learnt about the importance of exchanging business cards, and Lou Davies told me a wonderful story about his first experience with such matters. It occurred during the visit of a Japanese businessman to AWA in Sydney. They exchanged their cards, and then Lou turned over the one that he received, remarking, "That's interesting. It's got your name written in Japanese on the back."

The Japanese visitor pointed at the indecipherable script and said politely, "Excuse me please. This is the front."

On this trip, I had already spent about four weeks in North America. I flew from the West Coast through Honolulu to Tokyo, and then to Osaka on a domestic flight. I was therefore pretty travel worn by the time that I reached my destination. The AWA representative in that region, and elderly gentleman called Mr Okada, met me at Osaka airport. He was accompanied by an interpreter, although in actual fact his English was by far the better of the two. After I had checked into my hotel, Mr Okada insisted on taking me to dinner – something that I really didn't need because I was very tired after the long trip. We went to a very fancy western-style restaurant, and he ordered steak for us. It was cooked on a hibachi barbeque beside the table and was, I believe, the most tender steak that I have ever eaten. You could cut it with a fork. Regrettably, however, in my spaced-out condition the quality was totally lost on me.

I spent two or three days with Mr Okada and his interpreter doing business in Osaka. One day, he introduced me to the wonders of Kyoto. The beautiful shrines, palaces and gardens were breathtaking – I have revisited them many times over the years, and they never lose their charm for me. That evening, he took me to a Japanese-style restaurant. It was a totally new experience to me, right down to using chopsticks for the first time. We took off our shoes and entered a private room with beautiful timber walls and floors. There was an exquisite ikebana flower arrangement in an alcove, and the low table was set with Australian and Japanese flags. We sat down at it, crossed legged on the floor, something that has always been difficult for me to do, so that after a while my legs were completely numb. He poured beer, and I learnt my first Japanese word – *campai*, the equivalent of *cheers*. Then the sliding door opened to reveal a kneeling middle-aged Japanese lady wearing a traditional kimono. She shuffled into the room, and the feasting commenced. These days I am very fond of Japanese food, but at that time the raw fish and other unfamiliar things were quite a shock to me. The main meal was sukiyaki, cooked by our hostess on a gas-fired stove beside the table. She broke raw eggs into each of our bowls, put in the freshly cooked thin slices of meat, and then handed them to each of us. Each time, I would struggle with the chopsticks in my uncooperative fingers to get this delicious stuff into my mouth. Gradually, my hand started to cramp up as well. While all this was going on, we engaged in polite, but superficial conversation. Our hostess spoke no English at all, and I had no Japanese. However, when I showed her photos of my family, all communication barriers seemed to disappear. After a while, I started to fill up. Nevertheless, my two hosts were still stuffing the food down with undiminished enthusiasm. I reasoned that it would be impolite for me to be the first to refuse any more, so I kept going. After all, I felt that national pride was at stake. Eventually, to my great relief, our hostess collected our bowls, and emptied the dregs out. However, she then cracked fresh eggs into each one, and the whole thing started all over again. Finally, I was in a serious state of impending explosion. I put my bowl down, saying to Mr Okada, "I'm done! I couldn't eat another mouthful." His eyes glazed over and he let out a groan. I hadn't realised that, as the guest, it was up to me to call it quits first.

The next day during our business visit, I thanked him for his hospitality and remarked, "I ate too much for dinner last night, Mr Okada."

Smiling, but with a slightly sad look in his eyes, he replied, "I too, Dr Collins."

In many of the places that we visited together in Japan, the doorways were very low, and I frequently bumped my forehead on them, sometimes quite hard. As a result of these impacts, I developed a significant and obvious bruise. Whenever I suffered a collision, Mr Okada would himself wince as if in pain, and clutch his forehead. As my host, he was clearly feeling as much discomfort as I was. After three days in Osaka and Kyoto, I caught the Shinkansen (bullet train) to Tokyo. Mr Okada said goodbye to me at the station. He had tears in his eyes. Later, he sent gifts to Marilyn and our children, and we maintained a friendly correspondence for several years. Mr Okada gave me my first lesson about the importance of relationships when you are doing business in Japan.

During my first visit to Japan, the currency exchange rate was 400 Japanese yen to the Australian dollar. In the 1990s, the value of the dollar had declined by nearly an order of magnitude, to less than 60 yen to the dollar at one stage. The astonishingly weak yen in 1973 enabled me to do things that would be completely out of the question now. During my few days in Tokyo, I stayed at the Imperial Hotel! I was also able to buy things that I could not contemplate now. I visited a jewellery store in an arcade beside the Imperial Hotel, and purchased a beautiful gold and pearl brooch for Marilyn. The following day, something happened that, had I not experienced it, and told the story many times over the years to remind myself, I would find it impossible to believe. I was in my hotel room, and there was a knock on the door. I opened it to find the owner of the store from which I had bought Marilyn's brooch. In his broken English, he explained to me that he had found a discrepancy in his cashbox at the end of the previous day's trading, and he realised that he had not given me the correct change. He then handed me a 10,000 yen note! My recollection is that I started to protest, but he was gone. I don't think that I even got to thank him. I have no idea how he located me. I can only presume that I must have remarked to him when I was in his store that I was staying at the Imperial Hotel. I don't recall giving him my name, because it was a cash purchase in those pre-credit card days. I have to surmise that he sought me out by describing me to the staff of the hotel.

My Japanese experience started to intensify about the time that I joined the University of Sydney. A few months before my appointment commenced, the School of Physics received an unsolicited approach from Nitto Kohki Company Limited of Japan to license the evacuated solar collector technology that had been developed in the School. Two people from Nitto Kohki came to Australia to discuss this proposal, and I was invited to join the meeting. One of the visitors was Mr Hirosato Takeuchi, a director of the company, and a person with whom I later became good friends. After about six years, we actually got on first-name terms – Hiro and Dick! The licensing negotiations with Nitto Kohki took a year (in my experience, such matters always take at least a year) and the negotiations were at times very difficult. Eventually we signed off on a deal, and then the process of technology transfer commenced. Nitto Kohki sent two engineers to Australia – Fumito Degawa, and Tomori Koroda. I met them at the airport early one morning, took them to the School and installed them in an office. Almost immediately, they emerged wearing company jackets, and saying, "We must to work." And work we did, very long hours, Saturdays as well, and all through Easter. Right from the beginning, I informed them that, since they were in Australia, we had to use first names – Fumito and Tom. Many years later, I realised that this was going too far too fast, but they were too polite to tell me that at the time. After two weeks of very hard work, we had done all that we could, and they were due to fly back to Japan on a Saturday evening. That morning, I collected them from their hotel and drove them to the Central Coast where we had a splendid day off. We saw the sights, swam in the surf at Terrigal, and ate a picnic lunch on the beach. After lunch, we were relaxing in the warm autumn sun, and Fumito said, "Tom, when we get back to Japan, today is *Top Secret.*"

In 1981, I could see that I would be travelling to Japan quite frequently, so I decided to try and learn the language. With the permission of the lecturer (*sensei*), I sat in on the First Year Japanese language class at the University of Sydney. However, I found it very heavy going. In a typical class, the sensei introduced new words to us at the beginning, and we repeated them together. She then went on to other things. At the end of the class, she returned to our new words – everybody there would know them except me. I really tried to stay on top of these lessons. I purchased the book, and studied from it each day during my one-hour train trips morning and night, trying to stuff these unfamiliar words into my unreceptive brain. I also spent a lot of time in the language laboratory. Despite these very significant efforts, I invariably found myself behind everyone else in the class.

Around the middle of this year, I made a trip to Japan. I decided that it would not be appropriate to tell my colleagues about my embryonic skills in the Japanese language. In our meetings, I therefore tried to understand what was being said in the long and complex discussions in Japanese that took place between the relatively short English communications with me. Occasionally, I could pick up a word or two, and I was also able to tell when they were talking numbers, and even sometimes identify the numbers, but it was all virtually opaque for me. After a few days of this, I was travelling with Fumito Degawa in a taxi to our morning meeting. We were discussing something or other, in English of course, and I must have looked confused, because he said to me, "Do you understand?"

Understand was one of a few words of Japanese that I knew, so I thought that this would be a good time to spill the beans. I said, "Hai. Wakarimus."

Fumito stared at me, his eyes widened, and he went quite pale. "You … speak … Japanese!" he said.

He quickly extracted from me what I had been doing and,

even though I emphasised that I had barely begun, he would not have it. When we got to our destination, he rushed into the meeting room and, even before the introductions, he announced, "Professor Collins – he speaks Japanese!"

I still have colleagues and friends in Japan who think that my Japanese is considerably better than it is. I wish. Regrettably, however, I had to drop out of the class. Things came to a head immediately after my return to Australia from this trip. That very day, we had our first test in the Japanese class. Although I passed it with a mediocre B-, the pressures of other things in the School of Physics were bearing down on me to the extent that I felt I simply could not continue to give it the time that was necessary for me. I regretfully therefore ceased the development of what would have been a most useful skill. Over the years, I have continued to add a few words to my Japanese vocabulary, and I like to say that I have enough of the language to get into trouble, but not enough to get out of it. Learning Japanese was one of the things in life that I tackled unsuccessfully.

One of my most memorable trips to Japan was in the company of Jeff Symons, a research engineer from CSIRO. Our visit was one of a series, both to Japan and to Australia, that were part of a Government funded Japan-Australia collaboration on high temperature solar collectors. I had not met Jeff before, but we got on very well right from the beginning, and had a wonderful two weeks together. We visited many solar facilities and commercial organisations that were active in this field, in different parts of Japan. In addition, we were looked after splendidly. On one of our visits, in the company of a Japanese scientist, Sakae Tanemura, we visited two large solar power plants in Nio, west of Osaka. Sakae, now a good friend, had arranged for us to stay in a Japanese style inn, or ryokan. It was a truly wonderful and memorable experience. Amongst other things, Sakae took us through the protocol of the hot communal Japanese bath. After stripping, one first has to soap down and rinse off under a shower. There is a tiny stool on which you can sit during this process. After you are clean, you then get into the hot bath – and boy, is it hot! No towels were provided for drying off, but there was a little cloth for each of us. For a brief time, I contemplated trying to keep this cloth dry, but it was futile. It also turned out to be completely unnecessary, because we were so hot after the bath that the water evaporated almost immediately. Jeff and I found our first hot bath a truly amazing experience, and so the next night we persuaded Sakae to photograph the second one for posterity. After my return to Australia, I gave a talk to the School of Physics about the trip. Most of it was concerned with the solar installations and companies that we had visited. I thought, however, that I should end on a lighter note. At the conclusion, I therefore remarked that we had not neglected the cultural aspects of our stay in Japan. I then showed the slide that Sakae had taken of the rear views of Jeff and me, stark naked, sitting on the tiny stools and soaping ourselves. I had thought that this would get a good response from the audience but there was nothing – just a stunned silence, finally broken by hysterical laughter from one of the female staff. I had not judged my audience well.

Some of the things that happen during travel are quite extraordinary. One of these occurred during the 1975-76 trip that we made as a family to North America. We had driven to a place close to Yosemite National Park, and we all piled out of the car to play in banks of deep snow adjacent to a deserted car park. We had a wonderful time running, jumping and sliding down the snowy slopes. After a while, it was getting late and time to leave. I called the troops to order, and then put my hand in my pocket to get the car keys. They were not there. I experienced that awful sinking feeling that you have when you know that you are in big trouble. Before I could speak, however, Kathryn, who had insisted on having one more slide down the snow-covered embankment, felt something in the deep snow. She then held up her hand, saying, "Look what I've found." It was my lost keys. The chances of this happening were miniscule, yet that is exactly what occurred. I can't imagine what we would have done without the keys, as it was off-season, no one was about, and there was no nearby shelter.

Our family had another low probability snow-related incident during a visit to New Zealand in 1977. We had again stopped at a snow fight site, and were well into the battle when Marilyn decided that it was time to move on. She called us back into the car, and opened the door slightly to get in. One of us, the identity having been expunged from my memory for understandable reasons as you will immediately see, launched a large moist chunk of snow at the others. It went sadly astray. We all stood transfixed as the wet lump arced across the sky, and then slid without touching through the perfectly sized gap in the door, dissipating its kinetic energy inside. No skilled baseball pitcher could have achieved such perfect accuracy on purpose. It was not a good moment, and our frolicking was abruptly terminated. However, later on when the trauma had subsided a little, we recalled this *Shot of the Day* with great hilarity.

By definition, travel takes you to unfamiliar places. When you are moving around, many of the things that you accept without thinking in everyday living are not there, or at least their presence is not obvious. In some places, there is ample information available to guide the stranger. Other places make it so difficult that you are forced to conclude that they are deliberately trying to discourage people from coming there. I have found that one of the hardest things to do is to catch a bus in a strange city. Every place is different, and the way to buy a ticket is often kept top secret. Once Marilyn and I spent a week in Freiburg, Germany. At the beginning of our stay, our hosts gave us a handful of bus tokens so that we could get around. Towards the end, we ran out of them, and I needed to get two more so that we could travel back to our apartment. I went to a bus ticket office in the centre of town, the purpose of which is presumably to sell bus tickets. However, I was completely unable to communicate my needs to the gentleman there. In the end, we simply stole a ride on the bus.

Sometimes, the problems that I have experienced during travel had been my own fault. On one occasion, Marilyn and I were travelling in Europe. We flew into Zürich airport in the morning, and were met there by one of my former students, Dominique Jeker. We brought train tickets that took us into the city, and spent the day there on business. In the evening, Dominique took us back to the station, and we bought train tickets to travel west towards Basel. About halfway to our destination, we had to change trains. We were late for this connection, so we had to run from one train to another with all our bags. We only had time to scramble into the first available compartment, which turned out to be First Class, rather than Economy as we had purchased. I reasoned that this probably wouldn't matter. Soon the ticket inspector came along and he became very agitated when I showed him our tickets, and demanded an exorbitant sum of money. For once, I stood my ground. I could not see why we should be charged such a large amount for only a few minutes in a different Class. Our conflict was escalating towards boiling point where he finally made his objection clear to me. "These are tickets from Zürich airport to the city," he said. In my flustered condition, I had produced the wrong ones! The problem being resolved, he was perfectly happy to let us stay in First Class for the remainder of the trip. I was still in a pretty frazzled state by the time we left the train, however.

Of course, everybody occasionally has problems when they travel. I think that I get lost more than most. Marilyn has an excellent sense of direction, and mine is lousy. You would think that, after over four decades, I would know that she is always right and I am always wrong, but I am a pretty slow learner about some things. When we travelled as a family together, our kids used to refer to me as Mr U-turn! In Japan, people are particularly good about offering help to a stranger in need. Part of it is that many of them like to use opportunities to practice their English. I have been approached quite a few times by people on trains and asked if I would mind talking to them for this purpose. However, mostly it is because they have a genuine desire to help. You only have to stand on a street corner in Tokyo looking at a map and, without fail, someone will come up to you and ask if they can help. If you go further and seek directions from somebody, my experience has been that they will not only tell you the way – they will take you there themselves. It is a very endearing feature of the country. I have appreciated this type of help so much over the years that I have adopted the practice myself. Whenever I see someone looking at a map in Australia, I do the Japanese thing.

Every once in a while, I have had the opportunity to repay one of the innumerable kindnesses that I have received on my travels. Once I arrived back from overseas at Sydney Airport and, having passed through Customs and Immigration, I was making my way towards the taxi rank when a very worried individual approached me. He explained to me in broken English that he had just arrived from overseas and was expecting to be met at the airport, but no one had showed up. He said that he had no money, and asked if he could borrow some from me to travel to his friend's home. I didn't hesitate. I reasoned that if I were ever to find myself in a similar position, I would hope that someone would help me too. I gave him $20 and my business card, not expecting to see him or the money again. A few days afterwards, he showed up in my office at the University and paid the money back to me. That sort of thing gives you a nice warm feeling!

Interestingly, with all the travel that I have done, only once do I recall becoming seriously ill on the road. This occurred in Japan during a visit to Nippon Sheet Glass Company Limited. We had been working all morning and then went out to lunch at a fancy restaurant. We were about half an hour into the afternoon meeting when I suddenly felt icy cold, and then collapsed. My hosts carried me to the sick bay, evicting some poor woman who had been lying in there, and I proceeded to throw up, and do all the other unpleasant things associated with a severe attack of food poisoning. Every so often, an anxious Japanese face would peer around the corner and then disappear. I think that they feared they would lose me. A young Japanese girl came in and thoughtfully held my hand. Under other conditions, this could have been quite pleasant, but it made no difference at all to me at the time. In the midst of all this someone thrust a thermometer in my face. Obligingly, I put it in my mouth. The thermometer-bearer looked most alarmed.

"What's the matter?" I groaned.

"Excuse me, please," he replied. "We usually put it in our armpit."

I recall feeling much relieved. Later that evening, they took me to a doctor who charged quite a lot of money to tell me that I would live. In a very fragile condition, I took the next day's flight back to the safety of Australia. I certainly did not get my money's worth from the food component of that ticket, however.

For me, one of the major beneficial outcomes of my travel has been the friends that I have made, and maintained, in many different parts of the world. There are so many that I cannot possibly do justice to them all. Several of them appear in the last Chapter of this book. Here I will mention just two, both of whom, curiously enough, come from Switzerland – the Ludi family and the Jeker family.

My first contact with Hans Ludi was when he wrote to me at the University of Sydney expressing an interest by his company in licensing our vacuum glazing technology. For several months after this first approach, we carried on a lively and active correspondence. I had an overseas trip planned in a few months, so we arranged to meet. My trip to Switzerland was another one of those ball busters that seemed like a good idea at the time, but wasn't. I had been in South Korea, and flew to Tokyo, and then took a Swissair flight through Anchorage, Alaska to Zürich. I have no idea how long it took, but I arrived at Zürich at about 6am having had minimal sleep. Hans met me at the airport, and drove me to his company where I spent most of the morning. He then took me to my hotel where I rested for a while, and dozed for a bit. About 4pm I visited another of the company's plants, and then Hans and his wife Pia took me out to dinner. I can still recall feeling like death in the washroom of the factory just before we left. I remember splashing water on my face and smacking my cheeks in an attempt to wake myself up. Regrettably, I cannot recall anything at all about the dinner, but knowing Hans as I now do, it must have been pretty nice.

Soon after this first meeting, Hans visited Australia, and our travel roles were essentially reversed. Hans arrived at Sydney early in the morning without much sleep, and he and I worked together all day. In the evening, we went to Manly on the harbour ferry, and had a very nice meal together. When I noticed Hans drooping into the seafood platter, I realised that my hospitality had gone too far so we headed for his hotel. On the ferry back to Circular Quay, the lights of Sydney were at their spectacular best, and the sky even turned on a beautiful shooting star for us. Regrettably, I suspect that Hans doesn't recall any of that.

Our business relationship quickly grew into a strong personal friendship. Later on, I stayed with Hans and Pia in Switzerland on several occasions, and got to know their two lovely young daughters Sanna and Tina quite well. On one of my trips, Hans was away for most of the week that I spent there, and he let me drive his Audi to and from the factory. It was pretty nice. On another occasion, both Marilyn and I stayed with them for a few days. Even though the commercial relationship between Hans' company and the University did not survive, our friendship was maintained.

Several years later, Hans contacted me saying that he and his family planned to come to Australia for a holiday. He sought my advice about things to do. His idea was to visit us in Sydney, then fly to Alice Springs and do the Central Australia bit, fly to Cairns and rent a campervan and drive from there to Adelaide. He clearly had no idea about the size of our country. My advice was to do all of that, except the Sydney to Adelaide leg, and he planned his trip on that basis. Hans, Pia, Sanna and Tina stayed with us in Sydney for a few days while they did the sights, and then set off on their epic adventure. I understand that it was a great success. However, Pia tells me that, as they finally approached Sydney in their campervan, she said, "I'll bet you're glad we're not going on to Adelaide, eh Hans?"

My relationship with the Jeker family started out in a similar way. I received a fax from Dominique Jeker telling me that he was a student at the Swiss Federal Institute of Technology, and that he was looking to undertake his compulsory industrial experience in Australia. He added that he could meet all of his expenses himself. I always grabbed someone like that with both hands, and immediately wrote back encouraging him. Dominique later told me that he had written dozens of similar letters, and that mine was essentially the only positive reply that he received. After a fairly lengthy period during which we set up the formal arrangements for his visit, he made his travel plans. I went to the airport to meet him, carrying the obligatory sign, since neither of us knew what the other looked like. We hit it off right from our first moment together and became good friends. Dominique was a wonderful person to have working in my Department. He was keen, enthusiastic, and highly intelligent, and he achieved a great deal. He also had a fantastic social time here in Australia. As I heard it, the girls just loved him. Shortly after Dominique's arrival, I received a very nice letter from his father Josef, thanking me for looking after his son. I was quite chuffed by this, because such courtesy is rare.

Towards the end of Dominique's stay, Josef came to Australia to spend a few weeks with him, and they travelled widely together. As with Dominique, Josef and I also got on very well. Josef was absurdly grateful that I had gone to the airport to meet his son on his arrival in a strange country after a long trip. He told me that it would have been unheard of for a European professor to do such a thing. I insisted that it was no big deal, and that anyway the same courtesy had been extended to me when I first travelled overseas. Nevertheless, I had the feeling that Josef felt that he owed me something, and I always tried to persuade him that he didn't. After all, he had met all of Dominique's expenses during his time in Australia, so I had got a heap of work out of him without it costing me anything.

A couple years after Dominique's return to Europe, Marilyn and I visited Josef and his wife Marie-Thérèse in Switzerland. Their hospitality was overwhelming. They arranged visits for us to several educational institutions in Basel, and took us sightseeing in this lovely city, including a trip on the wonderful little cable ferry that is powered by the flow of the water in the river. Josef and Marie-Thérèse also had us to dinner at their home. As if this were not enough, they insisted on picking up our hotel bill. Not long after my retirement, Josef and Marie-Thérèse travelled to Australia to attend a conference and we were delighted to welcome them to our home.

I feel deeply grateful, and humbled, by the quality of the friendships that I have been fortunate to develop over the years because of the possibilities afforded by international travel. Despite all of the tensions and complexities associated with such travel, it certainly makes the world a better place.

The Mad Professor

The public image of a scientist is characterised by a curious dichotomy. On the one hand, the practice of science is seen as being highly methodical, requiring meticulous care, a logical approach, and great attention to detail. In contrast, scientists are often portrayed as being absent-minded dreamers, living in another world, and unconnected to reality. As a scientist myself, I believe that I am qualified to comment, although I would not pretend that my views are necessarily representative of those of all scientists. I actually believe that most scientists possess all of these characteristics. Indeed, I don't think that we scientists are too much different from the population at large. We are, after all, just people like anyone else, with all of the usual strengths, weaknesses and idiosyncrasies.

The fact that scientists can be precise and logical, and at the same time off with the fairies, is not that surprising when you think about the way in which science is practised. Some parts of our discipline require great care, patience and diligence, and meticulous observation skills. Other parts, specifically including the creative aspects and the generation of new ideas and concepts, involve lateral thinking, jumps in the logical thought process, and outrageous speculations. It is also highly beneficial to have an instinctive appreciation of whether something is correct or incorrect without there necessarily being a rational basis upon which to draw that conclusion. In my own career as a scientist, I have had periods where my work has been mind-numbingly boring, doing dull, repetitive and seemingly endless work grinding out data. I've also experienced exhilarating moments when novel concepts have emerged, often totally out of the blue, leading to a new understanding or a different way of looking at a thing – a piece of knowledge that is entirely new. Someone once remarked that the greatest excitement in being a scientist comes when you realise that you are the only person in the world who has a particular piece of knowledge. The moment of creation of a new idea is incredibly special, and it makes all of the tedious aspects of our discipline worthwhile.

When my daughter Jenelle was quite young, she was very

keen on a series of books about a character called Professor Branestorm. He was the archetypal mad professor, tall (like me), thin (like me), absent-minded (like me much of the time), and wore spectacles (like me, although he had a multiplicity of them because he was always mislaying them). Professor Branestorm is representative of the commonly accepted public image of a scientist. Over the years, I have given many fun Physics lectures to schoolchildren. One of the exercises that I used to run in these lectures was to ask some of the kids to draw a picture of scientist. I would then display their efforts on an overhead projector. Independent of whether the drawings were done by a girl or a boy, their scientists were almost invariably male, weird looking, and doing something bizarre.

Being a little weird, or at least knowing that the public expects you to be that way, is sometimes not such a bad thing. You can do things that are quite unexpected, or even seriously outrageous, without causing surprise, disappointment, embarrassment, or anger. I actually believe that scientists, and I might say academics in general, often use the expectation of such behaviour as an excuse for not complying with conventional societal norms. In my career, I don't think that I consciously worked at being odd in the sense that I did not try to act or look more strangely than what came naturally. To be sure, I have grown several beards, the first of which was at the suggestion of my spouse, and the rest were in the face of her vehement opposition. However, I always regarded these non-shaving periods as experiments to see what it would be like, rather than a deliberate attempt to place myself outside the bounds of conventional acceptability. At least one of my later beard periods met with very strong disapproval by the female members of my family, so that whenever I came near, they put on cutout cardboard kissing protectors. It is difficult to maintain enthusiasm in the face of such rejection.

Despite my assertion that I did not, as a general rule, set out to behave oddly, there are many things that I have done in my life that could only be so described. This chapter details a few of those incidents and behaviour patterns. In my defence, I must point out that many of the happenings reported here arose as a result of stimuli generated by other people. In only a few cases can my behaviour be truthfully said to be self-generated. I leave it to you, dear reader, to decide whether my daughter Kathryn was correct when she wrote to me in February 1999: "Dad, you have reached the point of eccentricity that you are beginning to push the bounds of normality."

Let's start with cooking. I like to cook. I enjoy the creativity of putting things together and producing something the characteristics of which are significantly different from those of the ingredients. However, I do not consider myself to be a good cook. I usually approach cooking in much the same way that I played with my Meccano set as a child. I tend to shy away from recipes, and to create food as the mood takes me. As a result, the outcomes of my cooking experiments have a certain unpredictability that, depending on your point of view, makes me quite unreliable as a cook, or adds spice to life. Nevertheless, despite the inevitable randomness in the outcomes of my cooking, my experimental approach sometimes leads to a beneficial evolution in the quality of the product. Take barbeques for instance. For decades, I always cooked them on an open wood fire and only since retirement have I graduated to the greater control of bottled gas. My early barbequing efforts were, quite frankly, appalling. I can still remember offering guests meat that had been totally dehydrated, sausages that appeared to have been at the holocaust, and potatoes in which virtually all of the hydrocarbons had undergone a complete chemical reaction to charcoal. I learnt from these disasters, however. I developed methods of combining modern technology (the microwave oven) with the traditional charcoal fire to produce meals that received wide approbation. I also invented my own marinades that were demonstrably good in the sense that my customers would make encouraging grunts of approval, and sometimes even come back for seconds. Regrettably, the development of my skills ceased many years ago, so that virtually all of the barbecues that I cook these days, while being more than adequate, offer few surprises compared with what came before. I have also diligently disseminated my barbequing skills to others. There are whole generations of students in the Physics Society of the School of Physics at the University of Sydney whom I have taught to cook sausages, so that they come out neither like burnt sticks, nor like raw vomit, but are nicely browned all over with not too much fat inside. Similarly, I have passed on to my children and their spouses everything that I know about barbequing. It is a great satisfaction to me as a teacher, albeit tempered by a slight twinge of sadness because I am no longer the top barbeque dog of the family, to see how their skills have developed well beyond mine.

Another of my few cooking specialities is macaroni cheese. The origins of this dish go too far back into the mists of time for me to recall, but I suspect that it might have been Marilyn who first cooked it, and then I took it over and made it my own. This is a great dish for a Sunday night, particularly in cold weather. Its base is macaroni, of course, with copious quantities of cheese, lots of vegetables, leftover meat and anything else lying around, and seasonings. Even though nothing is ever measured, the outcomes are consistently good. One reason for this is because the ingredients are always pretty much the same. However, once I cooked it for the Ludi family during a visit with them in Switzerland, and their cheese was completely different. I also miscalculated badly with the quantities. Although they were polite in their comments about what I served up to them, it was frankly speaking awful, and a great deal was thrown away.

I also like to cook lasagna. This is one of the few dishes where I follow the recipe moderately closely each time. I always cook a lot of this, so that some can be stored in the freezer for later. The outcomes of my lasagna exploits are therefore more predictable. I am not the lasagna king in our family, however. That title is held by our son Steven, who has lifted the creation of this dish to an even higher plane by learning how to make firkins of it for his many friends – without consulting a recipe, too. Despite the quality of my lasagna, my family usually gives me a hard time whenever I cook it, because of a long ago incident involving one of my thawed offerings. As we started to eat it, I noticed that it was a bit more crunchy than normal in parts. I decided that it would not be appropriate to share this observation with the others, but it soon became clear that they had also noticed. A few minutes of intensive forensic detective work and finger pointing followed, which revealed that I had forgotten to remove the plastic freezer wrap from the top of the dish before placing it in the oven. My loving family never lets me forget this. On another occasion, I launched into a lasagna cooking expedition, and was well on the way to my destination when I realised that I had used the cat mince. You have to take my word that this one never made it to the table, although it would have been an interesting experiment to see if anyone had noticed. I didn't have the courage to test their level of discernment, however.

There is another food-related incident that must be recounted, even though, in this case, I was not the cook. There is no doubt, however, about where the responsibility resides for what occurred. When we lived at Beecroft, we did most of our grocery shopping at a small supermarket just down the road. This store had the advantages that it was close, and relatively cheap. In every other way, however, it was an unpleasant place in which to shop. The aisles were narrow, and always seemed to be full of junk, so that passage along them was frustratingly slow. On more than one occasion, I saw an unpacked box of groceries fall from where it was stored high above the shelves. The range of goods was limited, the lighting was poor, and they often stocked out-of-date goods. I used to regard shopping there as a real health hazard. On one occasion after dinner at home, I was about to dispense ice cream to the masses. Upon removing the lid, I found that the ice cream had turned into a dirty-looking, yellow crystalline mass. I railed against our supermarket. Obviously, they had allowed the ice cream to melt, and then refrozen it. Typical! Marilyn returned the offending container to the supermarket, and obtained a replacement. Many weeks later, she was ratting around in our freezer, and asked, "Whatever happened to that chicken stock that I had in here?"

Before I finally get out of the kitchen, a word about washing up. For virtually all of our married life, I have been the evening washer upper in our home. It seems a little thing to do to get fed and, perhaps surprisingly, I actually like the job. Also I think that I am pretty good at it, although it hasn't always been that way. During the time that we lived in New York, I actually broke a complete dinner service, piece by piece, while washing up. Thankfully, over the years I have improved, both in reliability and technique. For example, I have developed and perfected a system of rinsing the dishes before they get into the detergent, and rinsing them again after it, so that they dry sparkling clean. Using this method, I can wash up a big pile of dirty dishes with just one load of water. I also find washing up quite therapeutic. It is mildly relaxing to stand there in solitude, thoughts ranging far and wide while my hands are immersed in hot water performing this mindless task. Also, it cleans your fingernails really well. Every so often, someone would come along and offer to wipe up for me but, although I appreciated the thought, I was just as happy to be alone. I recall one occasion when my two sons-in-law encroached upon my washing up space with tea towels. I like them both – they are nice guys – but they were getting in the way. Matters came to a head when I heard one of them say to the other, in a stage whisper that was clearly designed for me to hear, "Grab the plates as soon as he puts them in the draining rack and they are still dripping wet. It drives him crazy."

Since we moved into our new home at MacMasters Beach, we have acquired our first dishwasher. I reluctantly have to admit that it is an excellent thing to have, and I really don't miss my previous nightly chore. However, I certainly do not regret those countless relaxing hours at the sink, partially immersed in suds.

Outside of my family and my professional work, one of my greatest loves is wood, and woodworking. I cannot recall how this came about. My Father told me that when I was just a little boy he would give me a hammer and tin of nails, and I would sit happily for hours banging the nails into a piece of wood. I can even describe the hammer – it was a small ball pein model, which later on regrettably escaped my acquisitive grasp. I also have a vivid early recollection of an advertisement in a glossy magazine. I cannot recall what was being advertised – it was probably cigarettes or booze. However, the item in question was sitting on a wooden table, with the ocean and sailing boats in the distant background, and I can still picture the grain of this wood. I recall thinking how beautiful it was. I made my first piece of furniture, a record cabinet for my parents, while I was still in my early teens. Years later, I used to look at the quality of my workmanship and wince. However, my parents kept it in pride of place in their lounge room and, in the fullness of time, I of course came to understand why. About the time that Marilyn and I decided to become engaged, I told her that I would like to make a desk for her room – something that she did not have. I produced some sketch plans that, in hindsight, were totally lacking in style. Marilyn diplomatically suggested an alternative design that I then built. This first major piece of furniture is still with us over 40 years later, and going strong. This experience set a pattern that has been maintained over the decades. Marilyn has extremely good design skills, and I like to build things. It is an excellent basis for a team. Before we were married, I built a lot of the furniture for our house – chests of drawers, a dining room suite including table, eight chairs, buffet and china cabinet, some lounge chairs, and our bedroom suite. Some of these items have been superseded, but many still remain with us in excellent condition. As part of this furniture building exercise, I went to upholstery classes at the Eastwood Evening College and learnt something of the classical techniques used in this trade. I was particularly pleased, and a little touched, that Marilyn's Father, Stan soon joined me at these classes. Whether it was the case or not, I used to think of this as a tangible indication that he considered me worthy of his daughter.

My early furniture building also involved some elementary woodturning, and I used this method to produce many items that were satisfactory for their intended purpose, but were made totally without skill. Many years later, I went to woodturning classes, and learnt some of the correct techniques of this fascinating craft.

My early woodworking was done entirely with hand tools, except for an electric drill. Initially, all of the tools that I used belonged to my Father. Gradually, they were augmented by my own. Many of these I purchased. Right from the beginning, I adopted the practice of buying only good quality tools. The strategy has paid off, and I have had to discard very few of my acquisitions, even though many of them have been very extensively used for decades. Some of my tools were given to me, such as my first electric drill from Marilyn. Regrettably, after about 35 years of hard work and a mid-life rewinding, it finally died. One tool that she gave me about the time that we became engaged, and that I particularly treasure, is a large jointer plane. It has done a huge amount of work over the years, but remains in mint condition. Other tools that came as gifts include a beautiful set of Swedish mitre chisels from friends for my 21st birthday, and a very nice wood vice that was given to me in thanks for some Physics coaching that I gave to a friend and for which I would not accept any payment. In this case, what I received is valued far more by me than any money that might have changed hands. I also received a magnificent set of Sid-chrome engineering spanners as a farewell gift after I had spent several years as a director of a company. I chose to receive very little financial recompense for my work with this company, but again the value that I place on this gift surpasses any money that I might have been paid. I shamelessly have to admit that a few of my Father's tools made irreversible transitions into my keeping. At the time, I think that I rationalised that my need was greater than his. In general, however, I do not approve of theft, and I take a very dim view if anyone attempts to pinch one of my tools.

After many years of enthusiastic woodwork using hand tools, I started to acquire power tools. My first purchase was a router. I immediately discovered that I could do things with this machine that are far more accurate than is possible by hand. Perhaps more significantly given the way that my life was developing, I could perform specific tasks with it in vastly less time than before. I also designed and built a wooden router table, in which the machine is mounted upside down with the cutting bit protruding above the surface of the table, and the wood, rather than the tool, is held and manipulated, usually against a fixed fence. This enables highly accurate machining operations to be carried out on relatively small pieces of wood, and opens up new and exciting construction possibilities. I have also devised ways of using the router table to perform joinery that is quite difficult to make by hand.

The thing that really set the pattern for the future of my woodworking, however, was the acquisition of my Shopsmith in the late 1970s. The Shopsmith is a multifunction woodworking machine. It can be used as a circular saw, a disk sander, a wood turning lathe, and a horizontal or vertical drill press. I learnt about the Shopsmith through colleagues at AWA, many of whom possessed one. I had looked for a secondhand one for some time before I saw mine advertised one day in the Saturday paper. Extraordinarily enough, it was located only about two kilometres from our home at Beecroft. The fellow selling it had been forced to retire early due to ill health, and was intending to move into a retirement village where there was no room for it. Parting with it was breaking his heart. I was somewhat diffident about the amount of money being asked, but Marilyn encouraged me to go for it, so I drove over to see him. As soon as I saw the machine, I fell in love with it, and closed the deal immediately without haggling over the price. A few moments later, another chap arrived and offered more money, but the seller was a man of his word, and I had made my first significant woodworking machine acquisition. Several months later, the former owner contacted me, saying that his health had greatly improved, and asking if he could buy the machine back from me. Regrettably, I had to tell him that it was not for sale. It never will be – not by me, anyway.

My Shopsmith opened my eyes to the amazing possibilities afforded by well-designed woodworking machinery. Since I acquired it, I have gradually added additional pieces of equipment to my workshop, and I now have virtually everything in it that I need. People seeing my set up for the first time are pretty impressed, and I have to say that it is indeed wonderful. However, I have built it up over several decades. Moreover, all but two of my machines are secondhand, so I have actually spent a good deal less to equip it than would be the case had I acquired only new gear.

One of the things that attracts me to making things in my workshop is the challenge of designing the best way of constructing something, and of devising methods of performing the manufacturing operations so that the finished object will be as perfect as I can make it. To this end, I delight in inventing new ways of performing the manufacturing steps, and I am forever designing and making extensive use of jigs to hold the work and guide the cutting tool. I see in this interesting parallels with my professional work as an scientist, where I have observed how great progress can be made through clever, innovative experimental design. The skills needed to do well in both areas are complementary, and in each I get great satisfaction from the creativity associated with working out how to do something better than has been possible in the past.

Although woodworking is my first love, my last major machinery purchase was a metalworking lathe. Despite having done quite a lot of woodturning over the years, at the time of my retirement I had never actually used a metalworking lathe myself. In my professional work, I have designed countless objects that were manufactured on such machines. In addition, I have had quite a few foreign orders made that involved metal turning. I realised, however, that I would not have this luxury in my retired state, so I set out to look for a small secondhand metalworking lathe in reasonable condition. As it turned out, such a machine became available in the School of Physics a few months before I retired. As Head of School at the time and a contender for this machine, it was important that I followed the University procedures for disposal of surplus equipment to the letter. The Head of the School's workshop, Graham Mannes, therefore managed the sale of the machine completely independently of me. Graham called for tenders for the lathe, and I put in my offer. Extraordinarily, my bid was identical to that of one of the technical staff in the workshop, Terry Pfeiffer, so Graham gave Terry and me the option to submit a high bid. I thought carefully about the strategy of escalating my price. I increased my offer by 50%, and then added another $50 for good measure. However, Terry outsmarted me. His offer beat mine by $10, so I missed out on the lathe. No one could say that I used my privileged position as the Head of School to get the inside running. As luck would have it, a few months later some more pieces of workshop equipment became available in another department of the University. One of these was a metalworking lathe that was exactly the same model as the one that I had missed out on in Physics. Another was a band saw, the only other remaining machine that I lusted for. Both machines were quite old, but they were in excellent condition. I put in bids for both the lathe and the band saw. On my second last day of work, I learnt that I had been successful in both cases. It was a really nice way to finish up!

I am greatly enjoying learning the elementary skills of metal turning. There are some similarities in the principles of turning wood and metal, and some very significant differences in technique. My technical friends in the School of Physics have been very generous in the advice that they have offered, and I have read extensively on the subject. While my metal turning skills are still rather rudimentary, I get a great kick out of making things on this machine. It is yet another example of satisfaction that comes from creativity and achievement.

One of the main reasons why I chose to retire relatively early was that I wanted the time to do many things that were simply not possible with the demands of my full-time job. High on my priorities was to start to make some significant pieces of furniture again. It had been many years since I had tackled major work of this kind. Often, I would get into my workshop and then walk away without doing anything much because I knew that I would not have the time to come back on an ongoing basis and continue with a large project. At times, I actually began to wonder whether I still had the same passion for woodwork as had been there earlier in my life. My worries had been exacerbated by having observed workshops, even better than mine, which were never used by their retired owners. Having now successfully negotiated over three years of my retirement, during which I have created some fine new pieces of furniture to Marilyn's design, I am delighted to learn that it is all still there.

A woodworking shop is nothing without wood, and over the years I have managed to acquire a significant stock of this wonderful stuff, much of which has been previously used. Some people collect wine – I collect wood. It is interesting that once the word gets out that you are in this business, unsolicited offers tend to come in. On one occasion, I received a call from one of the technicians in the School of Physics who worked in a different building. Their laboratories were being refurbished, and he informed me that four large planks of Tasmanian oak, formerly shelving in the laboratory, were to be dispatched to the rubbish dump the next day unless I could collect them before 9am. They didn't get to the dump. Some of my timber has come directly to me as tree branches, and has been seasoning for many years. Pieces like this are superb for woodturning. Other bits have been given to me as presents. I have one large plank, now partially used, that I fell in love with at a timber yard one Saturday morning a few years ago. I had no immediate need for it at the time, but the quality of the piece was outstanding. However, it was quite expensive and I could not bring myself to buy it, so I walked away. The following Saturday, I went back and agonised over it again. Once more I walked away. The third week, I plucked up courage, and now it is mine, to be used and savored with delight as the years go by.

Of course, I have purchased a lot of the timber for my furniture from conventional timber yards. Very early in my career as a woodworker, I discovered that the blokes who manned the yards were usually as interested in timber as I was, even though they may not have been woodworkers. I also learnt that, if I told them that I was planning to use the timber for a piece of fine furniture, they were quite happy to let me go through their stacks and choose the best boards. I was always particularly careful, however, to ensure that I left the remaining material in good order and condition after I had selected my treasures.

Extraordinarily enough, I can look at almost every piece of wood in my store and recall where it came from. I don't have to write anything down in order to do this – I just know. There is an important lesson here for teachers in any discipline – if someone is interested enough in a subject, the learning becomes almost automatic.

Another of the great joys in being a woody is that you often have to go to the hardware store. I just love these places and can browse through them for hours. There is an old joke about the difference between men and women – women often go shopping together, but you never hear stories of men doing this. Well, it's not quite true. My son Steven and I have had countless happy hours together browsing through hardware stores and coming home with a prized item. On one occasion, I found myself with a spare Sunday in Japan. I was within walking distance of large shopping complex and, to my astonishment and pleasure, in it was a hardware store. I had a splendid time looking over the tools, many of which were quite different in design from their Western equivalents, and I even bought a couple of items that I still use and treasure.

Being involved in woodworking is not without its hazards. I carry on my body, and in my mind, many scars to remind me of times when I have not been careful enough, or have used incorrect techniques. On one occasion, I dropped a very large sheet of particle board on my toe that immediately responded with impressive blackness and pain. My daughter Kathryn recalls this event with great clarity. I hope it is not because I added to the breadth of her vocabulary, but there is a real probability that this is indeed the case. Kathryn is a very gifted artist, and she often produces excellent caricatures of everyone in our family. Being as tall and shiny as I am, she finds me quite easy to do but, in order to dispel any doubts, I am to this day depicted with one very black toenail.

Some of my self-inflicted injuries have left no visible scars, but their occurrence remains as fresh in my mind, and as painful to my memory, as when they happened. Quite recently I was using an electric drill to make a hole in a piece of steel on the concrete floor of my workshop. Because I was in a hurry, I had not properly secured the work, and the drill bit ran off the metal and onto the floor, and then snapped. In the process, its jagged stump went through my thumbnail. The pain was quite extraordinary, but the most memorable thing about the incident was the anger that I felt for my stupidity. After all, I have been in this game for nearly half a century, and to make a mistake like that out of sheer carelessness and incorrect technique was the height of foolishness. I also carry several significant scars on a few of my fingers, mostly arising from woodworking accidents. Again, they have usually occurred as a result of crass stupidity. In the few cases that they were due to ignorance, I have seldom made the same mistake again. Inflicting physical damage on yourself is a great learning tool.

Another time, I did myself a spectacular piece of self-harm with a chainsaw. Once more, I have learnt from the experience, but it should never have come to that. On this occasion, I was lopping some tree branches with my father-in-law, Stan Martin. I had climbed the tree with the chainsaw, and was using it above my head with only one hand. Our activities came to a rapid end when I cut through a branch that hit the chainsaw as it fell, and forced it down and into my leg just above the ankle. Again the emotions that I experienced are still very clear in my mind, and disgust was pretty high amongst them. Judging by the colour of Stan's face, I suspect that he felt a bit differently to me. Stan bandaged me up, and then drove me to the local doctors for stitching. As I lay on the table, still in my filthy clothes, I observed an inchworm measuring its way across my chest. Interesting. As it happened, I was scheduled to go overseas three days later and I was only just to be able to do that. A week or so into the trip, I got a colleague in the United States to remove the stitches from my leg using a pair of kitchen scissors.

You, dear reader, will doubtless have concluded that I have never grown out of my childhood *bull-at-a-gate* or *she'll-be-right* way of doing things, and I suspect that I never will. All too often, it appears that I transform DIY (Do It Yourself) into DYI (Do

Yourself In). I think that these attitudes are associated with an incurable optimism, and an inherent enthusiasm for getting on with the job. Without attempting to defend them, they often allow me to get things done that would not happen with a more prudent approach. Unfortunately, they also sometimes have unwanted and unfortunate consequences. On one much-reminded occasion early in our married life, we had arrived home with the grocery shopping, and I was unpacking the car. I piled up a lot of stuff in my arms, and I put a dozen eggs on the top. Marilyn told me to take them off, because they would fall. Of course, I didn't, and they did, causing a few to break. To compound the disaster, I then stepped onto the box, breaking most of the rest! I was furious with myself, and I think that I even half-believed that Marilyn's cautionary warning had somehow precipitated the disaster. I went into the garden for several hours and dug like a demented soul to work out my feelings.

Although wood is my first handyman love, I have lots of other interests and experience in home technology. Not all of the outcomes of my efforts in these areas have been entirely successful. When we lived in New York, our television set was a big chunky item with valves. It operated quite well, except that it would not receive two or three of the dozen or so New York channels. One evening, I misguidedly set out to fix it. My tools were a screwdriver, a pair of bull nosed pliers, and some manicure tweezers. I rationalised that the problem had to be in the tuner, and extracted that from the bowels of the set with relatively little difficulty. At that point, I moved rapidly down the slippery slide of disaster. As I started to take the tuner apart, hidden springs and ball bearings launched themselves out of it onto the lounge room carpet. I scrambled around collecting these items and tried to stuff them back into likely looking places. It quickly became evident that the task was way beyond my capabilities and equipment, and I reassembled the set as best I could. At the completion of my efforts, we could receive only two of the dozen or so New York channels. We were forced to call in the TV servicemen who, for a quite modest sum, transformed the set into perfect working condition.

It took me a long time to accept the idea of using a professional to do a job that should be achievable by a competent handyman.

Certainly, in the early days of our married life, our financial state was such that doing things myself was the only option. However, I also liked to try new things, and I enjoyed the challenge of understanding how systems were put together, and taken apart. On one occasion, I needed to replace the muffler in my car. What could be simpler? Well, it wasn't. I spent most of a beautiful Sunday afternoon under the car trying to loosen rusted bolts, get the old muffler off, and install the new one. In the end, I did indeed succeed in this endeavour, but at significant cost. I ruined a perfectly good pair of spectacles by scraping them on the underside of the car. The cost of the exercise greatly exceeded what I would have incurred by getting the job done profession-ally. In addition, I screwed up a lovely day. I resolved then and there that I would never again work on the insides of my car. The only manual work that I do now relating to car service is to move my right hand up and down slightly as I write out the cheque.

Being a handyman means you learn about lots of different technological systems. I actually think that I have a pretty good grasp of most of the relevant things in order to make running repairs on a house. Marilyn and I have also done a significant amount of building over the years, and we like to think that we can together do most things at least as well as tradesmen, and often much better. However, the learning path that we have walked down was not always smooth. I can do most plumbing things in a house now, but I have made some pretty significant mistakes in developing these skills. One of these occurred during the building of an extension on the top of our house at Beecroft. We had professional builders to do the bulk of this job, but I did a lot of the internal fitting and completion tasks myself. These included constructing three very large wardrobes in the children's bedrooms, and the entire fitting out of the bathroom. In fact, the bathroom was a real pain in the neck. It remained uncompleted for several years, sitting up there above my head like the sword of Damocles. Every so often, I would make a run at it, but I never seemed to finish it. On one occasion, I tackled the tiling. The wall tiles were easy, because they just had to be stuck on. The floor posed significant challenges, however, because the workmen had left the job with the levels of the floor drains all screwed up. I had to mix many barrow loads of cement in order to get the correct slope of the tiles to the drains in the floor and the shower recess. Eventually, I did this satisfactorily. Indeed, the tiling looked excellent. Many months afterwards, I finally finished installing the taps and shower fittings. It was with a great sense of relief that I realised that this miserable job was close to an end. How wrong I was! When I turned the shower on, the water went nowhere. I quickly realised that the cement-loaded water that had run into the P-trap of the shower recess during my earlier tiling exploits had solidified into an impenetrable plug. I therefore spent a couple of days working on the cement with quite strong acid. I eventually dissolved enough of it to enable me to crush up the rest and wash it away. All the time, I kept thinking how trivial it would have been to avoid this problem had I flushed out the P-trap with clean water before the cement set – something that any competent tiler or plumber would have known. The road to true enlightenment is not always smooth. For the record, I finished the bathroom just before we sold the house, and we never actually used it.

I had another most unfortunate plumbing experience during the building of an extension onto our house at Rouse Hill. (Do you get the impression that we were always putting on extensions to our houses? You wouldn't be wrong.) On this occasion, Steven and I were installing the plumbing for the new bathroom and kitchen. It was a reasonably complex job, involving a separate hot water storage tank, and a multiplicity of hot and cold outlets. I had borrowed a pipe bender from work, and we slaved together all day. I went to some trouble to ensure that, in addition to working properly, it looked good, even though the plasterboard and flooring would shortly hide the plumbing. We finally made our last solder joints late in the afternoon, and we were very proud of our efforts, with all of the pipes neatly running at right angles to the walls or the floor. We put our tools away, and I was removing the accumulated grime in a lovely hot shower when Steven came in and asked, "Dad, why did you put all of the hot water outlets on the right-hand side?"

My heart sank. I dried off, and then made a brief, but futile attempt to persuade Marilyn that it really wouldn't matter. The next day, we got stuck into the job again. This time, I abandoned all pretence at having things oriented neatly. The end result was a labyrinth of crossing over pipes, and connections in odd places, that had the sole redeeming feature that it operated according to the demands of convention. If ever the archeologists get to study this job, they will never be able to work out why it was plumbed up in that way.

For many years, I was also very keen on photography. I loved working in the dark room, and doing black and white prints. I even received an enlarger for my 21st birthday, and used it extensively. Much later, I went off taking pictures, because my eyes had deteriorated to the point that I had difficulty focusing the camera and it annoyed me that my pictures were not as sharp as they should have been. Modern electronic cameras overcome this difficulty, but I somehow have never got back into it. During the days when photography was big in my life, I volunteered to take the photos for the annual competition of our daughters' physical culture club. These physical culture competitions were pretty competitive. The mothers of these prepubescent nymphs spent hours tarting them up, with professional hairdos usually piled up high to make them look taller, complex makeup, new leotards and ballet shoes, and copious quantities of leg tan. They came out looking like little underdeveloped Barbie dolls. Photographing the extravaganza was therefore a pretty big deal because, after the event was over, the pictures were the only remaining record of these enormous preparatory efforts. The responsibility of a photographer at one of these physie dos was not dissimilar to that at a wedding. On the day of the big event, I fronted up with camera and flash, and did my thing. The next step was to develop the film, and I set about doing this in the evening. For reasons that are completely unknown to me, half way through the development process I inadvertently removed the lid of my developing tank. I have never done this before, or since. The film was ruined, and I had this dreadful vision of being hand bagged to death by the angry mothers of the daughters, the photos of whom I had ruined. Actually, it was even worse than this, because I did not *completely* ruin the film. It would have been much better had this been the case but there were some faint remains of the images within the darkness of the negatives. I therefore spent several evenings trying to produce prints of, if not acceptable quality, then at least with recognizable pictures. In the end, I had a bunch of very poor photographs that I simply gave away. I never expected to make any money out of this little exercise, but I did think that I might cover my costs. It was a sad, disappointing and stressful incident in my life.

I conclude this chapter with a few words about my ventures into the wonderful world of music. I never learnt a musical instrument as a child. Indeed, my only formal music education was in First Year at High School, and it was a subject that I came quite close to failing. Of course, I knew lots of songs, and later on I learnt to play many of them by ear on the harmonica. On the other hand, Marilyn is a very accomplished pianist, so quite early on we acquired a piano for our home. I made some attempts to learn it, without much success. As our children grew, they learnt piano, and they also joined bands, both at school, and in the community. I would often take them to band practice, and wait outside in the car reading a book. I used to watch wistfully as this procession of young kids went into the band hall carrying their instrument cases, and I recall thinking how great it would be to do that. I always rationalised, however, that because of the demands of my professional life, I would never have the time to learn an instrument. Then the Musical Director of the Hornsby Concert Band, Vic Grieve, announced his intention to start an adult beginner group. It was too good an opportunity to miss. I made a spur-of-the-moment decision to purchase a trumpet, because I thought that this was the instrument most compatible with my personality. Moreover, having only three valves, I reasoned that it might be easier to play than something for which you had to use all of your fingers. Marilyn acquired a saxophone, and together we started this new adventure. At our first meeting together as a band of very nervous mature novices, Vic started with the words, "Welcome to the wonderful world of music. Put your instruments to your mouth and make a noise."

Being a very late starter, the only way that I could make any progress at all was to work very hard at it. Almost every evening after dinner, I would therefore lock myself away, and do an hour's practice. Evidently, my earlier belief that I didn't have the time was not correct. The time is always there – you just have to give the matter in hand a high enough priority. Our children were very encouraging, and most tolerant of my incompetence. I actually think that it was very good for them to see me trying hard in an area where they were vastly better than I was. On one occasion, I took my trumpet down into the back paddock, and was playing away when something caught my eye. It was a large, red bellied black snake that had evidently been charmed by my sounds. Our mutual awareness of each other's presence caused us both to move rapidly in opposite directions.

Musician (late starter)

We had so much fun with this band. We very quickly learnt to play a few simple pieces, and progressed from there. Our first concert consisted of five numbers, and no encore, because we did not have a sixth. As a band of adult beginners, we were a bit of a novelty, and there were even a few articles about us in the newspapers, and little bits on the radio. In one of the radio features, a reporter asked Vic if we would ever get to be any good, and he replied, "Oh, they'll never be as good as the kids." I remember that several of us were quite put out by this comment. At first, I refused to accept that this was the case, but Vic was absolutely correct. Starting at our age, we could never become as good as somebody who began much earlier. It would be like pretending that a person could learn a new language in their forties, and speak it as well as a native. There are parallels in the scientific field in terms of developing competencies in new technologies. The most obvious example relates to computational skills. However, being as good as the kids was not the point. Our challenge was to be as good as we could.

Fairly early on, our adult beginner band took part in an evening concert that also included performances by several of the other bands in our organisation. For some reason or other, two of the other beginner-band trumpet players and I decided that we would do a turn at this extravaganza. With piano accompaniment, we stood up in front of the assembled masses and played a trumpet trio. It was pretty shaky all through, and the lead player lost the plot completely in the middle. (I was playing second.) However, we struggled on to the end and our performance was rewarded with thunderous applause. Later on, some of the really talented young players from the Senior Band came up, shook our hands and patted us on the back. I know that we were terrible, but we had a go, and they admired that.

When I started playing, my objective was to get to the point where I would be able to put on one of the yellow jackets that were worn by the "proper" bands at performances. I actually did that, at the national championships in Melbourne one year. After the championships, we even did a gig at the Melbourne Concert Hall. I experienced a real sense of achievement from this. After ten years or so, however, the pressures of my job became such that I wasn't practicing enough, and the quality of my playing was deteriorating. It is not much fun to go along to band practice knowing that you are not holding up your end. For this, and other reasons, we put our instruments away and they stayed there gathering dust for a decade or so. Recently, Marilyn found a nearby group of more mature players, who are generally of a standard that is compatible with ours. We have joined this group, Tempo Terrific, and are having so much fun, both in the music that we make, and through the social interactions.

Having started to play the trumpet at the age of 40+, I did not have the benefits of muscle and coordination development available to younger people. As a result, I always found it difficult to play the higher notes and the faster parts, no matter how hard and long I practiced. In hindsight, I formed the view that the trumpet might not have been the best choice for me, and that a lower, slower instrument would be more suited to my abilities. Again, I rationalised that I would never be able to pick up another instrument, because learning the trumpet had been so difficult and time-consuming. However, after six months or so with Tempo Terrific, a second-hand trombone became available. Encouraged by Steven, who says, "It's great to be part of the grunt of the band, Dad", I purchased it, and I have been amazed at how quickly I have progressed with it. Playing an instrument that is usually part of the accompaniment, rather than the melody, is a new experience for me, and I am enjoying it immensely. So much so, in fact, that I recently acquired yet another instrument – a euphonium. This instrument has the same fingering as a trumpet, and the same mouthpiece as a trombone, so I could play it immediately. However, some of the music for the instrument is written in bass clef, so I needed to learn that. To my astonishment, this again turned out to be surprisingly quick to do. Recently, I joined a second band, Brisbane Water Brass, which actually includes several professional musicians. The standard of the music that we play in this band is something else entirely! Brass band music is almost all written in treble clef, so I had to learn to play the trombone from such music. I was again surprised that this only took a couple of days. Indeed, I am intrigued to discover that I now have two quite independent memory banks in my brain for playing these instruments, depending on whether the music that I am reading is in bass or treble clef, and that they don't get confused. I have no idea how this works, but it does. I am now attempting to learn some pieces from memory, rather than reading them from charts. This is *not* proving to be easy. Nevertheless, I intend to persist – I have great admiration for those musicians who can play indefinitely without a note of music in sight, and can improvise in such a skilled and creative manner. I want to be able to do that.

I have many more things that I would like to get into before, in the words of one of my University colleagues, "it is too late." Our earlier retirement affords us the opportunity to travel more extensively, particularly in Australia. It would be nice to see lots of Australia's national parks without needing a walking stick or wheelchair. I am also attracted to the idea of learning about pottery, and developing some of the relevant skills. This discipline seems to me to be a very nice amalgam of artistic and scientific techniques, particularly in the design and use of glazing materials. I love writing, and I am intending that this book will be but the first of several. I get great joy and satisfaction from all of these things that I do. Indeed, I regard the pleasure that they give me as the experimental evidence that confirms an idea that I have developed over the years: *True happiness comes through continuing achievement.*

My Dear Students

For me, the best thing about being an academic is the students. I enjoyed virtually everything associated with my interaction with them, except for marking examination papers (more about that shortly). I found presenting lectures enormously exciting and stimulating. I considered it a great privilege, and an awesome responsibility, to be able to play a part in the students' development. I admired their fresh approach to life, their eagerness to learn, their lack of cynicism and their self-belief. They were having a good time at the University, and they welcomed me to share that experience, so that I enjoyed myself as well. I also found the teaching role enormously satisfying through the things that it taught *me*, including an increased understanding of the subject of Physics. Perhaps most importantly, my association with the students was refreshing and rejuvenating – it kept me young.

I didn't immediately feel as positively about my interactions with students when I first started to teach. This occurred during my Ph.D. studies at New York University, when I was a complete novice. I am aware of lots of occasions when my teaching was quite poor, even to the point that I said some things that were simply wrong. It's a bit like being a parent for the first time – you learn on the job, and those on the receiving end of your efforts have to survive the impact of your mistakes. Perhaps the biggest shock for me during my teaching at NYU was seeing how poorly my students did in their examinations. I often used to bring the exam papers home with me, and Marilyn would help me with the task of marking them. Marking these things is a soul-destroying experience. One by one, you have to work through a huge pile of scripts that never appears to get any lower. To me, it seems like walking through treacle (or how I imagine this feels!) The experience is made worse because you find that many of the students haven't understood even the simplest of the concepts that you were trying to communicate in your lectures. It's very hard to maintain a positive frame of mind under such conditions. My earliest reaction to the dismal performance of my students in their examinations was one of scorn. I felt that these kids must be really dumb if they couldn't understand such simple things. Over the years, however, my views have changed completely. Firstly, it is my job to make sure that they understand. If they dish up trash in the examinations, then clearly I have not communicated properly with them. And in any case, what were my own examination efforts like? I have always thought that it would be a wonderful learning experience for all teachers to go back and look at the examination scripts that they produced when they were students. Mine were probably no better than what many of my students gave me. Further, it is completely unreasonable to expect everybody to get 100% in every subject. Learning isn't like that. Much later on, my very humbling unsuccessful efforts to gain an elementary grasp of the Japanese language constituted a powerful learning experience for me. After all, I consider myself no dummy, yet within this class, I was right near the bottom. I realised that the difficulties that many of my students were experiencing in understanding concepts in Physics were directly analogous to my inability to remember all those Japanese words. Not everyone's mind is built the same way, and individuals excel in different things. Even though I hated to mark exam papers, I never went down the path of developing multiple-choice assessment alternatives. I strongly believe that it is important to read the students' unsuccessful attempts to answer your questions. It provides teachers with a window into their minds, and it therefore helps us to understand better the difficulties that they are experiencing, so that our teaching will be more effective next time.

Of course, when I was doing my Ph.D. in New York, I also took many courses myself. The combination of simultaneously being a student *and* a teacher was itself a very important learning experience for me, both in terms of helping me to understand the Physics better, and of appreciating the difficulties that my students were having in their own learning. Many of the topics that I was studying at an advanced level were also those that I was teaching at a more basic level. One really powerful learning experience from that time sticks in my mind. It occurred during the dreaded Preliminary Examinations at the end of my first year of study. Although I did very well overall in these exams, in one subject my performance was barely average. This was Electromagnetic Theory, which I later taught, and got to know quite well. In the exam for this subject, there was a question that I could have answered using very elementary principles that I knew well, because I had actually taught them. However, I attempted to answer it using some more advanced concepts that I had seen in the lectures that I sat in on during my preparation for the exams. I got a short distance into the answer, but could not complete it. Had I approached the problem at a more basic level, I would have solved it easily, and my performance in this part of the Prelims would have been much better than it was. My lesson, learnt the hard way, is that simplest is best, and I believe that this is applicable to virtually everything that you do in life.

It astonishes me how few people in the scientific field, and perhaps in academia in general, have failed to grasp the importance of simplicity in structuring their lectures and seminars. I first noticed this in the 1960s when I started to go to evening meetings of the Australian Institute of Physics. Although I enjoyed the interactions that I had at these meetings, I always found the talks quite impenetrable. Most of the talks were at such an advanced level that the only people in the audience who understood them were those few specialists in the same field as the presenter. For most of us, the whole thing was effectively a waste of time. I saw similar things at the weekly colloquia at the Physics Department at New York University that we graduate students were required to attend. Most of these talks were also impenetrable, but in those authoritarian days, we didn't argue – we were told to be there, so we went. And anyway, the only way to get cake at the afternoon tea that always preceded the talk was to stay on for the punishment afterwards.

Despite the fact that I often couldn't understand any of the Physics, I always tried to come away from such talks with something new, even if that was only an object lesson about lousy presentation techniques. Many years later when I had graduated to telling the students what to do, I tried to insist that they should come to our weekly colloquia at the School of Physics at the University of Sydney. Even though I was responsible for introducing the cake/bribe method before these colloquia, I was quite unsuccessful in persuading most of the students to come. Actually, I wasn't in any position to enforce my instructions to the students because, unlike at NYU, many of my academic colleagues in the School also refused to attend unless the topic was directly relevant to their particular field of interest. I found that quite disappointing.

Over the years as I obtained more lecturing experience, I tended to make my presentations progressively simpler and simpler. I don't want to pretend that this happened straight away. I can recall many courses that I taught at the University of Sydney in which I pitched the material too high, and the students did not get much benefit from my efforts. As I developed this philosophy of simplicity, however, I found that it was very effective, independent of whether I was giving a lecture course, a specialist presentation, or a talk to the general public. I also found that relating new concepts to things that are familiar to an audience is a very powerful teaching tool. In addition, I learnt how to use repetition, and especially humour, to bring people forward into new learning areas. I don't think that my status as a scientist has ever been diminished because I didn't talk above the heads of my audience.

One of my most enjoyable teaching experiences at NYU was the summer class of 1967. I taught this class at a time when things were very busy in several ways. Marilyn had just given birth to Jenelle. I had just completed my frantic efforts to obtain a critical amount of data from my experiment, and I was trying to get on top of this material, and also to master the relevant theoretical aspects of my topic. I was also taking a summer course myself in order to complete the requirements for my Ph.D. within my target three years. My teaching of this class therefore had to be fitted in amongst all of these other demands on my time, and I am surprised that I remember it so fondly. The class was quite intensive, and we met four times each week. I was required to mark the roll on each occasion, so I got to know everybody in the class. I worked very hard to bring the students up to a level that would enable them to enter a mainstream course at the commencement of the upcoming semester. They were a great bunch kids, and we got on very well together. At the completion of the course, they presented me with a piece of paper, signed by every member of the class, which carried this simple message:

We, the summer class of 1967, thank you for teaching us,
and wish you well in your future endeavors.

I returned to the world of teaching when I joined the New South Wales Institute of Technology in 1978. NSWIT required all new teachers to undertake some training. I remember feeling very negative about having to do this, even remarking to a colleague, "These people can't tell me anything about teaching." I was completely wrong, and I was very surprised at how much I learnt. The training consisted of a few workshop sessions given by the teaching development officer at NSWIT, Jackie Lublin. I found Jackie's classes immensely useful. For example, the simple idea of first determining aims for a course, and then structuring the content to meet these aims, was not something that I had ever thought about before. I even continued to go to a series of optional sessions after the completion of the compulsory ones. As things turned out, a few years later Jackie also joined the University of Sydney, and we often worked together as colleagues in teaching development initiatives.

In addition to the development of my undergraduate teaching skills, the two years that I spent at NSWIT gave me a significant new type of teaching experience – I supervised my first graduate student, Mike Riley, who was doing a research Masters degree. Actually, I wasn't his official supervisor, but I acted in that role for six months or so while his normal supervisor was away. Again, I learnt on the job and, even though Mike's research was in an area that was unfamiliar to me, I was able to help him quite a bit. More importantly, Mike and I developed a very close friendship, and this continues to this day. Soon after I went to the University of Sydney, Mike joined my group and worked with me for a year or so before going to the United States and undertaking his own Ph.D. He now lives there with his family, and I have visited them on many occasions. Mike is also a frequent traveller to Australia, so we still see each other from time to time.

My most memorable interaction with Mike was when he offered Marilyn and me two accommodation places at Arkaroola, about 600 kilometres north of Adelaide, at the time of the December 2002 solar eclipse. This was one of those once-in-a-lifetime experiences. We spent a week in South Australia, four days of which were in the magnificent, rugged and ancient Flinders Ranges around Arkaroola. On the day of the eclipse, we drove for about two hours to a place called Lyndhurst, which was within the path of totality. The sun was low in the sky in the late afternoon on a glorious clear day. When the moon finally blocked out the last crescent of the sun completely, the sky turned deep, deep blue, and the surrounding corona became visible. At this instant, the sun seemed to become much larger, and it appeared to me to jump out of the sky towards us. The bright white corona, surrounding the black central moon, was like nothing I have ever seen before. Most extraordinarily, the outer edge of the moon appeared to me to be deep red (perhaps because of small angle scattering of long wavelength sunlight from behind the moon due to the small amount of dust in the air?) After only about 25 seconds, the sun again became visible, not immediately as a crescent, but first as a point of light coming through a chasm between two mountains on the edge of the moon. Turning around, we then saw the shadow of the moon, as a dark vertical band in the deep blue sky, receding from us across the desert at about 6 kilometres per second. We drove over 3000 kilometres for that 25 seconds, but it was something that we will never forget! None of this would have happened had it not been for the generosity and thoughtfulness of my first graduate student, Mike Riley. I have a great deal to thank Mike for.

My love affair with students really took off after I returned to the University of Sydney in 1980. I immediately got into the teaching groove, and discovered that I enjoyed it immensely. I was particularly enthusiastic about my First Year teaching, even to such notoriously difficult classes as engineering students. Many of my colleagues found that teaching such groups could degenerate into an exercise in crowd control, but I never had any difficulties in this regard. I used to set the boundary conditions right at the beginning of each course, including my requirement that there be no talking, and no paper aeroplanes. I recall an occasion in the middle of one of my early lectures to engineering students when a paper aeroplane drifted silently down onto the floor. Everything went quiet, with the entire class looking at me expectantly. I asked for the person responsible to pick it up, but nobody moved. I immediately realised that I had painted myself into a corner. I had no alternative but to walk out, so I picked up my lecture notes and headed for the door. Before I got there, a very helpful young lady from the front row jumped up and removed the offending object, defusing the incident. I never had another paper aeroplane problem in any of my classes. However, I sometimes invited my students to have a paper aeroplane free-for-all at the end of the last lecture of a course. As a footnote, this was the only time during my entire teaching career when I came close to walking out.

Several years later, my son Steven was in one of my classes. At dinner one day we were talking about discipline, and he remarked that many of his classes were riots, but that mine were always quiet and orderly, and the students were attentive. He asked me how I achieved this, but I was unable to answer him. I do remember developing specific methods, however, for maintaining order. One very effective technique is to cease speaking abruptly, and to look attentively at a couple deep in conversation, or making love, the effect of which is that all the other students in the lecture theatre are soon looking at them as well. The power of peer pressure always causes them to desist. I never yelled at a class, or told them to shut up. It was just not necessary and for that I am most grateful.

Toward the end of my first year of teaching at the University of Sydney, I decided that I would like to give the students in my First Year class a treat in the form of some fun demonstrations. The idea of doing this went right back to when I was a student, and our First Year Chemistry lecturer, Mr Broe, put on a Chemistry spectacular in his last lecture. Joe Broe, as we called him, was a great lecturer. He reminded me of my high school Physics teacher, Percy Moss. He was right at the end of his career, but retained his enthusiasm for his subject and he really cared about our progress. As it happened, he had lectured to both of my parents at the University of Queensland a generation before – they remembered him as Jimmy Broe. I had also heard about similar lectures by some physicists in the United States. They called them *Physics is F = μN* – a word play on the well-known relation describing frictional forces. So I can hardly claim that the idea of developing my *Physics is Fun* lectures was my own. The lecture demonstration bloke in the School, Ray Anderson, was most enthusiastic about the lectures, and gave me a lot of help and offered many suggestions. My first effort was pretty rough, but we all had a great time. A few months afterwards, I was asked to give one of the evening lectures to the Australian Institute of Physics. They suggested that I might like to talk about the solar energy research in the School of Physics. I came back with the alternative suggestion of a *Physics is Fun* lecture, and this is what occurred. I even wrote the newspaper advertisement that they put out, that said, in part:

*So you think that Physics is dull, boring and uninteresting? Then come and hear Professor Dick Collins swing, slosh, whistle and bang his way through a series of exciting interactive experiments showing that **Physics is Fun**.*

The publicity was outstandingly successful, and acceptances for the talk were huge. We even contemplated doing two lectures to accommodate the crowd. In the end, we decided to jam everybody into the lecture theatre, breaking all of the safety rules in the process. The room was designed for 140 people and, as I recall, there were nearly 300 in there, sitting in the aisles, on the floor, standing around the sides and even behind me during the performance. At times, I actually had to move people in order to conduct some of my demonstrations.

As usual, I was packing death before the lecture, but once I got started, it went like a train. There was a lot of interaction, spectacular effects and, most of all, fun. Most of my experiments worked, but for those that didn't, I ran a Murphy's Law score on the blackboard that turned them into winners anyway. I had a couple of anxious moments, including my first, and last stoush with liquid oxygen. I had made the mistake of not doing a trial run, so I really had no experience with the use of this stuff. The demonstration of the magnetic properties of this remarkable material went off very well. It still astonishes me that this beautiful, pale blue, cold liquid is attracted by a magnet! The wheels fell off, however, when I used liquid oxygen to enhance the burning of steel wool. I placed the steel wool on a thick steel pan, and got it smoldering. I then poured a little of the liquid onto it. The rate of burning increased, but it was not very impressive. Ray was at my elbow, and helpfully whispered, "A bit more, Dick." This I tried to do, but what came out of the dewar flask was quite a lot more than a bit. The previously gentle flames were immediately transformed into an impressive roman candle, and the steel pan melted, causing the liquid, and bits of the floating flaming material, to flow in all directions over the surface of the lecture bench, leaving some small holes in my trousers, and even consuming part of my lecture notes. The audience thought that this was fantastic and all part of the show, but I nearly shat myself. The finale of the lecture was breaking a glass with sound, and this worked like a dream. After I got home late that night, I couldn't sleep.

My *Physics is Fun* lecture became something of an institution, and I gave it many times in different parts of the country. I once did it three nights running in Perth, with packed houses each time. I loved to give it – however, it was quite exhausting, both to prepare, and in the delivery. I came to wonder how actors managed to perform at a similarly intensive level night after night. In the early days, the Murphy's Law list of failures that I compiled each time was usually quite extensive. As I gained more experience, however, my batting average increased, so that I reached the point where almost everything worked well each time. There were some unexpected occurrences, however, that stuck in my memory. Once I was charging up a member of the audience with a Van de Graaff generator. This well-known demonstration works much better with a person who has lots of long, fine hair. (It saddens me a little to recall that there was a time when I could use myself in this demonstration.) Mostly, without being sexist, I chose a girl who was so endowed. On this occasion, my very comely young victim was quite nervous, so I reassured her quietly that she would come to no harm. I stood her on an insulating base, and placed her hand on the metal sphere that would be charged to high voltage. I then turned on the generator and she charged up very nicely, with her hair flying in all directions. As the voltage approached the highest levels, however, she started to let out some slightly alarmed squeals. From my vantage point behind her, I could see that her cute little butt had moved to be a bit too close to the ground plane of the generator, and the system was sparking from there, through her jeans, to what was inside. I quickly shut down the system, and no harm was done, or at least none that was visible to me.

Most of the experiments that I used in my *Physics is Fun* lectures are old standards. I invented a few of them myself, however. Perhaps the best known, and certainly one of the most impressive, of these was my *standing on eggs* demonstration. The idea for this came from something that I was shown as a boy – that if you hold a raw egg *end-on* between the palms of your hands, it is almost impossible to break it, even at the highest compressive force that you can apply. It took me quite a bit of work to figure out how to design the cups to hold three eggs in a way that would support my weight, and I broke many eggs on the way. I remember Marilyn commenting, "We seem to be going through an awful lot of eggs lately." Our dog got rather OD'd on raw eggs. Finally, I got it figured out, and I often used it as a spectacular finale to the show.

Lecture demonstration

One of the great things about my *Physics is Fun* lectures was that they appealed to folks aged from 8 to 80 (with the possible exception of those in their mid-teens.) Sometimes, however, I encountered unexpected problems associated with people at the extreme ends of this range. I was once giving the lecture to an audience that included quite a few boys who were less than ten years old. I was totally inexperienced in presenting to such a group, and very quickly observed that their behaviour did not conform to the usual norms. For example, they tended to move around the lecture room in an unpredictable and uncontrollable way. I thought it best to ignore this, and ploughed on despite these escalating distractions. In the middle of the lecture, however, and quite out of the blue, one of these little hoodlums said to me, "Do you know what?"

I was quite taken aback, but my Mother had always told me to be polite, so I said, "No, what?"

He replied, "I've got my shoes on."

The absolute irrelevance of this statement totally floored me. My daughter, Jenelle, who knows about children of this age, later told me that the appropriate response would have been, "That's nice," and then to move on rapidly. As a result of my inexperience in such matters, however, there was a significant discontinuity in my presentation until I got my nerve back.

Presenting my *Physics is Fun* lectures to the over 60s was also not entirely without its risks. One of the experiments that I did was an adaptation of the old grab-the-money trick. In this, you hold a bank note so that it hangs vertically down, and have someone place his or her fingers around the note, but not touching it, and positioned just below yours. You tell them that the money is theirs if they can grab it as it falls. You release the note without warning, and it passes through the victim's fingers before the human reflex system has time to operate. I developed this idea into a method of measuring the speed of a person's reflexes. After doing the bank note teaser with my volunteer (I only lost it once), I repeat the experiment with a metre stick. I hold the stick vertically, and get my subject to place their fingers around the bottom end, with instructions to grab it as it falls. For most people, they catch it after the stick has fallen about 20 centimetres, corresponding to a reflex time of a few tenths of a second. This is one of those wonderful Physics experiments that you can do with essentially no equipment at all. It is also a great one for kids, because usually they can perform better than adults. On one occasion, I was doing it at an International Science School in front of a large group of senior high school students.

Having measured the reflex times of a couple of the kids, I asked if one of the adults would like to have a go. The kids volunteered Harry Messel and he quickly agreed. Harry was always happy to become involved in anything competitive. I noticed that he did not look at the stick, but instead stared straight ahead, presumably because he thought, or maybe knew, that the reflex time associated with his peripheral vision was less. As it happened, he performed about the same as the kids. For reasons that I cannot recall, I then asked Professor Hanbury-Brown to try. Hanbury was pretty close to retirement at that time and had started to slow up a bit physically, although mentally he was still as sharp as ever. When I let the stick go, it fell right through his fingers to the floor. His response time was too long to measure! I was more than a little embarrassed, and I kicked myself for my insensitivity in putting him in such a position. Characteristically, however, Hanbury appeared to find the whole thing quite hilarious, for which I was most grateful.

The International Science Schools run every two years by the Science Foundation for Physics within the University of Sydney are something of an institution. Each School involves two stimulating weeks of lectures and interaction for the 140 or so 16-18 year old Scholars from many different parts of the world. Harry Messel started the Science Schools in the 1960s, and ran them for decades. He even held them every year for a while, an effort that I find quite extraordinary, given the amount of work involved in their organisation and raising the funds to support them. They are now called the Professor Harry Messel International Science Schools in honour of this remarkable man. I have given lectures to quite a few of the Science Schools over the years and, together with the Executive Officer of the Science Foundation, Jenny Nicholls, I ran them in 1997, 1999, and 2001. These days, all of the Scholars live in together at St. John's College at the University of Sydney. They have an absolutely fantastic time, both in the intellectual development that occurs, and through their out-of-class experiences. Many of them tell us that the Science Schools change their lives. The Scholars may not recognise it, but the Science Schools also have a very significant effect on many of the older people who are involved with them. For myself, some of my most memorable interactions with students have occurred at these Science Schools.

On the job

195

At the 1999 School, I chaired every lecture section, and also gave some of the lectures myself. I therefore came to know the Scholars quite well. I would start the first lecture session each day with a greeting that I had introduced to them on the first lecture: "G'day, mate!" (In actual fact, I pronounced it more like "G'die, mite!") They would enthusiastically respond in unison with the same greeting. All of the Scholars, but particularly those from non-English speaking countries, loved this little piece of Australiana, and I still get letters and emails that begin with these words. By the end of the first week, we were pretty good friends. On the Saturday evening in the middle of the School, the Scholars, lecturers and sponsors always get together on a cruise. With Sydney Harbour putting on its unique magic, this is a wonderful evening, and it provides the opportunity for close interaction between young and old – not to mention close interactions amongst the Scholars themselves, because by this stage, everyone seems to be in love with everyone else. On this particular cruise, one of the student helpers, Hong Nguyen, who had been a Scholar at the previous Science School, told me that some of the kids wanted to ask a favour of me. It seems that the Japanese Scholars had brought with them a new word: *Oss!* The word is delivered with both arms held high, the second and third fingers extended. They were not able to tell us exactly what it means, other than it is a bloke thing, and is used colloquially in Japan when good mates meet. I imagine that it could be roughly translated as Nina Culotta's *Owyergoinmateorrite?* The request was that I should use the word when we met at the first lecture the following Monday. I gave a non-committal response. On the Monday morning, there was an enhanced air of expectancy in the lecture theatre. I brought the Scholars to order and greeted them in the normal way: "G'day, mate!"

The reply thundered back: "G'day, mate!"

Dead silence. Then I raised my arms high and shouted the word: "Oss!"

The reply from 140 excited sets of young vocal chords was deafening: "OSS!"

What happened next was one of the most extraordinary moments in my teaching career. This group of highly intelligent senior high school students went absolutely ballistic. They screamed, cheered, clapped, whistled, stamped, and pounded the bench in an extraordinary spontaneous outburst of – I know not what – exhilaration, happiness, excitement, gratitude? And this went on … and on … and on. I stood there totally dumbfounded and highly moved. I remember looking across at Jenny Nicholls, and her face was a picture of confused disbelief. It seemed as if they would never stop, but gradually the noise subsided. Then Hong screamed out, "What have you done to him?" And it happened all over again. I have no explanation for this extraordinary event other than that the Scholars had become a tightly knit group who collectively had realised the value of the wonderful experience that they were having, and wanted to say so. The memory of the moment is something that I will always treasure.

A similar thing occurred at the 2001 International Science School. By the time that this School was held, I had retired from the University and we had moved to the Central Coast. I was still Director of the Science Foundation for Physics, however, and together with Jenny Nicholls, we had planned and organised the whole thing. Jenny, bless her heart, suggested that I should live in with the scholars at St. John's College for the duration of School. I was delighted to do this, because it solved the logistic difficulties of commuting each day. More importantly, it also enabled me to get much closer to the Scholars, and to see things from the inside. The whole two weeks was again an absolutely marvellous experience for me and I am delighted to have had this unique opportunity. I spent many long hours in the evenings chewing the fat with these wonderful young people and was quite humbled by the way that they welcomed me into their group. On the evening of the second last day of the School, the Scholars held a concert. Young people never cease to amaze me, and I was just blown away by the extraordinary musical and creative talents that they displayed. It is impossible to select a highlight, because all of the presentations were just so good. However, the effort of the group of Scholars from the United States is particularly relevant to this story. Before their performance, they asked me if I would be happy for them to do a take off of me. Of course, I was delighted, not only to be the butt of their jokes, but also because they were thoughtful enough to make the request. Their performance was hilarious, and they proved themselves to be keen observers of character. It felt like I was watching myself in a mirror. They had picked up many of my mannerisms and quirks, some of which were revealed to me for the first time. They also had a lot of fun with my morning introductory "G'day, Mate!" The next morning, the last of the Science School, everybody was on a high, with the memories of the previous evening's concert in their minds. Again, there was an air of expectancy as I brought the group to order. I know that several of them wondered how I would respond to the excellent take off that they had all enjoyed so much. I decided not to disappoint them so, instead of my normal greeting, I put on my best British accent and said, "Good morning, everybody."

It happened all over again. The group exploded into prolonged wild cheering, shouting and pounding that was both awesome, and immensely gratifying. When the dust had settled, I introduced the lecturer, Professor Greg McRae from MIT, and a former Scholar at an earlier Science School. Greg stood up, and also said, "Good morning, everybody." He then couldn't understand why he only received a normal polite response!

Exciting and memorable though the Science Schools have been for me, they were, in a sense, just the cream on the cake of my teaching as an academic. The main thrust of my interactions with undergraduate students was through the presentation of formal, conventional lectures. In fact, *conventional* is probably not a very good word to use in this context. In my early days as an academic, I certainly conformed to the norm for most university lecturers, which is *to do unto them as they did unto me.* As the years went by, however, I evolved my lecturing tactics significantly, to include much more one-on-one interaction with students, even in large classes. In addition, I progressively simplified the material that I presented, and made a conscious attempt to ensure that everybody there, including myself, had a good time. This last strategy could be seen as slightly self-indulgent, and in a way it is. I genuinely believe, however, that people learn more effectively when they are having fun, and are interested in the things that are going on around them. The fact that I was enjoying myself with everybody else in the lecture theatre just seems to me to be a bonus.

Over the years, I have taught many different courses across the undergraduate offerings of the School of Physics. Because I enjoyed doing this so much, I made sure that I continued to have as much involvement in the teaching as possible. On more than one occasion, I remember asking for more teaching than had been proposed. I take a very dim view indeed of the current tendency of many academics in Australia, particularly those with large research commitments, to follow the common United States practice of buying-out from their teaching. These academics are precisely the ones who should be ensuring that they involve themselves with students as much as possible.

I can't say that I had a particular favourite among my conventional courses, but I especially enjoyed teaching about electromagnetism. I initially taught this subject at First Year level and, after I had done it a couple of times, I felt that I had finally started to understand the Physics behind the mathematical equations which form the centrepiece of this part of our discipline. I was then given the opportunity to teach it to Second Year students. This had traditionally been the least popular of our Second Year courses, because it inevitably involved a very large amount of a complex mathematical formalism called vector differential calculus. The students found this quite difficult, as indeed it is, and had always responded very negatively to the subject. The course had traditionally been taught by introducing the mathematical formalism in the first few lectures, and using it where appropriate in the subsequent discussion of the Physics. I adopted a different approach, and went straight into the Physics. When I needed the mathematics, I introduced it, not formally, but in the context of the physical system that we had already discussed. The course was quite well received. Even after the first time that I taught it, the students' comments on the course assessment sheets were much more positive than previously, although they still said that they found the material very difficult. This was one of the courses in which I progressively simplified the material over the years, even though inevitably much of the complex mathematics had to remain. A particular source of gratification for me was that I gradually came to know this beautiful subject quite well.

My teaching of electromagnetism reached a high point at the 1999 International Science School, the topic of which was *Light*. I gave the first lecture at this School, in which I set out to provide the Scholars with the physical basis for virtually all of the material that would be presented in the following two weeks. That basis is electromagnetism, so I covered the essential concepts of this subject in the one hour available to me. This involved exposing the Scholars to all of the basic material in the Second Year Electromagnetism course. Naturally, I did not do this in a formal way – instead, I used lecture demonstrations, interaction and fun. Word about my one-hour electromagnetism "course" got out, and in later years, several groups of students asked me to give them that lecture.

As a student, you tend to think that your teachers know their subject material very well. As a teacher, you very quickly realise that often this is not the case. The tea room arguments that we had over the years about subtle points of so-called Elementary Physics are ample evidence of this. I used to wonder about our emphasis on teaching more and more complex and esoteric parts of Physics in the higher levels of our course, when both we, and the students, demonstrably didn't understand the elementary stuff completely. It had also been my experience that most of the Physics that I used as a professional in industry and research was at this basic level. I actually formed the view that one can be a very competent and successful physicist even if the only Physics that you know is what we teach in our First Year courses. These thoughts led me to develop what I believe was my most successful teaching initiative – a Third Year course that I called Energy Physics. The basic aim of this course was to show how elementary Physics could be used to obtain at least a partial understanding of quite complex systems. Because of my personal research interests, I chose energy-related topics for discussion. The same type of course could be taught with virtually any scientific theme.

To the best of my knowledge, Energy Physics was unlike any course that had been offered before within the School of Physics at the University of Sydney. Indeed, I have not heard anything like it described elsewhere. Initially, both the students and the academic staff regarded the course with some suspicion. If it just used simple Physics, they argued, then surely it would only be suitable for the less highly achieving students. In fact, the first time that I taught Energy Physics, only one or two of my students came from the upper levels of the Third Year class. The turning point came when we had an extraordinarily talented group of Third Year students, many of whom I had come to know quite well in the earlier years of their course. The best of these students decided to do the course because, I would like to think, they knew me well. Students like that will very quickly vote with their feet if they are not being challenged, but they stayed with me. We had a most stimulating time together, and afterwards several of them told me that it was the most demanding and interesting course of their degree program. The thing that pleased me most is that they said, "You made me think." When they completed their honours year, this memorable class asked me to give the talk at their graduation lunch. I was delighted, and humbled, that they chose me.

Recently, one of this group of students, Tanya Monro (she was Tanya Feletto when she did the course) reminded me of an incident from the Energy Physics course that had slipped from my mind. We were discussing thermal time constants, and I had asked the students how long it typically takes for a house to cool down at the end of a hot day. Tanya recalls being stunned when people started to give quite short times – say an hour or two. She said that the ground floor of her house takes days to cool down after hot weather unless you open all the windows and let the air flow through. I was very surprised at her comment, and asked for details of her house. She said that there was nearly a metre of concrete between the upper and lower stories. I am purported to have responded, "But of course, in proper Italian houses you need a lot of concrete to hide the bodies." I am sure that Tanya's recollection is correct, but I cringe when I think about it!

The content matter of the course is perhaps best illustrated by an assignment problem that I liked to set. It went like this:

Professor Snilloc retired from the University many years ago and lives in a mansion with his wife. He is quite mad in almost every way – the only thing that he always gets correct is the physics of what he is talking about. He likes to have a mug of tea (milk, no sugar) in bed each night before going to sleep in his room in the attic. He insists that the tea should be scalding hot, and his wife is always in trouble because, by the time that she brings it up from the kitchen downstairs, it has cooled off too much …

What instructions does the mad professor give his wife to ensure that the tea gets to him as hot as possible? Explain the physics associated with each one, as quantitatively as you can. Estimate the temperature of the tea that he would drink if she does everything correctly.

I still remember the first time that I handed this assignment question to the students. They found it hard to believe, because it was not what they had been used to – the problem was ill defined, the material that is needed to tackle it had not previously been covered in the lectures, and evidently there is no "correct" answer. As I pointed out to them, however, this is just what will occur when they work as practicing physicists. As I had hoped, they got into it with great enthusiasm. I have previously commented that marking exam papers is the least pleasant part of teaching, and marking assignment problems is usually not much better. In this case, however, reading the students' responses to my Professor Snilloc problem was an absolute joy. Over the years, I have received many memorable submissions, but two in particular stick in my memory. Interestingly, both of these came from girls. I wish that I could recall who they were, but regrettably my memory is empty on this point. Perhaps if they read this and remember, they can let me know.

One of the answers was actually written as a dialogue between Professor Snilloc and his wife Gwnnyth. The play format made the response most entertaining. Gwnnyth would ask a question, and Professor Snilloc would respond. At one point, the Professor was deep into the heart of his explanation, and was delivering a long diatribe involving many sophisticated concepts. All of this was highly relevant to the problem, but for one not familiar with the field, it would have been quite impenetrable. So this part of this assignment went something like:

> *Professor Snilloc: Rabbit on ... heat capacities ... heat transfer coefficients ... loss mechanisms ... minimise surface area ... rabbit, rabbit ... preheat the cup ... run like crazy up the stairs ... more rabbitting ... And so on for about half a page.*
> *Gwnnyth: "I love it when you talk dirty."*

I gave this young lady 100% for her answer.

The other memorable response was presented in much more conventional form, and contained a comprehensive analysis of the mechanisms that could cause heat loss from the cup, and techniques for decreasing these losses to the lowest possible levels. I could find no fault in anything that was written. The assignment concluded with a paragraph summarising the strategies that Professor Snilloc's wife should take to keep the tea as hot as possible. This paragraph concluded:

And so, if Professor Snilloc's wife follows all of these instructions, then finally he will be able to enjoy a nice hot cup of tea in his bed before he goes to sleep at night – the sexist pig!

I also gave 100% for this assignment. It did trouble me a little, however, that the problem *was* quite sexist even though (and I did not tell the students this) my idea for it arose from a comment once made by Marilyn that the cup of tea that I often make for her first thing in the morning was not hot enough. In order to redress the sexist balance, one year I therefore redesigned the problem around a young female graduate student, Flora, who is doing her Ph.D. in Plasma Physics. On the weekends, Flora lives with her hippie boyfriend Neil in a cave. Flora is always complaining that the cave is too cold, and Neil can't seem to do anything about it. What does Flora say to Neil? However, this did not strike a chord with the students, and all I got from them was straight, conventional responses. So I returned to good old Professor Snilloc, and I stuck with him over the years.

During my career, I have taught literally thousands of undergraduate students. Regrettably, I only learnt the names of a small proportion of them. While my memories of these students are almost entirely positive, they have tended to merge into an amorphous mass in which I have difficulty associating specific incidents with particular students. There are, of course a few exceptions. One of these is Jade Bond. I first became aware of Jade as a student in my Third Year Energy Physics course. I had made some comments relating to the application of physical principles to geological systems, and she politely took issue with what I had said. Subsequent discussions revealed that she was also majoring in Geology, and she clearly had much more expertise in that field than I did. Later, I got to know her quite well and, while I don't recall giving her any special assistance, evidently I did. As her graduation approached, I received a letter from her Mother, Lillian, that moved me deeply. It said:

My daughter, Jade, has greatly admired you and your love of teaching and of the Sciences since she first commenced studying at

Sydney University. You have made learning a pleasure for her and have encouraged her into a scientific career which has been her heart's desire for many years.

For her graduation (which is still a little away off) I am making her an "inspiration quilt" which will consist of blocks of fabric containing messages from people who have inspired her throughout her life to remind her, in the future, that there have always been so many people who have believed in her and supported her. I hope that it will also bring many happy memories of the great life that she has had so far.

... I know that Jade would be delighted and proud to have a message from you ...

Thanking you very much, in anticipation, and also thanking you for your understanding support of Jade and all the other students who come under your care.

With best wishes for a long and happy retirement – you will certainly be missed by the students.

Later, I had the pleasure of attending Jade's graduation ceremony, and being there afterwards when she was presented with the quilt. It was a great feeling.

Another thing that my students did that particularly touched me occurred during the last lecture that I gave before my retirement. Curiously, this was not a lecture in one of my own courses – I was standing in for someone else. The subject was my beloved Electromagnetism, so I really didn't need to do much preparation. At the conclusion of the lecture, I remarked to the students that this had been my last ever lecture as a member of the teaching staff of the University. Their response was immediate: "We know!" Each of them then produced a copy of a life-sized caricature mask of me that had been circulating around in the issue of the Physics Society magazine that coincided with my retirement. They all put these masks on, and I found myself staring at sea of exaggerated likenesses of me! I was then invited to sit in their midst, and a photo was taken of this memorable and moving moment.

Since my retirement, I seldom think about what I am missing by not interacting with the students as much as I used to – that would just be self-indulgent, and also it would make me sad. When the opportunity arises to go back, however, it is very special for me. I have returned to give several invited lectures to students, two of which were organised by Tim Bedding. My relationship with Tim has developed through the full range from undergraduate student, to colleague and friend. Tim tells me that I gave him his first ever Physics lecture when he started as a First Year student at the University of Sydney. I am touched that he remembers this, although quite evidently I do not. However, I do remember Tim's development as an undergraduate and graduate student, followed by his research work overseas, and then since he rejoined the School as a Lecturer. I was honoured to nominate him for his successful application for one of the University's Awards for Excellence in Teaching. Tim was recently promoted to Associate Professor, and I am sure that there is more to come. The lectures that Tim asked me to give were part of a course, The Practice of Physics, which we had developed together some years before. The course explores with the students the sort of things that professional physicists do in the practice of their discipline, rather than the Physics itself. The course involves a lot of interaction with the students, and contributions from them. I was thrilled to have the opportunity of returning to the University and talking with the students again. After the second of my lectures, one of the students in the class, Jackie Huber, came up to me and said that I was inspirational. I wanted to hug her, but you're not allowed to do that sort of thing these days. I had to work pretty hard to keep the tears from my eyes. Thank you, Jackie.

Formal undergraduate teaching in the lecture theatre and the laboratory constituted only part of the interactions that I had with students during my time at the University of Sydney. The other important involvement was with my graduate students. As I found during my time in New York, undertaking a Ph.D. is one of the most challenging things that you can do as a professional physicist. Unexpected crises and difficulties always emerge, both associated with the research itself, and also often of a personal nature. The role of a supervisor in helping the student to overcome these problems can be critical. I supervised 18 graduate students during my time at the University of Sydney, and I established a very close personal relationship with virtually all of them. In some cases, particularly with students from overseas, I found myself in the role of a surrogate father.

The first graduate student who worked on my vacuum glazing project was Tony Fischer-Cripps. Tony came to me as a mature aged student with a very impressive background. He had started his career as a mechanic, and then worked his way through a degree in Physics at the University of Technology, Sydney. When I first met him, he was employed at UTS as a Technical Officer. Because of his obvious practical skills, I saw him as a person who could make significant contributions to the experimental part of the vacuum glazing research. I therefore started him off in this area. It very quickly became apparent that he also had excellent computing abilities, and that he clearly enjoyed this type of work much more than being in the laboratory. This began to cause significant tensions between us, because I was forever dragging him off his computer and back into the laboratory, and he would inevitably drift back to his keyboard. I considered issuing him with an ultimatum but, as things developed, I am very glad that I took a softer approach. I suggested that we change the emphasis of his Ph.D. work to be more related to numerical modelling, and he accepted this with enthusiasm. It had been a classic case of poor communication. Tony had made up his mind that he did not want to do much experimental work, because he already had many of these skills through his earlier life as a mechanic, but he didn't tell me. I had been reluctant to pull him off the experimental work, because I thought that he might be offended, but I didn't tell him. This experience highlighted for me the need to be more proactive in addressing problems as they emerged, and not allowing them to fester and grow.

A little later in his degree, I proposed to Tony that we commence some collaborative work with an overseas group. My idea was that we would prepare the samples and undertake the experimental work, and they would do some associated numerical modelling using techniques with which they had considerable experience. Predictably (in hindsight) Tony did not like this idea at all. He argued that *he* should do the modelling, because the skills that he developed would be widely applicable after he had finished his Ph.D. By then, I knew him well enough not to argue. It was a case of the student knowing best. Tony proved to be very gifted in this area, and using these skills he has been responsible for some important and beautiful new science, both during his Ph.D. work, and in his subsequent career. He has now written several books about Fracture Mechanics and undergraduate Physics, and leads a successful research group at CSIRO. Not surprisingly, we are very close friends.

Another student with whom I became very close was Zhou Xian. Xian came to work with me in the mid-1980s, leaving his wife and baby daughter in China. He tells me that he arrived in Australia with only a few dollars in his pocket, and that I lent him some money to get him started, but I have no recollection of this. He experienced considerable difficulties during his Ph.D. program. The approach that I had originally suggested for his work was not successful, and he had to start again from scratch after a year. His research involved the construction and operation of an elegant and highly sensitive apparatus. It required a lot of time, and a high level of skill, to obtain data from it, and he did this very well. Fairly soon after he started, he managed to bring his wife Hong and daughter Lisa to Australia, and he somehow supported them on the very little money that he was receiving from his scholarship. I noticed that he used to have peanut butter sandwiches for lunch every day, and I correctly deduced that he was really struggling financially. The morning after the Tianamin Square massacre, Xian sat in my office with tears streaming down his face – he would have been there if he had been in China, and he had lost many good friends. Perhaps the biggest problem that Xian had during his Ph.D. was writing his thesis. Of course, English was not his first language, and he had enormous difficulties in developing his writing skills. I remember that he wrote over ten drafts of his first chapter. Each time, I returned it to him with the pages covered with red ink. We would then sit down together while I tried to explain why my words were better than his. Never once during this painful process did he object, and I don't think that I lost my cool either, but it was very hard going for us both. Imperceptibly, but steadily, Xian's English language writing skills improved. The second chapter was a little easier than the first, and so on. I took the final draft of his thesis away with me on an overseas trip, and spent many long hours going through it for one last time. I finished this task in Copenhagen when I sat in my hotel room reading it for a whole day during a weekend. When I finished, I wrote a quite long summary and critique, concluding with the words: *I am proud of you.*

At Xian's graduation ceremony, I sat on the stage in my fancy clothes watching the students come up one by one to the Chancellor. Just before Xian's name was called, I whispered to a colleague sitting next to me, "The next one is mine."

After Xian had received his testamur and saluted the Chancellor, he looked across at me and gave me a beaming smile.

My colleague remarked, "That makes it all worthwhile!"

I could only agree.

I believe that our country can do with many more people having Xian's work ethic and skills. During his Ph.D., I therefore helped Xian and his family in their application for Australian citizenship. As we went through this process, he promised me that, whatever happened after he obtained his Ph.D. degree, he would never go on the dole. When he finally graduated, he was unable to get a job that was relevant to his skills and experience. True to his word, he obtained work as a cleaner. A few months later, he was invited to a job interview in Melbourne. He asked me what he should say that he had been doing since he had finished his Ph.D. I advised him to tell it as it was. I do not know whether my advice helped (it would have, if I had been doing the interviewing), but he got the job. His work there was highly successful, and he became a valued member of the company. A few years later, he was headhunted to another company, and he has done very well there too. At the time of my retirement, his salary was a multiple of mine.

A few years ago, I was in Melbourne and we arranged to have a meal together. Afterwards, he insisted on paying for it. I argued with him, but he would not be moved. After I returned to Sydney, I wrote and thanked him for his hospitality, remarking that I felt a little uncomfortable that one my students had paid for my meal. He sent me an email that I stuck on the wall beside my desk. I used to look at it quite frequently, and I know it by heart:

Dear Dick

A Chinese phrase said "If your friend gave you a drop of water for helping you in your difficult time, you should pay back a river afterwards". You gave me a river, and I have just given back a drop of water.

Xian

Another of my graduate students with whom I had a memorable involvement was Cenk Kocer. Cenk first worked with me on a vacation scholarship while he was still an undergraduate student at another university. We got on together very well and he impressed me with his experimental ability. During his subsequent honours year, he asked to withdraw from a course because he considered it to be very poorly taught. He was not allowed to do this, and his participation was recorded as a Zero/Fail. As a result, Cenk obtained a lower level of honours than would be expected from his previous record. He was very keen to do a Ph.D. with me and, based on my previous interaction with him, I was happy to take him on. I also admired the strength of his convictions in taking the stand that he did during his honours year. Because of the grade of honours that he had obtained, however, he did not have a scholarship, and so he had to support himself throughout his graduate studies.

Cenk's Ph.D. project was concerned with the very slow growth of cracks in glass. This is important because the failure probability of glass under low levels of tensile stress over long periods of time is completely determined by such crack growth. In his work, Cenk used the venerable Hertzian cone crack system. These beautiful cracks occur when a hardened cylindrical or spherical indenter is pressed into the surface of a brittle material such as glass. The cracks form an almost perfect conical shape at a well-defined angle (22° in soda lime glass) to the surface of the material. They were first reported by Heinrich Hertz (the same Hertz as in electromagnetic wave fame) in the 1880s, and have been extensively studied for more than 100 years. Cenk developed a method of "marking" the position of the crack tip at any desired point of its advancement, by slightly altering the direction of its growth in a controllable way. After the completion of the growth sequence, measurements are made of the distance between these changes in direction, thus enabling the velocity to be determined. Cenk's work was outstandingly successful. He was able to measure the velocity of growth of cracks some five orders of magnitude smaller than had previously been achieved by others.

In this research, it was also necessary to relate the rate of growth of the cracks to the magnitude of the stress fields in the vicinity of the crack tip. Cenk needed to develop methods of calculating these stresses at all stages of the growth of the crack. In order do this, he constructed a computational model containing a symmetric cone crack. He initially chose the angle of the cone crack to the surface of the glass specimen to be the same as that of the pre-existing stress fields in the solid: ~30° from the free surface of the material. The assumption that the cone crack (and, indeed, any crack) follows the pre-existing stress fields was based on work going back to the 1960s, and had been used by all previous researchers who had investigated these aspects of Hertzian cone cracks. However, when Cenk calculated the stress fields near the crack tip, he always found that they were asymmetric relative to the pre-existing trajectory, rather than symmetric, as would have been expected. We did not understand this result at all. I advised him to refine his model and he did this, but the discrepancy remained. After several months of intensive work, he concluded that the results of his calculations were correct, and that the problem was in the assumption that the trajectory of the crack followed the pre-existing stress fields. My immediate response to him was that many people, including some of the best experimental and theoretical workers in Fracture Mechanics, had made this assumption for over 40 years, and they could not all be wrong. Cenk persisted with his arguments, and after about three weeks, he finally convinced me that he was correct. He further validated his ideas by developing a method of "growing" a cone crack in a computer. His first crack growth calculation took him over three weeks of intensive keyboard work, and is an extraordinary example of persistence and hard work. Later, he developed his method into what I believe is the first ever automated computational method of determining the trajectories of growing cracks. We published a couple of articles about this important work, one of which was described by a reviewer as *a landmark paper in the field*.

Like Xian, Cenk experienced enormous difficulties in writing up his thesis. He had somehow managed to get through school without learning most of the fundamentals of sentence construction and grammar. We had countless long and agonising sessions in which we attempted to grapple with these difficulties, and at times I despaired that his writing would ever get to an adequate standard. It seemed incongruous to me that this young man could do such beautiful scientific work, and yet could not write about it in an acceptable way. Nevertheless, we both persisted, and his writing skills are now very good.

I have told the story of Cenk's research in some detail because I regard it as perhaps the most beautiful piece of fundamental work with which I have been associated during my long career. It is rare indeed for a graduate student to overturn many decades of conventional wisdom. In the copy of his thesis that he gave me, he wrote the following:

> *Dear Dick*
> *Finally I have reached the end of this learning. I have much to thank you for, but most of all I'd like to thank you for showing me that 'it's' within me, to do and be as I choose.*
>
> *Cenk Kocer*

As I have remarked, the relationship between my graduate students and me as a supervisor has often become very close, sometimes quite similar to that between father and child. I conclude this chapter with a story about an interaction for which the relationship *was* of that kind – the student was my daughter Kathryn. Kathryn did her Ph.D. at the University of Western Sydney in the field of Social Ecology. Right from the beginning, it became clear to me, as an interested and concerned parent and an experienced supervisor of graduate students, that she was being shamefully neglected. She received virtually no advice or encouragement from her supervisor. Indeed, despite significant efforts on her part, she was hardly ever able to see him. Further, there seemed to be no mechanisms within her University to remedy the situation. She therefore had to do most of her research, and thesis writing, without supervisory assistance. Despite all of this, she persevered with her work and she finally completed the write-up of her thesis in the hardest possible way – as a part-time student in full-time employment elsewhere. I tried to help her as much as I could but, not having any experience in the field, my assistance was limited to looking at the line of logic in her arguments, and providing advice on the quality of her writing. Her Ph.D. thesis contained the following words:

Over my career, my students have done many things for me that have touched me deeply. One event that moved me more than most was a get-together that they organised just before my retirement. This was held at the home of Tony Fischer-Cripps and his wife Dianne, who was hugely pregnant at the time with their second child. Many of my former graduate students were there, including some who had travelled a long way. Marilyn and our three children also came, so it was a very special time for me. I received two gifts. The first was a large flag with a caricature of my face that for some days previously had been flown on the School of Physics. They also gave me a book in which each page contains a personal message to me from one of my many students. I regard it as perhaps the most valuable thing that I own. Of course, I had the opportunity of saying few words, and I had to plan my presentation very carefully to ensure that I did not get too emotional. I hope, however, that I did convey to them all how much their presence meant to me, and the depth of my appreciation for everything that they had done for me.

When I look back at my long involvement with universities, first as a student and later a teacher, the thing that pleases me most is the extent to which the relationship between teacher and student has become closer over the years. During my university studies, I got the distinct impression that many of the academic staff regarded themselves as being in an adversarial position to the students in the learning process. Mind you, even by then things had moved a long way from the situation when my Father was at university. As I have mentioned, he was extremely deaf. In one of his University classes, the lecturer had assigned a particular seat to each student, and my Father found himself located at the back of the room. He approached the lecturer and explained about his hearing difficulties, saying that he would be able to lip-read better if he sat closer to the front. He requested permission from the lecturer to swap places with another student. Permission was denied. During my teaching career, it has given me enormous satisfaction to see how the relationship between teacher and student is now so cooperative and close. I believe that most academics now have a genuine concern for the welfare of their students, and work very hard to help them to learn more effectively. May it ever be so.

As you can see, I am passionate about my interactions with students, and I take my associated responsibilities very seriously. It was therefore a great thrill and honour for me when, in 1993, I received one of the Awards for Excellence in Teaching from the University of Sydney. I am more proud of this than of any other achievement in my professional career.

Relations and Relationships

No life occurs in isolation. Rather, the things that we do, and the person that we become, are influenced by those with whom we interact – the family that nature gives us, and the friends, acquaintances and, in my fortunate case, the students that we deliberately or accidentally get to know. In my life, I have experienced many rewarding relationships with others. This concluding chapter of my book deals with a few of these.

I begin where I started, with a friendship that goes back further than any other – Robin Farrow, the boy with whom I played before I was five years old. At the end of the war, the Farrow family moved to England, and the trajectories of our lives separated. My parents were both great letter writers, and over the years they used this method to keep in touch with their many friends, both in Australia and overseas. When I was a boy, it was the norm in our house each evening for one of them to sit at the desk in our lounge room and write letters. Decades later, after my Father's retirement, they undertook several overseas trips together. My Mother used to say that the highlight of these trips for her was when they stayed with their former friends and neighbours, Morris and Mary Farrow. She really enjoyed sitting in their garden in the English countryside talking about old times. After my Father died in March 1989, I discovered that he had continued to maintain an active correspondence with many people. Indeed, I wrote over 100 letters telling of his passing. One of these was to Morris Farrow in England, with whom my Father had corresponded the previous Christmas. I was delighted to receive a reply on his behalf from his elder son David. In his warm letter, David told me a little about what had happened in their family, and invited me to visit them should I come to England. Soon afterwards, I arranged to meet first with Robin, and later with David and their families.

I know that Robin and I both felt some mild apprehension before this first meeting. After all, we had not seen each other for over 50 years and, apart from our close relationship as sub-five-year-olds, we had essentially nothing in common. We were, however, both looking forward to getting together. In one of his letters to me before I left Australia, Robin said he was keen to learn how I had evolved from hoodlum to professor. When I read this, I felt that this was the sort of bloke that I would like. I wasn't wrong. On a fine Sunday morning, Robin picked me up from my accommodation in London, and we had the most fantastic day together. Curiously enough, although our conversations ranged over many topics, I don't recall that we talked much about our earlier times together. For me, the most memorable experience during the day was when his car broke down in the very busy Brompton Road, right outside Harrods. He called for road assistance, and then we sat together in the vehicle for an hour talking about countless things, oblivious to the surrounding chaos that our vehicle was causing (although nobody complained). In the evening, I had dinner at Robin's home with his partner Paula, and brother David and his wife Liz.

Starting with this tenuous link, we are frequently in touch through the wonders of email, and we have become good friends. I stayed with both David and Robin on a subsequent visit to England, and Marilyn and I hope to have the opportunity to return this hospitality here in Australia soon. I find it immensely gratifying that these good friendships can exist at the two ends of my life, even though in between we were barely aware of one another's existence. They have happened, however, only because our parents maintained contact from opposite sides of the world, and over so many decades, through the simple act of writing letters.

Although I don't think that I was directly influenced by my parents' letter writing propensities, I have long recognised the importance of maintaining friendships through regular contact. In many cases, this has been as simple and basic as an annual Christmas card. I cannot recall a single year in which I have failed to send Christmas cards, often more than 100, although on several occasions they departed after the event. The reason for such delays was that I always wrote something personal, and reasonably meaningful, in every card that I sent and, until recently, I did each one individually by hand. I remember on more than one occasion travelling to Japan in December during which I spent the whole plane trip writing Christmas cards. I never regarded this as a chore, however, and I certainly did not dislike doing it. I always believed that quality friendships could be maintained over long periods of time in this way, and events have proved me correct.

One of my very close friends is Jim Slevin whom I have seen only twice in the last 35 years. I first met Jim and his wife Fran when I was a graduate student in New York in the 1960s. They were from Ireland and Jim was also doing a Ph.D. in Physics, but at another University. My interactions with him were entirely work-related until after Marilyn and our two girls returned to Australia and I remained behind alone to complete my degree. Jim and Fran then clearly recognised how I must be feeling, and were extremely kind to me. I spent several warm and friendly Friday evenings in their apartment, and they introduced me to the splendors of Jewish food and Irish hospitality. In due course, we both completed our work in New York and returned to our homelands. In the following years, we wrote to one another, quite frequently initially, and ultimately at every Christmas. For a short while, our correspondence fell into disrepair, but it was reactivated when a mutual friend informed me of Fran's tragic death, and I wrote to Jim to express my sympathy and to thank him once again for the kindness that they had both given to me during a very difficult time. Jim responded, and I learnt that he was a Professor of Physics at St. Patrick's College (now National University of Ireland) at Maynooth, close to Dublin. At that time, we resolved to get together. After several unsuccessful attempts, I flew from London to Dublin where he was to meet me at the airport. As I was collecting my bag before proceeding through customs, I recall wondering how I would recognise him because I did not have the faintest idea what he looked like. All that I could remember was that he had red hair, hardly a distinguishing feature in Dublin. When I emerged, I saw a white-haired gentleman about my age standing there. I walked up to him.

"Jim?"

"Richard?"

It was as if the years since our last meeting had never existed. We had a wonderful few days together during which I stayed at his home, visited his department, and gave a talk about my work. The Irish are famous for their hospitality, but I was quite unprepared for the depth of my feelings on this visit. Marilyn and I have since been back to see Jim and, once again, we stayed with him and met his new wife Frances. We remain in frequent contact. My friendship with Jim is very precious to me, and I am most grateful to have it. Even more satisfyingly, Jim is just one of several people that I am privileged to call *friend* because of similarly tenuous interactions over many years.

It appears to me that many good friendships grow out of chance encounters. That's the way it happened with our neighbours at Beecroft. We found ourselves living amongst a group of wonderful people who all got on together very well. Right from the beginning of our time there, it seemed that we had just been made to be friends. Shortly after we moved into our house in 1964, Marilyn and I had our neighbours in for drinks on Christmas morning. It was stinking hot, and Marilyn was hugely pregnant with Kathryn. The party went off like a bomb, and I still have a clear memory of our lounge room, stuffed full of happy people, celebrating the day and each other.

During our absence in New York, we could not attend the 1965 and 1966 Christmas morning celebrations, but we were not forgotten. Our neighbours across the street, Charlie and Johnnie Simmons, had the parties at their place and each time they made a telephone call to us using multiple extensions so that several people could participate in the conversation at the same time. We therefore had the pleasure of talking to our neighbours from far away. It was a very special thing to do for us. The party for Christmas 1967 was also at the Simmons' place, and Marilyn was back in Australia with the girls. Once more, the Simmons did their stuff, and I had the enormous thrill of talking to everyone from the United States. On this occasion, they gave Marilyn a phone extension of her own so that she could listen in during the entire call. These people were such good friends. The tradition of neighborhood Christmas get-togethers that we started in 1964 continues to this day. We were recently delighted to attend one that was held at our former home by John and Karen Carroll who had bought it from us in 1982!

Perhaps our closest friends amongst the neighbours at Beecroft were the Skinners. June and Ross Skinner lived two houses up the street. They are about half a generation older than us, so their three children, Janet, Philip and Debbie, were primary school age or thereabouts when we first met. Many of our early interactions were through these kids. We were natural targets for them in their fund-raising activities at school. Each year, our house became the repository for Santa Claus' handiwork, and on Christmas Eve we would smuggle this loot up the street in the dead of night for the opening next morning. As our own children came on the scene, I was intrigued to see how the roles reversed, and were extended a little. A few years on, our kids started to put the touch on the Skinners during school fund-raising. Being a little older, Janet became the favoured baby-sitter for our children when we went out. The Skinners' place was where Santa Claus stored his stuff for *our* kids.

We could always rely on the Skinners to be there whenever we needed them. On the night that Steven was born, we phoned them about 11 o'clock and asked them to come down and sleep at our place while I took Marilyn to hospital. A few hours later, June was the first person with whom I was able to share the news about the birth of our son. Nearly 30 years on, Ross proposed the toast to the bride and groom at Steven and Katrina's wedding. He recounted this happening, and said that June often used to laugh about the fact that she had spent a night in Richard's bed. In my subsequent speech at this occasion, I missed a golden opportunity, so I will say now what I should have then: "June, the night that you spent in my bed was one of the most memorable of my life."

The Skinners are the nicest people that one could ever hope to meet, and we feel very lucky to count ourselves to be among their many friends. They did have a problem, however – whenever they went on holidays, the rain would bucket down upon them without fail. The Skinner's ability to attract bad weather when they went away became legendary in our neighborhood, and we used to give them quite a bad time about it. Once after a period of particularly severe weather during one of their holidays, we sent them a *Welcome Home* card that read:

When the Skinners depart on vacation
The neighbours are filled with elation
For each of us knows
That we won't need a hose
For all the vacation's duration.

On another occasion, we sent a typed letter to them with a hand-drawn (but, if I might say, impressively professional-looking) logo from an organisation that we had invented called Rain Makers International. The letter was from the President of RMI, Mr Noah D Rainmaker, and he congratulated the Skinners on being elected to Life Membership of his erstwhile organisation because of their perfect track record of having caused it to rain on all of their annual vacations for a whole decade. We were quite proud of our creation. When June opened this letter, she at first thought that it was fair dinkum. She hadn't got too far into it, however, before the light dawned, and she didn't need any advice to figure out who were the culprits: "Those Collins'!"

We were invited to the Skinner's place for Janet's 21st birthday party and the invitation from them contained a poem that maintained our little in-joke about the weather:

A party at Skinner's? You're thinking
The weather is sure to be stinking.
So if there's a flood
Just wade through the mud
And join in the eating and drinking.

Writing doggerel was something of a tradition in our family, and we often did it for ourselves, and to inflict upon others. In fact, we have a book of family poetry that we have composed. I have extracted from it just two more pieces, each again written for the Skinners. The first was on the occasion of the engagement of Janet to her now-husband David. Our present to them was a cleaning implement for their house, and our card read:

Since Janet and David have tarried
A bucket they'll need when they're married
For you'll find lots of stuff
From vomit to fluff
That in it quite well can be carried.

Later, we went to a cellar tea for the young couple shortly before they were married, and our gift was accompanied by:

When, shortly we see from the pews
The end of life's freedom for youse
We'll wish you good luck
But, if things get unstuck
May you find happy solace in booze.

One of the highlights of our times with June and Ross Skinner was when we helped their children organise a surprise party at our place to celebrate their 20th wedding anniversary. The whole thing was a carefully planned exercise. We located some of the people who had played key roles in their wedding, and many of their newer friends and neighbours, and secretly spirited them into our house by getting them to park in a back street and walk through a neighbour's yard, rather than coming in our front door. It was one of those operations that really worked, and we got the guests-of-honour right into our lounge room before turning on the lights to reveal the assembled masses. It was a great night.

We continue to see the Skinners from time to time, even though we now live some hours drive apart. Recently, we were honoured to attend a function for their Golden Wedding anniversary. When we thanked June for including us in their family celebrations, she gave us perhaps the best possible compliment: "It wouldn't be a party without the Collins'."

I will finish this chapter, and this book, with a few words about the thing that is most important to me in whole world – my family. During the time that I was writing this book, most people that heard about it naturally assumed that it was an autobiography. If you have made it this far, you will obviously have realised that it is not. Rather it just chronicles a few loosely connected incidents that I have remembered, perhaps because they are humorous, or a bit unusual, or whimsical, or maybe because they have moved me deeply. So it is with what I have to say about my family. This is not a history of my family life. Rather it's just a few of the things that are memorable enough that they have stuck in my mind over many decades.

As I mentioned in the first chapter, Marilyn and I were in the same classes throughout infants' school, although neither of us has any recollection of the other. Not an auspicious start, you might say, for an affair that is still plugging along after nearly half a century. In fact, although I took another girl out to a couple of high school dances, Marilyn was, and is the only girlfriend that I have ever had. We met up in second term during our First Year together at the University of Sydney. I liked what I saw, and made a play for it. As I have often remarked to my students, when you see something that you really want, go for it with your ears back, and repel all boarders – it worked for me. The thing that astonished me was that she reciprocated my feelings. I just couldn't believe my luck and, so many years later, it still strikes me as wonderful and extraordinary that I am so fortunate to have shared my trip through life with such a person.

Marilyn and I were only 17 years old when we first went out together. I know that all of our parents thought that this was much too early to be serious, and I do recall that we were not given much encouragement. In particular, Marilyn's Father, Stan, was fairly stern with me and, as a father myself many years later, I can understand exactly what he had in mind. We fathers take a very proprietary attitude when young blokes start sniffing around our daughters. Nevertheless, I was welcomed into their home and, over the years, our relationship has strengthened into something that is very close. This whole thing very nearly didn't get off the ground, however. I recall an occasion early on when we were celebrating a fireworks night in the back yard of Marilyn's home. I lit a bunger, threw it high in the air, and then watched with horror as its trajectory headed directly towards the top of Stan's head. If the fuse been one millimetre longer, I would have been on my bike. As luck would have it, however, it exploded harmlessly just above him, and he didn't notice. One's course in life really is determined by chance occurrences.

My own Mother was similarly less than encouraging about my relationship with Marilyn. I don't think that she approved of it at all, even up to the time that we were married, although later on she accepted Marilyn completely, and came to rely on her when she needed assistance. Again, in hindsight, I believe that she was reflecting her concern about how young we were. At the time we certainly didn't appreciate the discouragement that we received. After we had become engaged, we planned to go on a weekend hiking trip with another engaged couple that were good friends, Peter Field and Jan Benson. I can put my hand on my heart and swear that the whole thing was a straight up and

222

down kosher deal – the boys were going to sleep in one tent, and the girls in another. When I raised the subject with my Mother, however, you would have thought that I had proposed triggering the end of the world. She objected so strongly that we abandoned the whole plan. Many years later, our daughter Jenelle moved in with her future husband Jason. I remember my Mother talking to me about this and saying, "I'm really pleased that Jenelle and Jason are living together."

I exploded. "Mum, what a hypocrite you are. Remember how you forbade us from going on that hiking trip when we were engaged?"

"Oh," she said, "Things are different now."

They certainly are.

Marriage is a wonderful institution, and I am extremely fortunate for all the marvellous things that have happened to me in it over the years. Right at of the top of the list are our three children Kathryn, Jenelle and Steven. Of course, bringing up kids always has its moments, and there were times when they drove us crazy. However, if I add it all up, I have to say that the experience of seeing them grow, from before they were born into the splendid people that they are now, has been fulfilling beyond description. I do not believe that I deserve to be so lucky to have been part of it. The things that give you joy out of your relationship with your kids change as the years go by. Early on, I remember thinking that absolutely the best time as a parent was when the kids are going to bed and you're sitting there with one on each side, perhaps a third in the middle, reading a book. When they were quite young, I discovered Dr Seuss, and he was my favourite author in these reading sessions. I know several of the Dr Seuss books off by heart, including The Sleep Book. Indeed, I have used quotes out of this book on several occasions in my professional lectures and writing. These days, our kids continue to give us equivalent pleasure, even though our relationships are now as adults to adults.

Not that it was always plain sailing, mind you. Shortly after Jenelle arrived, we noticed that Kathryn was occasionally a little concerned that someone else had entered her previously exclusive domain. Although she was very fond of Jenelle, we suspected that she would sometimes put in a bit of a poke when we weren't looking. One day, just by chance, I happened to see this occur and determined to stop it once and for all. I said sternly to her, "Did you just hit Jenelle?"

She thought for about one second and replied, "Look – I don't want to say 'Yes' right now."

This cracked me up so much that whatever punishment I had planned went out the window.

I remember with great fondness the Santa Claus runs that Marilyn and I used to do for virtually every Christmas. It appeared that we would always plan some major construction project for the kids at this time. We loved the excitement of putting something of ourselves into the gifts for our children, even though there was considerable strain and tension associated with getting everything finished in time. On several occasions, I had to complete a painting job squatting on the timbers above the ceiling of our house, in order that the children would not discover their presents. Our Christmas conspiracies reached their high point the year that we built them a cubby house in our backyard without their knowledge. In fact, the cubby was attached to a workshop for me that I also constructed at the same time. We had a stepped concrete slab poured, and then I built the frame on this. The lower part of the slab with the full height ceiling was to be my workshop – the adjacent part with the stepped-up concrete and correspondingly lower ceiling was to become the cubby. As the building progressed, the kids would climb all over the frame and one of them even remarked that this bit here would make a great cubby. Once again, I lied to them. I finally got the structure to lock-up stage one week before Christmas. Marilyn and I then set about doing the internal finishing of the cubby part. Because of the need for secrecy, this could only happen after the kids had gone to sleep. So every night around 9 o'clock, we would get onto the job, often not finishing up until midnight. On one of these late evenings, I was kneeling in the doorway of the cubby facing inwards when Marilyn came down the yard to say that it was time to knock off. In the shaft of light coming out of the doorway, she noticed a very large funnel web spider sitting right behind my bare foot. I would probably have been bitten if I had moved further back.

Finally, after the kids had settled on Christmas Eve, we fixed on a little awning over the window, put a *CUBBY* sign on the door, and hung curtains that Marilyn had made. Come Christmas morning, the final present for the kids was an envelope. Upon opening it, they read the message:

Dear Kathryn and Jenelle
Here is the key to your Cubby House
Love
Santa

Kathryn's response was predictable: "But we don't have a Cubby House."

"Well," we said, "Why don't we go and see."

I can still picture them in their nighties walking down the yard, and getting more and more excited as the realisation of what was there dawned upon them. It almost seemed as if they were not touching the ground. Marilyn and I were extremely pleased with ourselves. Even our ever-tolerant neighbour who watched the whole thing called over the fence, "Well, it was all worth it, wasn't it?"

You need a lot of skills to bring up kids, and they don't offer courses on the subject. Inevitably, therefore, you make the odd mistake. When they are young, they tend to accept everything that you say to them at face value. (The disbelieving phase comes later.) On one occasion, their trust in what we said backfired on us. We had been travelling in the United States, and had found a marvellous little gadget called a Square Egg Maker. This consists of two plastic pieces into which you put a freshly hard-boiled egg that has been shelled while it is still hot. The egg is compressed, and then chilled so that it sets in the cubic shape of the plastic mould. Marilyn and I decided to have some fun with the kids, so we prepared a salad with some square eggs, and served it up without comment. The kids were absolutely intrigued and asked how they happened to be like this. "We don't know," we lied. "They just came out that way." The kids thought that this was pretty cool, and we thought that this was the end of it. However, a couple of days later, Kathryn came home and informed us that she had told her class tutor at Hawkesbury Agricultural College about the square eggs. She was quite upset that the tutor and her friends had doubted that the eggs could have come out square. She was quite adamant that they indeed had done just that, because that's what her parents had said.

Inevitably, I suppose, they got their own back. Perhaps my favourite story about this starts a long time before the actual retaliation. We were invited to the 21st birthday party for one of our friends called Simon. The theme of the party was *Come as the letter S*, so there was much consideration about dressing up as soldiers or sailors, and the like. Always one to be different, I tried to persuade Marilyn that we should go as Sonny and Cher, with long tall me as Cher, and cuddly little her as Sonny. She declined, so I worked on Jenelle's boyfriend Jason who was in the process of establishing himself in the family, and therefore perhaps felt that he couldn't afford to refuse. Jason is a chunky, hairy bloke, so the type-casting was perfect. Our girls fitted him out with a shirt open to the waist, the flariest pair of white flares that you are ever likely to see, and a guitar with no strings. The outfit that they made me was a bit more subtle. It was a backless, and nearly frontless dress made from a leopard skin patterned fabric, and split one side up to the waist. I was also provided with a long black wig, and they tarted me up with lipstick, and painted nails, both top and bottom – very understated. As I drove to the party, I remember hoping that I wouldn't get stopped by the booze bus. The party was a great success, and Jason and I won the prize – it was no contest. For many years afterwards, the occasional person in our area would stop me and say, "You were Cher!"

The story continues. During his Engineering degree at the University of Sydney, Steven was in my Second Year Electromagnetism class. My recollection is that he wasn't much interested in what I taught him, and got an average pass in this subject. It hasn't slowed him down, however. As I have remarked, I had exceptionally good discipline in all of my classes, and this one was no exception. One day, however, there was an undercurrent of unrest in the lecture theatre, and I couldn't figure out why. That evening at dinner, I asked Steven if he knew what had been going on. He looked at me with a wicked grin, and pulled from his pocket a photograph of me as Cher. Who needs enemies?

A couple of years before this incident when Steven was in his final year at high school, he gave me one of those memorable object lessons by demonstrating, yet again, the astonishing things that young people can achieve due to their extraordinary and uninhibited confidence. In return, I taught Steven a bit about electronics – it hardly seems like a fair exchange. Steven had always been into music and electronics, and had assumed responsibility at his school for managing the public address system, and associated equipment, in the school hall. He had formed the view that the mixer in this system was inadequate. He therefore proposed to the school that they purchase a new one, and specified what was needed. They said that the cost was beyond them but, like all good negotiators, Steven had a fall back position. He said that he would be prepared to build an equivalent mixer from a kit if they bought it for him. They showed remarkable faith in his ability by doing just that, with the expenditure of many hundreds of dollars. Steven got stuck into building the kit with great enthusiasm, and very little understanding about what he was doing. Within the first day or so, he had blown up several components in the power supply by unknowingly connecting it up incorrectly. We figured out what bits had been destroyed, and then went to Dick Smith's and purchased replacement parts. He then commenced work on the operational amplifiers, and soon there were several more fried components. Down to Dick Smith's again. As the building progressed, I taught him the fundamentals of how the circuit modules operated. When the mixer was properly connected and working perfectly, he knew a great deal about the way the circuits worked, and the assembly techniques. Together we made a nice wooden box and mounted the circuit in it. Steven presented it to his school, and it continued to be used for many years. A very nice touch was that his school had a little plaque engraved and fixed to the mixer, recording that Steven had made it. During this exercise, Steven even persuaded the school to let him rewire their sound system, and it all worked well after he had finished. It never ceases to amaze me how much young people can achieve if you give them the opportunity. I was always grateful that the teachers at Steven's school were prepared to show confidence in him, even though it was clear that the task was way above him. But then again, it obviously wasn't. And Steven was always a good talker, anyway.

I think that I was probably exhibiting a similar sort of fearless and foolhardy confidence the first time that I took my family out for a sail in our Mirror dinghy. I had never sailed as a boy, and did not have much interest in it until I saw a Mirror dinghy on the beach at Terrigal one day. The Mirror is a beautiful little boat, designed by Jack Holt from the UK, and has been extremely popular over the years. With Marilyn's encouragement, I bought a kit and started to build it. I'm pretty handy with tools, but I made lots of mistakes along the way. The worst was when the boat was nearly completed, and I stood it on its end in our carport to apply a final coat of polyester resin on all of the seams. Unfortunately, the wind blew it over. Mine must be the only Mirror dinghy ever to have been holed *before* it actually got into the water. That summer, we took the dinghy away with us on holidays, and I was busting to put the family into it and head into the wide blue yonder. We did this for the first time under a fairly brisk off-shore breeze on Tuggerah Lake one morning. All went well with the wind behind us. The problems began when we had to start tacking, and I realised that I had only the faintest idea about what to do. Necessity is a great teacher, however, and we somehow managed to stay upright due to some deft manoeuvres by the crew, and a great deal of good luck.

On another early sailing adventure, we took the Mirror dinghy out on Pittwater. In those days, the kids were quite young, and we used to sail five-up, although the boat was really only designed for two adults. All went well until we passed from the reasonably still water close to the shore and into the fairly stiff on-shore breeze. The combination of this wind, and the restricted area of Pittwater, had worked up a viscous chop, causing our little boat to buck and plunge most unpleasantly. The bow soon started to submarine, and large amounts of green water came into the cockpit. It quickly became clear that this was not a good place to be, so I turned around and headed for the shore. Running before the stiff breeze, the boat started to yaw from side to side in a most alarming way. At this point, Kathryn announced her intention of abandoning ship, and swung her legs over the side. As Captain, I sternly forbade this mutinous act and, to my surprise, for once she obeyed me. Deep in the recesses of my mind, I recalled reading that running before the wind goes better if the centreboard is up and the crew is located at the stern, so I gave the appropriate orders. The boat immediately ceased its suicidal behaviour, and we progressed towards safety in a more orderly way. It seemed to me that this was a nice example of the application of theory to practice. I thought that this was the end of our problems, but the fickle onshore wind was not quite finished with us, and we collided with a wharf on the way, leaving a small hole in the hull. We were all happy to abandon sailing for the day, and to head for home.

We sailed our Mirror dinghy many times. My favourite place was in the ocean, out from Terrigal Beach. It is possible to do this without having to take the boat through the surf, because at the south end of the beach there is a small body of water that is protected by a reef on the ocean side, and a headland on the other, so that the water there is essentially free of large waves. We could therefore launch the dinghy from here, and sail out between the reef and the headland, arriving at the open ocean beyond the breakers. We had such a lot of fun there, including doing capsize practice with unsuspecting, and unwilling crew.

Our most memorable sailing excursion at Terrigal occurred on a windy summer afternoon. We were on holidays at the time, and a young lad named Wally had arrived unexpectedly just before lunch. I think that he had some sort of vague and unspecified interest in Kathryn, although it was clear that this was not reciprocated. A problem therefore existed – what to do with Wally? Why, we could take him sailing, couldn't we? We took the Mirror down to Terrigal, and rigged her. The wind was blowing strongly and the ocean waves were quite large, but it looked manageable to me. I put Kathryn and Wally in the boat, and together we headed out from the sheltered beach and into the open ocean. It was an exhilarating ride with the boat skipping along, and quite a few whitecaps on the waves. Eventually we turned and headed back to shore. Jenelle and Steven then wanted a turn, so out we went again. The wind was noticeably stronger, but we managed to handle things without problems. At this point, I should have been smart enough to call it quits. Alas, I was always the slow learner, and anyway, we still had Wally on our hands. I therefore agreed to take Kathryn and Wally out for one last time. We hadn't got too far beyond the protection of the reef when it became abundantly clear that conditions had deteriorated dramatically. We should not have been there, and I told the kids that we had to head for home immediately. The waves had other ideas, however. A huge one broke over us, capsizing the boat and turning it completely upside down. By this time, I knew quite a lot about how to handle a capsize. Of course, we all had life jackets on, so I really wasn't worried about anybody getting drowned. I first checked the crew – Kathryn was in the water beside me, but there was no sign of Wally. I went underneath to discover him inside the upturned cockpit of the dinghy. I dragged him out, and then set about righting the boat. Getting the bow into the wind was not too difficult. Keeping it upright turned out to be virtually impossible. Every time that I would pull it up, a wave would knock it over again. This was starting to get serious. Bit by bit, the wind and the waves were pushing us towards the huge breakers that were pounding on the beach. Again, I felt that we could get through them if we had to, although they would have knocked us about a bit, and the boat would have been wrecked. Eventually I managed to get it upright for long enough to put the kids on board. The Mirror dinghy has a lot of built-in buoyancy, but even so the cockpit was deep in water. I climbed over the transom, and told them to bail as if their lives depend on it. Kathryn went at it like a demon, but Wally, who had turned an interesting shade of green, appeared to be able to do no more than cling onto the mast. We were on the wrong tack, and heading out to sea. By an extraordinary stroke of good luck, I managed to get the boat around without capsizing and, aided by Kathryn's demented work with the bucket, we slowly made our way back to safety behind the reef. They say that experience is a great teacher, and I learnt a couple of things on that day. We never saw Wally again.

This experience with Wally appeared to set the pattern, and any young fellow who showed an interest in either of our daughters was subjected to the full force of the Collins hospitality. Mostly, they ended up thinking that the pace was too hot, and just faded away. A few stuck it out a bit longer. One who was particularly interested in Kathryn was a fellow student at Hawkesbury Agricultural College. I did not know his real name – he was universally referred to as Stud. Any father reading this will know exactly how I felt about a young man with the nickname of Stud showing an interest in my daughter. To make matters worse, Stud was quite well built, and knew it. I suspect that he worked out pretty hard in the gym. We started him into work one afternoon on the usual manual stuff. As it happened, a large tree had come down, and I needed to cut it up with a chain saw. We gave Stud the job of carting the logs away. This would normally have been pretty heavy going for even quite enthusiastic suitors, but it was just bread-and-butter stuff for Stud. Indeed, on more than one occasion I saw him heading off with the huge lump of wood under *each* arm. Clearly more subtle treatment would be needed for this one. After dinner that night, we got on to card tricks. I know several quite simple card tricks that, when presented properly, make it look like I can read minds. Our kids are all onto this, and it makes quite a good show when you can get a victim to choose a card, apparently at random, and then have someone else who is outside the room identify it. Stud was quite impressed, and he told us how he had known other people who could read minds. I then did something that I had never tried before, and never will again. I spread the cards out face down, and asked Stud to pick one at random. He selected, and I then correctly told him what it was. The astonishment on our kids' faces was quite memorable. They had never seen this one before. I was pretty impressed myself, too – after all, I had taken a 1 in 52 chance, and it had paid off. For Stud, however, it was the last straw. Here was conclusive evidence that the woman for whom he lusted had a father who could read his mind. This was not a good place to be. Goodbye Stud.

The relationship between child and parent is a very special one, and is different from any other. For a while, this relationship with one of my kids was broadened into a professional interaction when Kathryn became my secretary at the University. I think that we both initially felt some reservations about having a father-daughter relationship that was also a boss-secretary one, but it worked out extremely well. Kathryn was very professional in her work, and ran the office extremely efficiently. Actually, she was not totally professional in everything. She was the only secretary I ever had who took off her shoes at work. Because she used to put powder into them each morning, the carpet in my office had little white footprints all over it. It looked like a midget yeti had been around. Everyone in the School knew that Kathryn was my daughter, but nobody seemed to mind. At the beginning, however, I was quite concerned about sending the wrong message, so I told Kathryn that, while we were at work, she should address me in the same way as everybody else did there.

"I can't call you Dick," she said.

"Well, you have to," I replied.

And so she did, but I know that it didn't come easily. Then one day, I was down in the laboratory and a telephone call came in for me. She walked out of her office on the upstairs mezzanine and called to me.

"Dick."

No answer.

"Dick!"

Nothing.

"DICK!"

Still nothing.

"Dad."

"Yes?"

That was the end of the Dick thing with Kathryn.

Interestingly enough, my other daughter Jenelle also did something memorable for me at work that involved my name. Jenelle is very talented with arts and craft, and is particularly good at what is known as Folk Art. After I became Head of the School of Physics, she made me a nice wooden sign for my office. In beautiful flowing script, surrounded by little flowers, it reads:

Dick – Head
of
School

I was very fond of this sign, and it occupied a prominent place in my office. I found it quite amusing to have visitors in there, and to see them get put off in the middle of their spiel when they suddenly noticed it.

No account of our family life would be complete without some reference to the animals that have shared it. Over the years, we have had an almost continuous series of relationships with cats (up to five in permanent residence at one stage, most of whom arrived by chance or simply walked in the door and decided that this was a good place to be), two marvellous dogs, and Kathryn's lovely Palomino gelding, Tom. Perhaps the most interesting, and certainly the most bizarre interactions, however, have been with the animals that the children have brought home. One of these was a butcherbird chick that had fallen from a nest, and was rescued by Kathryn on her way home from school. When Butch first arrived, he was very young, and had no feathers. We initially had some problems getting his diet correct, and as a result he seemed to have difficulty standing. After obtaining professional advice from the Zoo on how to avoid rickets, he thrived and grew into a lovely bird. Butch was a real character, and considered us to be his own family. At night, he slept in his cage at one end of the house. Early in the morning, he would demand to be released. When I opened the door, he would fly down the kitchen, negotiate several sharp turns at high-speed, and land on the end of our bed. Chattering all the time, he would hop up the bed, and snuggle in under Marilyn's neck as she lay in bed. He never messed on the bed, but he left his marks almost everywhere else in the house. As he got older, we used to let Butch fly freely outside during the day. In the afternoon after she arrived home, Marilyn would call for him, and he would swoop down from high in a nearby gum tree, negotiate the sharp turns through the back door into the kitchen, and demand to be fed. We took Butch away with us when we went to North Avoca on holidays, and he similarly enjoyed the freedom of the bush there. By this time, he was quite mature and had become skilled at catching insects on the wing. One morning, he woke earlier than usual, and demanded to be let out. We never saw him again. However, a couple of years later, a neighbour told us about this marvellous butcher bird who would bring his family to their balcony to be fed. We are sure that this was Butch, and that he and his progeny live on.

Kathryn was always the one who brought animals home. Some of the more memorable did not come from the wild. Once after returning from an overseas trip, Marilyn and I were somewhat surprised to find a dozen or so young chickens living in the stable. While not exactly approving of this development, we let it run its course. The birds grew, and soon reached the stage when they needed to be turned into meals. I had often watched my Father kill a Christmas chook and subsequently pluck and gut it, but I had never actually performed these acts myself. I found the killing and plucking reasonably straightforward, but I was quite uncertain about how to proceed from there. It turned out, however, that we had a very useful book called *Surviving in the '80s* that was full of information about maintaining a self-sufficiency lifestyle. Sure enough, there was a section in it about gutting a chook. So Kathryn and I took the corpse and, squatting down on a concrete path with me holding the chook, Kathryn holding the book, and our dog drooling hopefully close by, we began.

Kathryn read the instructions. "First make an incision from the back opening up towards the breast."

"Done that."

"It says be careful not to sever the bowel."

"Aarh! Too late!"

And so we proceeded until the job was done, the chook was thoroughly hosed out, and the dog was happy. One by one, the chooks were eliminated, until there was just a single individual left. However, on the morning of her planned execution, she laid an egg. Well, you couldn't kill someone's Mother, could you? So she survived for several years, eventually being transferred, as an arthritic old lady with huge gnarled legs, to a chook retirement home close by.

Before our Mother chook left us, she went clucky and Kathryn, ever being the one to seize the moment, acquired a dozen or so day old chicks to satisfy her maternal instincts. (I leave it to you, dear reader, to decide whether "her" in the previous sentence refers to Kathryn, or the chook.) Again, Marilyn and I were not thrilled by this development, but we let it go. As this set of chooks grew, it became apparent that they had not been past the chicken sexer, because about half of them were male. Young male chooks make a very peculiar sound when they are learning to crow. Initially, we found this to be quite amusing, but it quickly lost its charm. One morning, I was outraged to be woken about 4.30am by one of them insistently croaking in this immature and maddening way. I got out of bed, put on my boots, went up to the pen, extracted the offending creature, chopped off its head, hung it from a tree, and then went back to bed. These male chooks seemed to become even more antisocial as they grew, and I was horrified to see the things that they attempted to do to their foster Mother. One of them became very aggressive, and would attack us as we walked around the yard. He was quite unsubtle in his methods, and you could hear the thump, thump of his feet coming up behind you before he launched himself into your legs with violent impact. We got to learn what was happening, and I in particular would turn around and drop kick the little bastard so that he would wander away dazed and reeling. Eventually, all of these animals made it into the cooking pot. We then laid down the law that the chook thing had to end and, as far as I am aware, it did.

It will be obvious to anybody reading this that Marilyn and I have received great pleasure from our children. In addition to our direct relationships with them, we were always very pleased that they were happy to bring their friends into our home. We feel exceedingly fortunate that they wanted to share their friendships with us and, through this, we have broadened our own relationships, not only with the younger generation, but also with their parents. Steven, in particular, made many friends at school who have impacted on our life for various ways, and continue to do so. While he was still at school, Steven and some of his friends formed a band. The membership was augmented by the mates of mates, and it eventually grew to become the Squid Munchies – "the best cover band in Sydney," as once modestly described by one of them.

The first gig of an early version of the band was held at a local hall and, as I recall, the lads did it because they wanted to provide an evening of fun for their friends. They charged about $2 entry, and stopped collecting money when they had enough to pay for the rent of the hall. As time went by, the Squid Munchies got to be very good, and they did lots of gigs around Sydney, and a few in more distant places, some of which paid very well. On one occasion, I got dressed up in a dinner suit and acted as bouncer – a role that I felt comfortable in only because I had Steven's athletic mate, Mick Brown, standing next to me. We went to quite a few of the Squid Munchies gigs, as did many of their friends and relatives, particularly Mick Brown's parents, Bob and Sonia, who were probably their most loyal groupies. As the band developed, Mick and his brother Rick became their roadies. Mick did the sound stuff, and Rick was the lighting expert, and they were both very professional in the way that they carried out their responsibilities.

The Squid Munchies always practiced at our place, and it was a great pleasure to have them there. We were happy for them to come and go as they pleased, even if we were not there. Never once do I recall having a significant problem associated with their presence. To be sure, one evening we had a nice visit from a couple of friendly policemen who asked them to turn it down a bit, and from time to time we needed to get them to tidy up. However, overall we were thrilled that these fine young people chose to spend time in our home. As the years went by, the membership of a band evolved and now, although the Squid Munchies live on, none of the original players remains. I understand, however, that they all do stand-in jobs from time to time.

The relationship between the blokes in the band, and their mates, was exceedingly close. Indeed, we used to wonder how there could ever be any room for girls. Inevitably, however, they came along and formed part of the group. In due course, marriages and children ensued, and so our circle of friends was continually broadened. Most significantly for Marilyn and me, Steven won the heart of Katrina, who had obtained the advertised job as lead singer in the band. For the record, I should note that I did not give Katrina a hard time, as I had done with all the fellows who were interested in our daughters. I didn't want to do anything to risk losing her! Katrina and Steven are now married, so the legacy of the Squid Munchies is now permanent through the augmentation by Katrina of our immediate family. We couldn't be more pleased about what has happened, even if Steven did advertise for his wife.

Obviously, having the band practice at our place was good for them, but Marilyn and I never expected anything in return. However, they once did something for us that we found quite moving. As a gesture of thanks for the use of our place over the years, they took us to dinner at Centrepoint Tower. We had a splendid evening together, and its memory lives on through the autographed and framed Squid Munchies poster that they presented to us during the evening, and that hangs with pride in our home.

Two memorable Squid Munchie gigs warrant brief mention here. The first was for Jenelle and Jason's wedding, that we had at home. The reception evolved into a swinging party that never seemed to end, with the Munchies in full cry. The other was a farewell party that we had at our home at Rouse Hill shortly before we moved to MacMasters Beach. We had many of our friends there and, of course, the music was classic Squid stuff. Needless to say, on both occasions, the band provided their services gratis. This farewell do had an unexpected ending that had been carefully planned and that everyone, except me, was obviously in on. It was about 12.30am, the band had finished for the night, and we were winding down and packing up. One of the lads came up to me and said that Steven wanted to see me out the back. Innocently, I sought him out, and walked straight into a face full of cream pie. As the oracle said, *There is no fight like a pie fight*, and it was then on for young and old. We had always threatened our daughters that we would turn their weddings into a pie fight, but somehow sanity had prevailed. On this occasion, however, no one had any such inhibitions, and very soon Steven, all his mates, and I were coated with large amounts of sticky muck. I was unfortunately a bit nobbled by the preemptive hit that I had taken. My spectacles were coated with cream, so I couldn't see through them, and if I took them off, I still couldn't see anything in the poor light because of my myopia. So that made me an excellent target, and all those present took full advantage of the opportunity. I was, in fact, absolutely delighted that the blokes felt able to show their respect and affection for me in this uninhibited way, and will always recall this pie fight with fond memories.

Obviously, the nature of the relationship between parent and child changes as they grow. For us, this is perhaps no better illustrated than by the experiences associated with our holiday house at North Avoca. We had acquired this house with the money that I received from cashing in my superannuation contributions when I left AWA in 1978. I had proposed that we use it to reduce the size of the mortgage on our home. Marilyn suggested the alternative of investing in a holiday place, and that is indeed what we did. And what a good investment it was! Financially, I suppose that it did all right, but the real benefits were in our family experiences there. We had such a lot of fun at North Avoca. Over of the years, we renovated the house, and added to it, so that eventually hardly any part was left untouched. Early on, we always went there as a family, and had some wonderful times together in between all of this work. As the children moved along in their teen years, they became less enthusiastic about going away with us to North Avoca. The word *boring* was used in the discussions on more than one occasion, as I recall. So often Marilyn and I would leave the kids behind and head off there by ourselves. A little later, the tables turned. The kids would say to us, "You're not using North Avoca next weekend are you, by any chance," and then stay there with their friends. After she had completed her Higher School Certificate, Kathryn started a tradition, which was maintained by Jenelle and Steven, of taking a group of friends away there for a week's holiday by themselves. I know that they all had a fantastic time during these symbolic transitions to adulthood.

Steven in particular made a lot of use of North Avoca with his friends. We understand that, on occasions, a very large number of people stayed there together, although we never enquired too closely about how many there were, or how they all managed to fit in. After an initial short learning period, the place was invariably left spotlessly clean, with no evidence of the hilarity that had obviously ensued during their stay. On one of these periods there, Steven and his mates made a movie that they called *Predatator*. This was a loose takeoff of the Arnie action thriller with a similar name, and featured Steven's mate, Mick Brown in the starring role. I recall that our neighbours were quite bemused by the antics of the mob as they cavorted through the bush shooting this masterpiece. This was the first of two movies made by Steven and his friends. The other was another Arnie takeoff, starring Dave Byrne, the base player in the Squid Munchies, and was entitled *Davebo*. As it happened, Marilyn and I also got to play bit parts in this movie. The kids put a lot of effort into the whole production, and even had a world Premiere launch. Naturally, this star-studded event was held at our place, and people came in dinner suits and evening dresses. Our two daughters looked very fetching in shapely cigarette girl outfits, and their blokes were done up in red coats and tails. There was a gala supper after the screening, and the whole event had more atmosphere than the real thing. It was a wonderful and memorable evening, and the movie was hilarious, too. We were presented with our own personal copy, which we treasure.

One of the inevitable dilemmas in raising a family is finding an appropriate balance between the time that you spend at home, and the time that you must give to all the other essential things in life, including your job. In one sense, it is much easier to spend time at work than with the family. Things are usually more ordered at work, and you often only have to pay attention to just one matter at a time. Involvement with the family requires multitasking of a high order. I know that when our children were young, I spent much less time with them than I should have. I am extremely fortunate to have a wife who diligently reminded me of the necessity of spending enough time with our kids, and who encouraged me to try and make this happen. Often the things that she said to me were not very easy on my ego, but they were true. Did I give enough attention to my family over the years? Almost certainly not. However I did spend much more time with them than would have been the case had Marilyn not emphasised the importance of doing this. You only get one go with your kids – growing up is a one-way trip, and it happens extraordinarily quickly. I am immensely grateful to Marilyn for the time that I spent with our children that, but for her, I would never have enjoyed.

I find it most gratifying to look back on our many decades of family life and to reflect on the things that have happened between then and now. I consider myself to be astonishingly fortunate to have had so many wonderful experiences as my family has grown. It is a marvellous thing to see babies develop from total dependency through to maturity. Kathryn, Jenelle and Steven are now all making the own way through life, with happiness and distinction. Jenelle and Jason have recently given us even more pleasure through the acquisition of our two dear adopted grandchildren, Gareth and Georgia. Having the privilege of participating in their development is a joy beyond description. And I know that there will be more grandchildren to come. One of the things that gives me most pleasure is that our children obviously still enjoy being with us. Whenever there is a birthday, or a family function, they all make a real effort to come, without our asking. We are indeed fortunate that our children are also now our friends. In my life, I have probably achieved a few other things that have been more difficult and challenging. For me, however, no outcome has been more important.

Epilogue

I have observed that, as most of us grow older, we appear to be unable to resist offering advice to those younger. It is almost as if we have to get it off our chest before it is too late. I am no exception. My advice consists of a few epithets that I have drawn from experiences during my life, and that have been useful to me. Most of them are well known – a few are my own. This material actually formed a concluding slide at some presentations that I used to make at development workshops in the University, and people seemed to like it. So I now offer it to you, dear reader, to do with what you will:

Think positive
Lead by example
Empower your people
If worry won't fix it, don't worry
You can't right all the wrongs of the world
If it's worth doing, it's worth doing well
Fortune favours the brave
Make the world a better place
Never lose your Nerve

Now that's all done, I am going to get stuck into the rest of my life.

Marilyn and Richard